P9-AFM-773

Since the publication of his celebrated first essay on Shakespeare, "The Avoidance of Love: A Reading of *King Lear*," Stanley Cavell has continued to explore radically new and provocative interpretations of a number of the plays. This volume collects those writings for the first time and includes pieces not previously published: the Introduction, which culminates in an extensive discussion of *Antony and Cleopatra,* and essays on *Hamlet* and *The Winter's Tale.*

The essays are bound together by a concern for skepticism. In Coriolanus's disdain, Leontes' and Othello's jealousy, Hamlet's inertia, and Lear's exorbitance, Stanley Cavell sees Shakespeare as offering, for the first time in European letters, a profound diagnosis of the skeptical refusal to acknowledge truths about oneself and one's relations to others, and as exploring the motives and tragic consequences of that refusal. His readings of the plays are subtle and challenging, and the insights they contain often startle by both their originality and their familiarity. As a whole they present a unique point of view on the plays.

Disowning Knowledge

To David Franklin Cavell

Disowning Knowledge

In Six Plays of Shakespeare

STANLEY CAVELL

The right of the
University of Cambridge
to print and sell
all manner of books
was granted by
Henry VIII in 1534.
The University has printed
and published continuously
since 1584.

CAMBRIDGE UNIVERSITY PRESS
Cambridge
New York   New Rochelle   Melbourne   Sydney

Published by the Press Syndicate of the University of Cambridge
The Pitt Building, Trumpington Street, Cambridge CB2 1RP
32 East 57th Street, New York, NY 10022, USA
10 Stamford Road, Oakleigh, Melbourne 3166, Australia

© Cambridge University Press 1987

First published 1987
Reprinted 1988

Printed in the United States of America

Library of Congress Cataloging-in-Publication Data
Cavell, Stanley, 1926–
Disowning knowledge.
Includes index.
1. Shakespeare, William, 1564–1616 – Criticism
and interpretation. I. Title.
PR2976.C336   1987   822.3'3   87–10874

British Library Cataloguing in Publication Data
Cavell, Stanley
Disowning knowledge: in six plays of
Shakespeare.
1. Shakespeare, William – Criticism and
interpretation
I. Title
822.3'3   PR2976
ISBN 0 521 33032 7 hard covers
ISBN 0 521 33890 5 paperback

Coriolanus and Interpretations of Politics,

EXCERPTED FROM:
THEMES OUT OF SCHOOL, © 1984 by Stanley Cavell.
Published by North Point Press and reprinted by permission.
All rights reserved.

Contents

Preface and Acknowledgments

Suppose that philosophy is pursued either according to the myth or wish that one may know everything, or else according to the myth or wish that one may know nothing – defenses against the philosophical defeat of claiming to possess some privileged access to or measure of truth. In our century the names of Heidegger and of Wittgenstein are reasonably clear instances, respectively, of these modes of defense. By instinct and training my mode has been that of careful ignorance, but nowhere more than in my reading of Shakespeare have I been more aware of the liabilities and hazards of this course, hence nowhere more needful of timely aid and encouragement.

From the first of these essays I have counted on the friendship and the work of Michael Fried, of John Harbison, and of the late Seymour Shifrin; especially in recent years on that of Janet Adelman, Jay Cantor, Burton Dreben, Marc Shell, and Judith Shklar. I think also with gratitude of the vivid lift in particular exchanges with Paul Alpers, David Bevington, Carol Neely, Norman Rabkin, Amelie Rorty, Edward Snow, Meredith Skura, and Richard Wheeler. And throughout there have been the students – from those in the General Education course at Harvard for which the material on *King Lear* was prepared, to those in the two discussion seminars I have offered on the other plays represented in what follows here, to those generations of philosophy graduate students on the third floor of Emerson Hall willing to listen and to question as I sought to follow out my irregular sense of philosophy's bearing toward and from Shakespeare, conversations many of which – I am blessed to know – continue now years later.

In the months since the present work was sent off to the publisher, I have, as part of a third Shakespeare discussion seminar, begun studying recent criticism of Shakespeare composed from the perspectives of the new historicism or cultural materialism, and from that of deconstruction, and from that of feminism. Much of it seems to me to bear on what appears here, but for me to say how is something for other occasions. I had, in any case, for my part, to come to feel that this sequence of readings or measures has been accomplishing the staking out of a certain reasonably early and reasonably consistent perspective; otherwise the bearing on it of others would have no particular point.

That there is some such perspective whose staking out it was for me to accomplish I glimpsed consciously as a result of an exchange whose special role for me I wish to record explicitly. It took the form of a telephone call to me during the spring (as I recall) of the year I was in residence at the Center for the Humanities at Wesleyan University, so in 1970–1, from C. L. Barber in Santa Cruz, California. He said that students of his had been recommending that he read my essay on *King Lear* and that having now done so he wanted to invite me to share a symposium with him (I no longer remember for what institution) in which we each would undertake to say something about the complete body of Shakespeare's work and then to compare this achievement with that of another writer (I gathered in any other language and I imagined in any other mode). It seemed to me a remarkable stroke simply to recognize that the time had come again in which a project of that character could be well conceived, or reconceived. I said so, moved as much by the tone of the invitation and by the idea of it as by the fact that they came from a scholar I had not then met but whose book *Shakespeare's Festive Comedy* I had, with so many others, profited from. But I went on to decline the invitation, arguing that preparation for such an undertaking would require from me, at a guess, about ten years. More than half again that span has now passed, and my sequence of essays or measures takes up no more than a sixth of the corpus of the plays; but however incomplete the extent and limited in scope the accomplishment, the idea in it of Shakespeare as a writer of human consistency, developing a particular problematic in and of a world, and in and of a language, shared with and faced against other writers, is part of whatever good there is in it, and that idea began to become active for me from the time of Barber's invitation.

After the Introduction, the essays to follow appear, with one reversal I shall note, in the order of their writing. That on *King Lear* was completed in 1967 and appeared as the concluding essay of

Preface and Acknowledgments

Must We Mean What We Say? (first published in 1969, reprinted in 1976 by Cambridge University Press). The pages on *Othello* conclude *The Claim of Reason* (published in 1979 by Oxford University Press). The paper on *Coriolanus* was prepared at the invitation of Janet Adelman for the Shakespeare Congress held at Stratford-upon-Avon in the summer of 1981. I was unable in the event to attend that Congress, but two subsequent invitations gave me opportunities to present the paper and to profit from its discussion. The first, at the invitation of Philip Holzman, was to read a paper to the Rapaport–Klein Study Group at the Austen Riggs Center in Stockbridge, Massachusetts, in June 1982, and the second, in the following September, to participate in a colloquium on *Coriolanus* at The Humanities Institute during its meetings at Stanford University. The paper first appeared in *Representations* for Fall 1983 and then in my collection of essays entitled *Themes Out of School* (published in 1984 by North Point Press). I am grateful to Oxford University Press and to North Point Press for permission to reprint. The *Hamlet* piece was part of a symposium held at the American Shakespeare Association in April 1984; it is to appear in the forthcoming issue of *Hebrew University Studies in Literature and Art*. The essay on *The Winter's Tale* is printed here for the first time. It was written as the last of four Mrs. William Beckman Lectures given at Berkeley in February 1983; a revised version was presented as a Louis O. Mink Memorial Lecture at Wesleyan University in February 1984; and a similar version at The Humanities Center at The Johns Hopkins University in October 1985. The Beckman lectures were entitled *In Quest of the Ordinary: Lines of Skepticism and Romanticism,* and the opening and closing moments of the essay on *The Winter's Tale* show the marks of its links there. They are links of value to me and I have not wished to hide them. I hope to see this essay also appear in its place as the last of my Beckman lectures when that sequence is published as a group, indicating more freely and clearly paths of the Shakespeare material and of the romanticism/skepticism material across one another. The chronological reversal I mentioned is of the final two essays, made because the study of *The Winter's Tale* seemed better able to stand up to ending this sequence than the somewhat later piece on *Hamlet,* so conscious of its brevity. As it turns out, however, the book still contrives to end on a thought of Hamlet's.

Editing has for the most part confined itself to syntactical clarification and to bringing the material into stylistic consistency. The *Lear* essay is the exception. It bears scars of our period in Vietnam; its strange part II is not in control of its asides and orations and love letters of nightmare (once casting America's shame and wrath as Lear's). Then its period-piece, male-centered use of pronouns I had thought to let stand, not out of a desire for rueful self-humiliation, and not to brazen out the obvious human obligation sometimes to take the bad with the good, but for two other reasons. First, I am in fact there often concentrating on the male inflection of the world, Lear's and ours, one in which, from which, I felt I suffered as much, no doubt, as I profited, my expression of which will eventually have to enter into the balance of whatever credit may be mine for whatever feminism was mine early, forever. Second, the male inflection cannot be undone, needless to say, by altering a few pronouns, and the essay has meant too much to me to dismiss, without more care than I can exercise now, the possibilities that the inflection was the condition both of worse things and also perhaps of some better things, say more progressive, than show up at a glance. Yet I could not after all let the pronouns, all of them, stand. The effect of tone was sometimes simply too grating, so I have accordingly here and there rephrased. That feminism is in these years a movement of such depth that its pressure on, say, pronouns poses a continuous stylistic pressure not to be answered with the use of certain set formulas but to be decided in each case does not surprise me. But I was I guess surprised, reading over the essay with this particular question in mind, by the experience I called grating. For a political experience to have moved back out from the mind onto the skin and into the senses means that in these twenty years something like a new set of natural reactions has formed, which means a new turn of history.

I am grateful to my production editor at the Cambridge Press, Mrs. Jane Van Tassel, for her eye, tact, conscientiousness, and forbearance; and to my research assistant Jim Conant for, among other things, the making of the index.

References to Shakespeare's texts are according to the respective Arden editions.

1

Introduction

I HAVE resisted earlier suggestions that the few essays I have devoted to individual plays of Shakespeare be put together as a book.
I did not want to give the impression that I felt I had arrived at a
stable view of Shakespeare's writing from the limited perspective
I work from and the limited sample of plays I have worked on;
and I did not feel the justifications I have for my intrusions into
this fearful territory would make themselves felt taken in isolation
from the philosophical bearings that led me to them. But with the
completion of the two hitherto unpublished essays included here,
on *Hamlet* and on *The Winter's Tale*, I began to wish to assess what
happens to the essays in the face of one another, or backed against
one another, and to let them find their weight with just the philosophy that clings to them in their individual emergencies. The
misunderstanding of my attitude that most concerned me was to
take my project as the application of some philosophically independent problematic of skepticism to a fragmentary parade of
Shakespearean texts, impressing those texts into the service of il-
lustrating philosophical conclusions known in advance. Sympathy
with my project depends, on the contrary, on unsettling the matter
of priority (as between philosophy and literature, say) implied in
the concepts of illustration and application. The plays I take up
form respective interpretations of skepticism as they yield to interpretation by skepticism. To indicate as much for each of these plays
is the task of this introduction.

There is a further reason for agreeing to this collection. It seems
to me that I have done the best I can do in justifying and exem-
plifying my sense of an epistemological reading of Shakespearean
tragedy and I want now to be able to encounter the Shakespearean
corpus with a free mind. So I shall let this introduction go on at

further length than I had at first proposed to do. Those who have some interest in what I have so far written may be glad of this; others may find the results needlessly difficult and obscure. Since conviction in its pertinence must depend on the convincingness of the handling of individual plays, a reader unfamiliar with how I look at the work of the plays might find it efficient to turn at once to one or another of the individual readings and then come back here.

Because I foresee that these introductory remarks are not going to constitute the simple words of welcome I had meant to produce, I am hoping they will provide help to those who themselves welcome, or are prepared to welcome, the company of philosophy in reading works of, let us say, literature; and vice versa. (I know the company is sometimes restive, difficult, occasionally quite impossible. If you do not find it so it may be that you are too much conceiving of philosophy as a well-behaved and well-explored function of literature, or of literature as treating independently well-known philosophical ideas.) I become perplexed in trying to determine whether it is to addicts of philosophy or to adepts of literature that I address myself when I in effect insist that Shakespeare could not be who he is – the burden of the name of the greatest writer in the language, the creature of the greatest ordering of English – unless his writing is engaging the depth of the philosophical preoccupations of his culture. I guess the insistence comes from a sense that English philosophy is characterized, in distinction from, say, that of France and of Germany, by its relative distance from the major literature of its culture. Compared with Kant's or Hegel's or Schelling's awareness of Goethe or Hölderlin (or Rousseau or Shakespeare) or with Descartes's and Pascal's awareness of Montaigne, Locke's or Hume's or Mill's relation to Shakespeare and Milton or Coleridge (or Montaigne) amounts to hardly more than that to more or less serious hobbies, not to the recognition of intellectual competitors, fellow challengers of intellectual conscience. (I do not speculate here about why this is so. It is, among other matters, surely some function of the differences in the relations of these philosophical cultures to religion, or perhaps rather to what the West calls the Bible.) Sensing this difference makes me sorely aware of my American fate.

Is there an American difference in philosophy? If there is, it will look one way if you think of its source as Peirce's and Dewey's pragmatist empiricism or experimentalism; it will look another way if you think of its source in Emerson's and in Thoreau's transcendental experimentalism. Because I yield to the latter (perhaps sometimes too stridently just because of its oddness to reigning philosophy) and therewith to the side of philosophy that edges against literature, and because I do not therefore feel free of the former, of the side of philosophy that edges to science, I have a thirst for a question that motivates the writing of this introduction: Is the issue of communication between philosophy and literature itself a philosophical or a literary issue? Something mannerly and no doubt something unmannerly in my prose is caused by my acceptance of such a question and by my refusal to decide it prematurely, to decide it judiciously ("It is both"), or to decide that it is undecidable ("It is neither quite"), before closing with it, keeping it open, enacting it, experimenting.

My intuition is that the advent of skepticism as manifested in Descartes's *Meditations* is already in full existence in Shakespeare, from the time of the great tragedies in the first years of the seventeenth century, in the generation preceding that of Descartes. However strong the presence of Montaigne and Montaigne's skepticism is in various of Shakespeare's plays, the skeptical problematic I have in mind is given its philosophical refinement in Descartes's way of raising the questions of God's existence and of the immortality of the soul (I assume as, among other things, preparations for, or against, the credibility of the new science of the external world). The issue posed is no longer, or not alone, as with earlier skepticism, how to conduct oneself best in an uncertain world; the issue suggested is how to live at all in a groundless world. Our skepticism is a function of our now illimitable desire. In Descartes's thinking, the ground, one gathers, still exists, in the assurance of God. But Descartes's very clarity about the necessity of God's assurance in establishing a rough adequation or collaboration between our everyday judgments and the world (however the matter may stand in natural science) means that if assurance in God will be shaken, the ground of the everyday is thereby shaken.

If Shakespeare's plays interpret and reinterpret the skeptical problematic – the question whether I know with certainty of the existence of the external world and of myself and others in it – it follows that the plays find no stable solution to skepticism, in particular no rest in what we know of God. Being Shakespearean texts they test, as well as test themselves by, their sources, so that in incorporating, let us say, a philosophical problematic, they test, as well as test themselves by, philosophy. What interpretation a text finds of skepticism is, accordingly, not knowable apart from what interpretation the text finds of itself; and in particular philosophy's own interpretation of skepticism (or skepticism's self-interpretation, namely as discovering that we cannot achieve certainty in our knowledge of existence on the basis of the senses alone, hence on no human basis) is denied privilege.

I do not command the learning to argue seriously on historical evidence that the shaking of the ground of human existence, in what philosophy calls skepticism, finds its way into Shakespeare's words – call this ground authority, or legitimacy, in the realms of religion, of politics, of knowledge, of love, of family, of friendship – hence to argue that the unique endlessness of the Shakespearean order of words is a function of that shaking. My conviction, or evidence, is in something of the reverse state. Given my intuition of the occurrence of skepticism in Shakespeare, it is from him that I would have to learn, were I a historian, what to look for to give his history. In calling my guiding theme an intuition I am distinguishing it from a hypothesis. Both intuitions and hypotheses require what may be called confirmation or continuation, but differently. A hypothesis requires evidence and it must say what constitutes its evidence. (I know what it means to say that lighter objects fall to earth at the same rate as heavier objects, though it may be no easy matter to collect the evidence that determines this one way or the other.) An intuition, say that God is expressed in the world, does not require, or tolerate, evidence but rather, let us say, understanding of a particular sort (and it may be no easy matter to talk someone out of the idea that the only need for statements of such a sort is, or was, as hypotheses). Emerson says in "Self-Reliance": "Primary wisdom [is] Intuition, whilst all later teachings are tuitions." He is accordingly called, not incorrectly, a philosopher of intuition. For some reason it is typically not noticed that he is at the same time a teacher of tuition. But in such a statement declaring the importance of intuition, Emerson is at the same time grounding the necessity of tuition. I read him as teaching that the occurrence to us of intuition places a demand upon us, namely for tuition; call this wording, the willingness to subject oneself to words, to make oneself intelligible. (Tuition so conceived is what I understand criticism to be.) This is something Descartes means in looking to express clear and distinct ideas; for example, in finding that his idea of God is a function of his sense of himself as dependent, finite.

In looking for words for Shakespeare's interpretations of skepticism I may well from time to time, in my experimentation, speak incredibly or outrageously. For me this is no more serious, though no less, than making a mistake in computation – if the words do not go through they will simply drop out as worthless. My aim in reading is to follow out in each case the complete tuition for a given intuition (tuition comes to an end somewhere). This has nothing to do with – it is a kind of negation of – an idea of reading as a judicious balancing of all reasonable interpretations. My reading is nothing if not partial (another lovely Emersonian word). Yet some will take my claim to partiality as more arrogant than the claim to judiciousness.

A full decade elapsed from the time I completed my first Shakespeare essay, "The Avoidance of Love," on *King Lear,* in 1966–7, to the moment, a third of the way through the last part of *The Claim of Reason,* at which I recognized that bringing the thoughts of that book to a conclusion would depend on formulating the significance to me of the fact that that *Lear* essay, in concluding *Must We Mean What We Say?* follows an essay on what the Anglo-American tradition of philosophy calls the problem of other minds, "Knowing and Acknowledging." I had seen that the extreme precipitousness of the Lear story, the velocity of the banishments and of the consequences of the banishments, figured the precipitousness of skepticism's banishment of the world, and I had surmised at some length that not only was tragedy obedient to a skeptical structure but contrariwise, that skepticism already bore its own marks of a tragic structure. (This surmise is registered in the section on the tradition of epistemology interpolated into the *Lear* essay. I note the surmise there as both obscure and as relying on my doctoral dissertation. This reliance was a principal motivation for my continuing measures to preserve what I could of the dissertation in what became *The Claim of Reason.*) But not until the working out of the end of *The Claim of Reason* with a reading of *Othello* could I claim that tragedy is the working out of a response to skepticism – as I now like to put the matter, that tragedy is an interpretation of what skepticism

5

is itself an interpretation of; that, for example, Lear's "avoidance" of Cordelia is an instance of the annihilation inherent in the skeptical problematic, that skepticism's "doubt" is motivated not by (not even where it is expressed as) a (misguided) intellectual scrupulousness but by a (displaced) denial, by a self-consuming disappointment that seeks world-consuming revenge.

That the study of tragedy can and should entail reconceptions of what drives skepticism – of what its emotion is, of what becomes of the world in its grip, its stranglehold, of what knowing has come to mean to us – is, in retrospect, hinted at when I first show my awareness that a reading of *Othello* is called for, and I begin steering toward it, for some reason, along routes of romanticism. Romanticism aside, the opening moments sound this way:

> Over and over, an apparent symmetry or asymmetry between skepticism with respect to the external world and skepticism with respect to other minds has collapsed, on further reflection, into its opposite. . . . It would not hurt my intuitions, to anticipate further than this book actually goes, were someone to be able to show that my discoveries in the region of the skeptical problem of the other are, rightly understood, further characterizations of (material object) skepticism, of skepticism as such. So that, for example, what I will find in Othello's relation to Desdemona is not just initiated by that phase of its career in which the human being makes to secure or close its knowledge of the world's existence once and for all, only to discover it to be closed off forever; but also that their relation remains to the end a certain allegory of that career. The consequent implication that there is between human existence and the existence of the world a standing possibility of death-dealing passion, of a yearning at once unappeasable and unsatisfiable, as for an impossible exclusiveness or completeness, is an implication that harks back, to my mind, to my late suggestion of the possibility of falling in love with the world.
>
> (*The Claim of Reason,* pp. 451–2)

In that context I continue for a moment by touching a certain vision of film comedy, as if merely to stake the claim that some way remains through this tract of denial. Now I note certain veins of implication I have since come to expect from that stake.

Introduction

Most immediately, what philosophy knows as doubt, Othello's violence allegorizes (or recognizes) as some form of jealousy. Now, whatever philosophy's dissatisfaction with its own understanding of doubt, it will scarely accept this step to jealousy as a help. Because whereas jealousy shares with doubt the idea of suspicion, it shifts the philosophical balance in two ways: It makes the project of assurance or appropriation less cognitive, so to speak, than philosophy takes it to be; and it makes the object of suspicion uncomfortably, let me say, animate. But the shift of philosophical balance seems to me to uncover the animism, so to speak, in the philosophical idea of doubt itself: Doubt, like belief, is most fully, say originally, directed to claims of others, of speakers; an appropriate reaction to, for instance, rumor, Iago's medium. If you tell me that there is a table in the next room I may or may not believe you; hence I may say I believe or do not believe there is a table there. But philosophers are led to say that they believe that there is a table *here* (the presence that is for all the world *this* table), before the very eyes. The context is one in which the philosopher is talking, so to speak, at most to himself: He is not speaking to someone whose position is inferior to his with respect to the table, so he is not telling anyone anything; nor is his position with respect to the table inferior to anyone else's, so he cannot be denied, from outside as it were. It is the position that reveals us humans to be in the same human boat of sensuous endowment, fated to the five senses, the position from which alone the skeptic's doubt demands to be answered. It is (therefore) equally alone the position from which the skeptic's radical question demands to be raised, in which *the best case* of knowledge shows itself vulnerable to suspicion. We may say that what it is vulnerable to is the transformation of a scene of knowing for oneself into a sense that true knowledge is beyond the human self, that what we hold in our minds to be true of the world can have at best the status of opinion, educated guesswork, hypothesis, construction, belief. The concept of belief is turned from its common course. I say, in *The Claim of Reason,* in a phrase from, and as part of an interpretation of, Wittgenstein's *Philosophical Investigations,* that in such a case a word is being used outside its language game(s), apart from its ordinary criteria. It is essential to language that words *can* so be turned. But there are consequences. In turning the concept of belief to name our immediate or absolute relation to the world, say our absolute intimacy, a relation no human other *could* either confirm or compromise, the philosopher turns the world into, or puts it in the position of, a speaker, lodging its claims upon us, claims to which, as it turns out, the philosopher cannot listen. Everyone knows that *something* is mad in the skeptic's fantastic quest for certainty. Philosophers from the beginning, in Descartes and in Hume, have taken the madness into account. I am here merely picking up a different corner of the veil. The glimpse is of an internal connection between skepticism and romanticism, of a sense of why skepticism is what romantic writers are locked in struggle against, writers from Coleridge and Wordsworth to Emerson and Thoreau and Poe (and for future reference I single out E. T. A. Hoffmann); and specifically in struggle for some ground of animism, which may take the form of animation (as emblematized in Hoffmann's automatons, in Coleridge's figure of life-in-death in *The Ancient Mariner,* perhaps in *Frankenstein*), a struggle as if to bring the world back to life from the death dealt it in philosophy, anyway in philosophical skepticism.

Skepticism's results pass themselves off, before all to itself, as specific claims, as expressions of particular beliefs – as if "The world exists" were one more belief among others, the world one more object among others. It is the object so conceived, as representing the world, the world as object, that in response to the skeptical interrogation is put in the position of inaudible speaker. Here one would one day have to look at the philosopher's extraordinary treatment of objects, as in Descartes's wax that is melting, in Price's tomato with nothing but its visual front aspect remaining, in Moore's raised moving hands, in Heidegger's blooming tree, to explore the sense of hyperbolic, unprecedented attention in play. It is not just careful description, or practical investigation, under way here. The philosopher is as it were looking for a *response* from the object, perhaps a shining. And of course one may not sense this; the skeptic exactly would not. It is in taking tragedy as the display of skepticism, and skepticism with respect to other minds as allegorical of skepticism with respect to material objects, that in my experience the treatment of the object forces its attention upon us. (If this were meant as an *argument* for the presence of this issue of the object it would be a terribly poor one.)

What specifically for me is at stake epistemologically in the allegory of Othello and Desdemona is my finding that Othello's radical, consuming doubt is not caused by Iago's rumoring. Othello rather seizes upon Iago's suggestions as effects or covers for some-

Introduction

thing the object has itself already revealed, and claimed, despite its most fervent protestations to the contrary. In this way Othello's jealousy itself is an unstable, turned concept. He seeks a possession that is not in opposition to another's claim or desire but one that establishes an absolute or inalienable bonding to himself, to which no claim or desire *could* be opposed, could conceivably count; as if the jealousy is directed to the sheer existence of the other, its separateness from him. It is against the (fantasied) possibility of overcoming this hyperbolic separateness that the skeptic's (disappointed, intellectualized, impossible, imperative, hyperbolic) demand makes sense. (Othello's capacity for eloquence or incantation comes in here. It is the counter to that drive of skepticism I have called the fear or anxiety of inexpressiveness. This drive should particularly be borne in mind when we take up Cleopatra's powers and motives of self-presentation.)

With his "jealousy," Othello's violence studies the human use of knowledge under the consequence of skepticism. This violence in human knowing is, I gather, what comes out of Heidegger's perception that philosophy has, from the beginning, but, if I understand, with increasing velocity in the age of technology, conceived knowledge under the aegis of dominion, of the concept of a concept as a matter, say, of grasping a thing. In Kant this concept of the concept is pictured as that of synthesizing things, putting together appearances, yoking them, to yield objects of knowledge: Knowledge itself is explicitly, as opposed to the reception of sensuous intuitions, an active thing – Kant says spontaneous; intuitions alone occur to us passively. (In a motto, there is no intellectual intuition; or, there is no world without the suffering, the sensuous reception, of intuitions together with the active emplacement of concepts upon them.) I have claimed elsewhere that Emerson contests Kant on this fundamental ground of the *Critique of Pure Reason*. Or if Kant is himself ambivalent about this matter, then Emerson may be seen to contest the ambivalence, putting his weight on the side of receptiveness, of, say, intelligible intuition. What this means for Emerson, however, is not to be taken at face, or Kantian, value – as my linking of what Emerson sees in intuition with what he expects from tuition should indicate. I add that the suggestion of a masculine/feminine contest over the nature of knowing, over, say, the economy as between activity and passivity in knowing, is not to be missed here, however difficult it will be to develop usefully.

It shows up, or fails to show up sufficiently, in the habitual citing of the biblical use of the term "knowing." The term is always, so far as I recall, used (and always in the past tense?) to name the man's access to the woman, not hers to him. (*The Winter's Tale* is pertinent here and I shall come back to it.)

The violence in masculine knowing, explicitly associated with jealousy, seems to interpret the ambition of knowledge as that of exclusive possession, call it private property. Othello's problem, following my suggestion that his problem is over success, not failure, is that Desdemona's acceptance, or satisfaction, or reward, of his ambition strikes him as being possessed, as if he is the woman. This linking of the desire of knowledge for possession, for, let us say, intimacy, links this epistemological problematic as a whole with that of the problematic of property, of ownership as the owning or ratifying of one's identity. As though the likes of Locke and Marx, in relating the individual to the world through the concept of laboring, and relating the distortion of that relation to the alienation or appropriation of labor, were preparing a conceptual field that epistemology has yet to follow out. "Appropriating" seems to have the same stress put on it in relating the individual to the world through the ownership of property as "belief" has in relating the individual to the world through the acquisition and power of knowledge. As with belief it seems clear what the relation of appropriation is as between persons. I have no more conceptual hesitation over the possibility of one person appropriating something from another person than I have over one person believing another. But as it seems unclear, or ought to, what it is to (feel driven to) establish the relation of belief between me and the isolated (say, private) existence of this object or place, so it seems unclear what it is to (feel driven to) establish the relation of appropriation between me and this isolated (say, private) object or territory.

A metaphysically desperate degree of private bonding, of the wish to become undispossessable, would seem to be an effort to overcome the sense of the individual human being not only as now doubtful in his possessions, as though unconvinced that anything really belongs to him, but doubtful at the same time whether there is any place to which he really belongs. It remains to be assessed how the institution of law takes its bearing here, particularly in relation to the demand for consent to a social contract. I assume that if there is a skepticism with respect to belonging and to belongings, the

fact of law will not settle it, any more than the existence of science
will settle skepticism with respect to the external world. On the
contrary, what we call law and what we call science would themselves have become modified as part of the historical trauma that
sets the scene for skepticism (or for which skepticism sets the place),
the scene in which modern philosophy finds itself. And it remains
to be assessed what the role of God was, and what compensates
for it, in these dispossessions in question. In Cartesian epistemology
God assures the general matching of the world with human ideas
of it by *preserving* it, its matching and its existence; in Lockean society
God assures our general human claims to possession and dominion
of the world by having *given* it to us.

A word, before leaving this backward and forward glance at my
thoughts concerning *Othello,* about my method (poor thing) in the
way I went about composing the pages on *Othello* that close *The
Claim of Reason* and that are extracted here as Chapter 3. Those
dozen-plus pages are moved forward by words and clauses that had
been given place in that book in the hundreds of pages of argument
and description preceding the turn to Shakespeare. Words and
clauses such as these: the problem of the other as the replacement
of the problem of God; the body and the mind as each everything
the other is not; the search for a best case for knowing the existence
of others; the consequences of the failure to know and to acknowledge a best case, with respect to objects, with respect to the other;
the stake in skepticism; its precipitousness; its emotion; an opportunity to believe; wanting to believe; the torture of logic; a voice
in one's history; false public and false privacy; denial of sight; fighting not to awaken; the human guise; am I identical with my mind?
with my body? with neither?; the marks of finitude; unstable certainty; the denial of the human is the human; thinking to escape
human nature from above, and from below; what it is we take to
express skepticism, to express knowledge; to interpret a metaphysical finitude as an intellectual lack. In saying that these couple
of dozen sets of words, among others, have been "given place" in
the earlier work of *The Claim of Reason,* I specifically do not mean
that they have received some special definitions there but just that
they are, as words of ordinary language, recurrent and essential to
the stories I tell in those pages about skepticism and knowledge,
about privacy and publicness, about the inner and the outer, about
ordinary language philosophy and its position in a philosophical

tradition, about philosophy as the education of grown-ups, about language and the world, about myself and others. So while those sets of words play a kind of theoretical or shaping role in the book as a whole, I count on them as no more, but no less, clear and convincing than the stories are to which they are essential. In what I called "moving forward" my pages concerning *Othello,* say motivating them, they are in principle unremarkable. Empirically this means that I require that the words that I state have been given place in the prior working of the book enter into the reading of Shakespeare without having to reproduce their credentials. Theoretically this means that I claim my text on Shakespeare's text as an enactment of (illustration of? evidence for? instance of? model for? image of? allegory of?) the theoretical movement of *The Claim of Reason* at large, but to no greater extent, and to no smaller, than the convincingness of the reading of *Othello* in its own terms; I mean to no greater extent than the capacity of the terms thus brought to the play to sustain themselves under pressure from alternative, competing readings of the play.

The material collected here on *Coriolanus* has elsewhere received its own introduction,[1] so I note now, in passing, just the specific difference of its contribution to the perspective and project of the present collection of essays. The point of responsiveness to skepticism I hit on in thinking through *Coriolanus* I might place as follows. The skeptic can be cloaked as the thinker wishing to bring assertion to its greatest fastidiousness, refusing our knowledge as of the world, so refusing the world, because he cannot satisfy our apparently *pure* demand for certainty, or demand for pure certainty ("You don't see *all* of the object but at most part of the surface facing you, so you don't strictly see *it*"). But Coriolanus's enactment of disgust with the world suggests that the skeptic's search for purity is not originally in response to the failure of intellectual certainty but before that a response to a vision of intellectual vulgarity, of commonness, call it a vision of communication as contamination, the discovery that human existence is inherently undistinguished. That Coriolanus's disgust is, as I read it, directly and emblematically a disgust with language, with the vulgarity of the vulgar tongue, seems revelatory of something in skepticism that Descartes and Hume, for

[1] See "A Cover Letter to Molière's Misanthrope," which precedes the *Coriolanus* essay in my book *Themes Out of School* (North Point Press, 1984).

instance, were not able quite to thematize; so revelatory of philosophy, or of a major strain in philosophy, quite generally. Coriolanus is thus a particularly vivid portrait of (one form of) *living one's skepticism,* a matter that is brought forth as an issue by Descartes and by Hume, each of whom, perhaps too hurriedly, takes his way back from the skeptical discovery to some more sheltered, if still unstable, ground.

Hamlet overlaps Coriolanus's disgust, and also, in the context of the denial by her, the discovery that his mother is not his to dispose of. I express Hamlet's response as the refusal to admit himself to life, rather than, as with Coriolanus, the banishment of life (of public life, I should rather say, since he is, critically unlike Hamlet, married), an opposite or contrary end of the refusal to partake and to be partaken of. I bring denial by the mother here in juxtaposition with the denial of the world in order to mark, without following, the possibility of a direct psychoanalytic interpretation of skepticism, one that would not exact what may seem the detour through literature. The interpretation would be to the effect that what philosophy registers as uncertainty in our knowledge of the existence of the world is a function of, say an intellectualization of, the child's sense of loss in separating from the mother's body. A philosopher a bit suspicious of psychoanalysis must be a deal suspicious of this interpretation, or of its spirit, say the spirit of explanation; for one might equally say that the appeal to the loss of the mother's body is a sentimentalization of the grown-up task of philosophy, call this the acceptance of finitude, the assumption of our separate existence, that is, the recognition of the (separate) existence of the world and of others in it. My essay on *Hamlet* makes the issue of my relation to Freudian thought more explicit than the others on Shakespeare, at least by way of suggesting why the relation cannot be simple.

One who finds that essay sympathetic is apt to find it awfully short, almost too swiftly producing a return of the (repressed) familiar. It is an effect I welcome, so that I would consider it the soul of witlessness on my part to destroy its brevity by expanding it with what evidence I might collect of its soundness. Either it has an initial plausibility or it is, and must remain, nothing; and my commitment to it is such that I leave as naked as I can the difficulty of accepting it. It strikes me as sufficiently undeniable, and nervously enough located, to change and to enter into every way I see the play. But this just means that because of the thoughts in the essay everything in the play for me needs to be gone back over.

Take, for instance, Hamlet's remark to Rosencrantz: "Sir, I lack advancement." Hamlet encourages Rosencrantz's taking up of his remark to mean that his succession to the throne is doubtful; then upon being encountered by the Players with recorders Hamlet turns on Guildenstern with his parable of knowing another – plucking out the heart of his mystery, knowing his stops, sounding him bottom to top – as the skill of playing him, as if this knowing just is being able to (re)produce the origins and combinations of all that comes from him. Since Hamlet's demonstration of Guildenstern's and Rosencrantz's transcendental lack of skill at such playing is ground home with repetitious urgings to play a recorder, repetitions as boring as they are bullying in their obviousness, it may occur to us to ask whether we, who claim to know characters top to bottom (or, what is hardly different, to know where their mysteries begin), know, for example, what Hamlet means by lacking advancement. That phrase combines stops whose particular mystery to these acquaintances produces Hamlet's manic outburst of contempt for their powers of penetration. One may reason that a worry over the succession is the very truth and that it popped out to Rosencrantz from Hamlet's very exasperation with his prying, so that the parable of knowing others is meant as a distraction from this inadvertent revelation; or one may suggest that advancement is a cover story produced because he was forced to say something or other to satisfy these agents. Neither seems the sound of Hamlet's stops.

In cultivating my perplexity here, in terms of my reading of Hamlet as resisting birth, holding back from existence, from entrance into such a world as awaits him, I take lacking advancement as indeed the truth leaping out, but as the expression of a fantasy, one of remaining in his mother's womb, as if always buried alive, or caught in the passage out. (This is not incompatible with a worry over political advancement. On the contrary, it might explain the worry.) It would not be the only time Shakespeare has imagined and interpreted the physical facts of birth. Of course there is no thought of proving the truth, or existence, of such a fantasy on my part – I mean of proving that it is conveyed to me from Hamlet (surely I mean *Hamlet?*) – but it is again the kind of glimpse of derangement in oneself that reading Shakespeare, perhaps more

Introduction

readily than with other writers, is apt to cause.[2] The point of expressing it here is to repeat and enforce my implied warning about taking too inflexible a line in thinking of the connection of skepticism with tragedy: There is no antecedent limit on the form of representation the response to skepticism may take, in this case a response to its refusal of the world in disgust, and the consequent opening of the question whether the disgust or the refusal comes first.

It was upon exiting (so I thought) from the path of reading through *The Winter's Tale* that I felt the idea of Shakespearean tragedy as interpretations of skepticism had reached a clearing at which consolidation might prove worth while, a turning at which some regrouping is called for. The interpretation of skepticism in *The Winter's Tale* questions the universality or radicalness of skepticism altogether.

This possibility had been for me a recurrent, but unpresentable, premonition. Like Othello, Leontes obeys the structure of skepticism expressed as a form of insane jealousy; but whereas Othello's skeptical astonishment, or nightmare, is represented as a horror of feminine sexuality, Leontes' state is represented as the torturing sense that his children are not his. Now, nothing could more painfully be clear in this play than that this openness to doubt over the provenance of his children is not shared by his wife Hermione, that on the contrary this openness expresses his most extreme isolation from this woman with whom his existence has been shared; it is internal to the doubt that it is taken *against* the wife, the mother. The tuition in this observation seems blatant enough once it is voiced, but I resisted saying it, kept it a premonition, as if for the pleasure of continuing to scare myself with it, even for a while after getting clear of the play. Because the premonition or suggestion threatens the insight I had found and refound so guiding for two decades in

---

[2] Derangement: And yet when on a long walk I described this fantasy of advancement to Marc Shell, he was for a moment startled (I thought) but then adduced theories of the Sphinx's embrace of her victims, and then drew with a twig on the ground a diagram of Oedipus's approach to her – matters that I have not yet followed out for myself. But he has followed them out, surely not just for himself, in an extended essay on *Hamlet*, the manuscript of which he sent to me in the spring of 1986, that continues the work he had broached in his commentary on *Measure for Measure*, entitled *The End of Kinship*, forthcoming from Stanford University Press.

pondering human finitude, that human language is inherently open to the repudiation of itself. The premonition or suggestion or tuition of the play of Leontes' opposition to his wife is – or seems to be, within the initial resistance to any such tuition – that skepticism is a male business; and accordingly that the passion for knowledge as such, so far as it is motivated in skepticism (hence in a certain strain of modern philosophy as such, since Descartes and Hume and Kant), is inflected by gender difference, that the economy of knowing is different for men and for women. (Is this news?)

Then are we to conclude that the issue of skepticism does not arise for women? (I do not want this question now to expose the apparently more general question whether philosophy as such arises for women. I note merely that the logic of this further question seems just to repeat certain obvious opening moves in gender dispute as such. For example: If philosophy does not arise for women then which term suffers, women or philosophy; which is worse off? Or again: If you perceive that philosophy does not arise for women this shows just that you do not recognize all the forms in which philosophy can arise. The more specific issue of skepticism allows the postponement of, I hope the better preparation for, these questions.) But I know some women for whom I do not doubt that the skeptical issue does arise. One might here speak not of men and women but of the masculine and feminine aspects of human character generally, and explain the instability of the appeal of skepticism, and variation of its distribution, as meaning that the masculine side of human character doubts while, or doubts exactly what, the feminine side assures (the relative strength of the sides, and of the struggle between them, may then vary in their distributions). Something of this sort may at some stage become irresistible; but here it seems defensive, evasive. A conclusion clearly called for from *The Winter's Tale* is that, *so far as* skepticism is representable as the doubt whether your children are yours, skepticism is not a feminine business.

Many directions are thereby opened. It may be that skepticism on the feminine side is representable as doubt over one's relation to an object other than a child, say a woman's doubt over the identity of the father of her child. (Here I am thinking particularly of Kleist's tale "The Marquise of O." I do not mean to skip the speculation whether or where skepticism is related to doubts about the identity of one's own parents. But this speculation does not on the face of it invoke gender discrimination, either on the part of the child in doubt or with respect to the parent under doubt. Work is to be done, and a place to begin is with tales in which one parent is notably and suspiciously absent, a mother in *Lear* and *The Tempest,* a father in *Hamlet* and *Coriolanus.*) Then the issue becomes whether the economy of the representation of the question of the father of the child is the same as that of the representation of the question of the doubt and denial of the child. "Economy" here takes up what I call the stake in skepticism, its presentation of the collapse of a "best case" of knowledge.

Again, skepticism on the feminine side might bring into focus not, or not only, a different object but a different passion. And different not as doubt is different from jealousy – these still share the sign of negation – but differently as negative differs from positive. Take the origin of skepticism as an intimation of, in Kant's concept, human conditionedness. Then what philosophy calls skeptical doubt is a drive to reach the unconditioned. Philosophy may think of the unconditioned, the inexplicable, or limit of the explicable, as the "given." Empirical philosophy will think of it as empirically given, say sensuously given; rational philosophy will think of it as the givenness of reason. Ordinary language philosophy seems, intuitively, linked with certain recent developments of French thought – I am thinking mostly of Lacan and of Derrida – in conceiving of the given as language. Wittgenstein explicitly identifies the given as "forms of life" (*Philosophical Investigations* [Macmillan, 1958], p. 226), but I find that is not different: The human form of life is the life of language. (This is obscure, and I do not know that it is elsewhere said. One might think of it, after Kant, as life not only in accordance with rules but in accordance with the concept of rules, a fate pertaining only to the human, not to the bestial or to the angelic. But then Wittgenstein famously contests philosophy's understanding of "accordance with rules.") Then a feminine passion toward the unconditioned, construed as a drive toward the given, may be representable not as doubt but instead as love. And what masculine philosophy knows as skepticism feminine philosophy will know as fanaticism. Fanaticism is explicitly one of Kant's names for a distorted expectation of reason, one form taken by the desire to refuse human limitation, the limitation of finitude; hence it is exactly measurable with skepticism. This affinity is what permits me to describe Leontes as a portrait of the skeptic as fanatic.

The idea of the fanaticism of unconditioned or hyperbolic love as a contrary face of the skepticism of unconditioned or hyperbolic doubt – skepticism under a reverse sign – takes me to some concluding thoughts about *Antony and Cleopatra*. In sketching my present access to this play, in suggesting from it a certain new light in which to consider the plays to which I have devoted the essays collected here, I mean to give new earnest that the work of these essays is provisional, continuable.

I have sometimes hinted that I see the concluding moments of *Antony and Cleopatra* as matching those of *The Winter's Tale* in presenting a new ceremony (or new sacrament) of marriage. Before now going on to follow this hint I owe it to the pleasure and the instruction the study of film has been for me to say that it is because of the idea of remarriage in the great Hollywood comedies of the period of the advent of talkies that I came to think of the conclusion of *The Winter's Tale* as a vision of (re)marriage, of the bonding of marriage as the willingness for remarriage (hence contrariwise, to see *The Winter's Tale* as a source of those comedies). This is the thought of *Pursuits of Happiness: The Hollywood Comedy of Remarriage* (Harvard University Press, 1981).

It is, I assume, the sense that Cleopatra's concluding ecstatic transcendence may be effective, that is, may effect her marriage with Antony – a sense at any rate that marriage itself is here under the pressure of no less radical a rethinking than it is in *The Winter's Tale* – that drives admirers of this play past responding to its events as simply tragic. Its detractors, for whom the issue of effective transcendence is settled, in the negative, take (or took? but I assume they still exist) Antony as seduced and abandoned by a sorceress; for them the effect of the play does not reach the tragic but stalls at the pathetic, a story not of the achievement and costs of lucidity but of the deserts of delusion. What is at stake in the effect, as in the case of *The Winter's Tale,* is the state of our participation in this ceremony of theater, a participation I claim in the essay on *Coriolanus* as well as in that of *The Winter's Tale,* that shows the Shakespearean corpus as in competition with religion. I suppose this is why the idea of Shakespeare as producing "secular scripture" does not quite satisfy me. Thoreau in *Walden* produced a scripture. Whether or not it is useful to call it post–Judeo-Christian, it is surely a testament of no known religion. Yet to call it "secular" might leave out its aspiration, and achievement, of some mode of transcendence, the

Introduction

competition with – Thoreau's concept for competition is that of revising – what we have known as religion. Besides, in a secular age, Scripture itself is apt to be no more than secular, say a work of literature.

What has made the invention or reinvention of marriage necessary? When I can motivate that question with sufficient philosophical perspicuousness, it should become the question What has caused the radicalization of the threat of skepticism, such that a ceremony of single intimacy is what we have to oppose to the threatened withdrawal of the world – of the realms of the natural, the social, the political, the religious?

The expression "withdrawal of the world" promises the following of various paths into and out of the collapse of the "best case" in the skeptical interrogation: the sense, as in the case of Descartes's wax or of C. I. Lewis's apple, that "if I cannot know this then I cannot know anything"; and the sense that here the object stands for, enacts the position of, the world as such; and that this elicits, as in some metaphysical parody, the animism (and loss of animism) of the world; and that these paths presume that the best case of acknowledging another mind works itself out similarly to and hence differently from the best case of knowing a material object. Such are the itineraries of *The Claim of Reason*. In these introductory remarks I am less traveling these paths than staying with aerial views of them. The remarks are meant to indicate why I so much as get the idea that a map of the territory of skepticism provides, or is, a map of Shakespearean regions, leaving open the extent to which maps of such regions, to be discovered within the region, are themselves among the treasures of the region.

In Shakespeare's measures of the withdrawal of the world we are offered a picture of, let me say, the privatization of the world, a picture of the repudiation of assured significance, repudiation of the capacity to improvise common significance, of the capacity of individual human passion and encounter to bear cosmic insignia. The tragic and the pathetic beckon one another. "Is this the promised end? Or image of that horror?" (Is *this*? This play. Now.) "To be or not to be." "A tale told by an idiot." "Are you fast married?" "Look down and see what death is doing." "Then must you find out new heaven, new earth." After such words, in their occasions, there is no standing ground of redemption. Nothing but the ability to be spoken for by these words, to meet upon them, will weigh

19

in the balance against these visions of groundlessness. Nothing without, perhaps nothing within, Shakespeare's words could discover the power to withstand the power Shakespeare's words release. Is this, since then, the demand we place, to greater or lesser extents, on all writing we care about seriously?

To indicate the stakes I see at play in *Antony and Cleopatra* I wish to take the play, to begin with, uncontroversially. (I owe to a reading some years ago of Janet Adelman's superb book on *Antony and Cleopatra,* entitled *The Common Liar* [Yale University Press, 1973], my sense of a way into the play, and the sense that I would not have earned my say about skepticism in Shakespeare without taking the issue to that play.) It is not controversial to conceive the play as belonging as much with Shakespeare's histories as with his tragedies; and, since it is a Roman play, to sense in it a freedom of speculation not quite available in the English histories, where a particular care is required in handling the historical events and in suggesting their pertinence, as precedent or parable, for contemporary events. And not controversial, I believe, to find for the play a setting of world catastrophe. (The editor of the first Arden edition of the play, R. H. Case, in 1906, accepts the idea of world catastrophe as from Georg Brandes; the later Arden editor, M. R. Ridley, in 1954, does not quarrel with it; Frank Kermode, in the Riverside Shakespeare of 1974, cites the idea as familiar and specifically attributes it to Bradley.) And I suppose I am counting as well on a sense in the play's conclusion of some aspiration and achievement so powerful as to align the play with Shakespearean romance. What is, or should be, controversial thereupon arises in these terms: What is history in this play? What world is experiencing catastrophe? What is Rome? To what may we aspire?

If this play is Shakespearean history, then the events of its Rome must form some precedent and parable of the events of the contemporary world – Shakespeare's world, I mean, but I assume it is the beginning of ours. But this means that our world is perceived as undergoing, not to say experiencing, catastrophe. What could this be? Something about the succession or the passing of Elizabeth, or about her predecessors or her successor? These events seem, if not the wrong size, a poor shape for the events between Antony and Caesar and Cleopatra. But this depends on what we take these events for. The catastrophe I anticipate, controversially, is of course the event or advent of skepticism, conceived now as precipitating

Introduction

not alone a structure each individual is driven by, or resists, but as
incorporating a public history in the modern period, in principle
awaiting a historical explanation for its specific onset in, say,
Shakespeare and Descartes. Such a history will doubtless include
the matter of the rise of the new science; the consequent and precedent attenuation or displacement of God; the attenuation of the
concept of Divine Right; the preparation for the demand for political
legitimation by individual consent – call this the exaction of a personal willingness to be governed in common, as if one is becoming
responsible for the political world, unless one abdicates. Hegel says
that with the birth of Christianity a new subjectivity enters the
world. I want to say that with the birth of skepticism, hence of
modern philosophy, a new intimacy, or wish for it, enters the world;
call it privacy shared (not shared with the public, but from it). I
suppose this is registered, among other places, in the history of
marriage, in the shift from politically arranged to romantically de-
sired marriage. Here is a reasonable opening way to consider what
is enacted in *Antony and Cleopatra* in the shift from Rome to Egypt.
To consider it simply a shift from political honor to romantic passion
leaves out the erotic of Rome (importantly in the domination between males) and the political in Egypt (in the equality, or, say,
role reversals, between lovers).

But even supposing for a moment that such things can add up
to world catastrophe, what has it to do with Shakespeare's Rome,
I mean his Roman world? What I know of (what I take to be) this
Rome I learned from the thinking that enters into my essay on
Coriolanus. There I found Rome haunted by the event of Christianity, as if it is a place between old and new, not knowing whether
this event, or advent, has or has not yet happened. Continuing this
feeling into *Antony and Cleopatra,* we are given, so it strikes me,
not a picture of the preparation for Christianity (such is, I gather,
the usual interpretation of Caesar's prediction and promise that "the
time of universal peace is near" [IV, vi, 4]), but a picture of Christianity's presence, such as it is, abstract as it may be (the picture
and the presence). These will not be just different pictures, if the
idea is that Christianity is something in its very presence that is to
be expected, that exists only in expectation, say in faith. Then the
absence or refusal of Christianity is a constant possibility of its offer
or presence. In a play about, and of, the subjection to mood, it
may appear that faith itself is no more than a mood. Then there is

21

no religious faith. And then what we fail to know is not whether Christianity is present or future, but whether it is past, gone, whether the present state of Christianity is such that expectation in it is lost. The time of universal peace is near – but if this is *our* peace, and it remains a Roman peace, it is not the (nearly imagined, the ironically, maddeningly near) peace of heaven. That peace will have not happened, its time may be near as always just gone, ungrasped. I do not mean to deny Frank Kermode's finely perceived and placed description of Octavius as *"fortunatus,* the man of destiny; the future lies with him." I might indeed put my further thought as taking Shakespeare's reading of these famous events to contest the idea that Rome prepared for and will accede to Christianity, to suggest rather that the *final* victory may also be Caesar's – to pry open the issue whether the death of Antony (whoever that is) prepares the way for Christ (whatever that is) or prepares the way to contain and overcome Christ. If this is still Shakespeare's issue then it is still ours. And if this issue is the catastrophe or crisis before the Western world posed by the play, it is evidently not confined to a crisis in the authority of knowledge represented in skepticism; but then I do not think that the crisis of skepticism is confined. And if one feels that the catastrophe must be a function of the succession of Stuart over Tudor then this might name not a crisis within politics but a crisis of the succession of politics over religion. And even this – as a weird parable of that historical present derived from the map of *Antony and Cleopatra* conceived as a history play – is partial, confined, omitting nothing less than the theme of love.

Mostly these abstractions on my part arise from a dissatisfaction with the abstractions this play already causes. For example, it is said that Shakespeare divides the world of *Antony and Cleopatra* between the realms of the political and of the erotic, or between war and love. Of course this is not wrong, but it slights the way in which in the play love takes, for example, the form of war and war the form of love, slights the ways these events go beyond a Roman, public understanding of the conflict of honor and desire, or of public and private life, and propose a more private, let us say Christian, understanding of rendering unto Caesar the things that are Caesar's and unto love the things that are love's.

Love or God, it turns out that the problem is not known to be solvable. Antony's story is of love from beginning to end. Plutarch describes him, in an early paragraph of his biography, as "given to love":

> Furthermore, things that seems intollerable to other men, as to boast commonly, to jeast with one or other, to drinke like a good fellow with every body, to sit with the souldiers when they dine, and to eate and drinke with them souldier-like: it is incredible what wonderful love it wanne him amongest them. And furthermore, being given to love: that made him the more desired, and by that means he brought many to love him. For he would further every mans love, and also would not be angry that men should merily tell him of those he loved.

And Cleopatra's story is of contest and legitimacy from beginning to end. Antony's problem in its outer face is to combine desire (he sometimes calls it pleasure) and honor; but its inner face is to relate desire and marriage (whatever that is), the humbler problem the rest of us have also had occasion to become familiar with in recent centuries. What precipitates his departure from Cleopatra, after many false attempts, say ambivalences, is the news that his wife Fulvia is dead, news that he and Enobarbus and that he and Cleopatra hammer home to one another:

> ANT. Fulvia is dead.
> ENO. Sir?
> ANT. Fulvia is dead.
> ENO. Fulvia?
> ANT. Dead.
> . . . .
> ANT. My more particular . . . is Fulvia's death.
> CLEO. . . . Can Fulvia die?
> ANT. She's dead, my queen.
> CLEO. . . . Now, I see, I see,
>   In Fulvia's death, how mine receiv'd shall be.

And Antony will return to Cleopatra only when he is once again safely married – conveniently arranged as a political maneuver, hence as if without erotic significance. With Fulvia dead the way to Cleopatra is not for him cleared but clouded and closed; since no longer

Disowning Knowledge

externally prohibited (which he knows how to overcome), it becomes internally so. His political and military honor he finds it reasonably easy to protect when he feels it jeopardized.

And, although professors seem to find otherwise, it does not appear from Shakespeare's account that Antony's generalship is impaired. For all the warnings to him about his fighting at sea, and for all the desertions of small kings, Antony was right to believe his final battles militarily winnable. He would have prevailed at Actium, except that without Cleopatra to see it there were no victory, nothing remarkable. And what defeated him at Alexandria was indeed love, not however love prevailing over his honor or prowess but the opposed soldiers' love of one another. It is hard to say the world would have been better off if the soldiers had vanquished their feeling for one another in favor of their general's battle. It was Caesar who as a military, or rather managerial, strategy had former friends placed in the front ranks where they would see and be seen; a manipulation not of arms but of love. Next time some Caesar may manipulate these positions otherwise, not through affection to effect peace, but through disaffection to cause war. Nor has Antony's position been surmounted by the world that has passed him by, but made general, democratized. We shall all inherit the passing, the withdrawal of the world; all are "lated in the world." It is up to each to interpret whether this means that it is we who are tardy or the world, in whose trust we are disappointed, disaffected; the choice appears as one between nostalgia and revenge. I say democratized, and I think of Antony's initial presentation of the mutual love of Antony and Cleopatra, pitching it against kingdoms ("Let Rome in Tiber melt" [I, i, 33]); and now when I hear him cry, "The world to weet / We stand up peerless" (I, i, 38–9), I do not (simply) hear the claim to have no equal, but the claim that there are no peers, no separate class, the claim accordingly to be first among equals, first because the first to put mutual love first, before kingdoms, "the nobleness of life" before the nobleness of birth and rank, which belong to the Roman nobleness of death.

Besides the withdrawal of Antony from Cleopatra shown in *Antony and Cleopatra,* the play shows one and describes two further mysterious, or, say, mythical, scenes of withdrawal from Antony, scenes that shape my sense of the play as of the withdrawal of the world (from Antony) – that of Hercules from Antony as his precedent and guardian spirit, and those from battle, Cleopatra from the engagement at Actium, the soldiers from that at Alexandria. Antony interprets the scenes of military desertion as betrayals, on Cleopatra's part, but he is both times fairly quickly talked out of this idea, as if he never really believes it. Then what does he believe? Somehow, surely, that his love has been betrayed, but somehow not by anyone, and not to anyone, but as if the investment of his love in the world is no longer returned, or returnable, on the same scale as it was meant, as if love now matters less than it should, to the world and to him. Everything known to him as the world recedes; call it Rome and call it Egypt. The play offers no explanation for this, for, let me say, the shrinking of the world, from him, from itself. What explanation could there be? The recession of the world is this play's interpretation of what I have called the truth of skepticism, that the human habitation of the world is not assured in what philosophy calls knowledge. (Again I intervene to express my puzzlement over the way, or the place to which, to address this question. Certainly no one could accept it who feels that the events of the play are pretty well explained by the personal faults of Antony and of Cleopatra or by the public faults of Rome and of Egypt. All surely *have* impressive faults.)

The soldiers think they hear Hercules leaving Antony, "whom Antony loved" (IV, iii, 15), and though there is some question for them whether the sign is good or is bad, their sense is ominous. Being soldiers they feel the change in their godlike commander as a loss of power. But we are free to wonder whether spirits or half-gods leave except on the appearance or invocation of a greater god. Does Antony have an interpretation of the hidden music in the night, the pervasive, wandering sounds of desire and rumor? If he does it will be shown in the preceding scene, his invitation to supper that last night with his "servants" where he tells them, "I look on you / As one that takes his leave" (IV, ii, 28–9). He denies, when Enobarbus shows that his manner and words are discomfiting them, that he meant anything but comfort to them; and he says he means to lead them to where he expects "victorious life" rather than "death and honor." It is all exactly as mysterious as a last supper in which a death is announced through which hyperbolic victory is to be expected in the place of death, and in the expectation of a transformed reappearance. Cleopatra asks Enobarbus, "What does he mean?" and receives no answer, save from within Enobarbus's now tortured sensibility, for Enobarbus replies only, "To make his followers weep" – but of course we already know that he is looking for some way to leave an Antony who has become incomprehensible.

Antony's own incomprehension of what is happening to the world he still represents is shown in his persisting in looking for an explanation. When he gives up ideas of Cleopatra's betrayal and of his own dishonor, he is intellectually and spiritually finished. He cannot do the thing of forgoing explanation and letting his powers of representation represent the suffering of human contradiction, in a world in which there is no solution to the human contradictions of honor and desire, giving and receiving, plenitude and lack, liberality and greed, publicness and privacy. How can a hero represent the recession of heroism into the conduct of ordinary life, exemplify the fact that we are now without universal example, on our own, assuming ourselves, from each of whom the world is equally, peerlessly, withdrawn? (It is the fact I call living one's skepticism, or living the threat of skepticism.) Cleopatra does, I find, manage a representation of this sort.

(I pause, before concluding on her note, to make explicit my unwillingness either to say or to leave unsaid Antony's figuring of the figure of Christ. I know that what I have said about Coriolanus is pressing me here, that he is in some competition with Christ, as one may say Rome was; but Antony in his narcissistic intimacies seems even less plausibly to invoke Christ than Coriolanus with his narcissistic distances. If one is caught by the self-presentation in the anticipated scene of supper; and by Antony's task as one of standing for, as against Caesar, something Antony thinks of as an incomparable love; and by Enobarbus as moving from the imagination of the supper to a place in which he is imagined as denying Antony [ANT: "Who's gone this morning?" SOLDIER: "Who? / One ever near thee: call for Enobarbus, / He shall not hear thee, or from Caesar's camp / Say 'I am none of thine' " (IV, v)]; and by Antony's thereupon sending Enobarbus's treasure after him [the soldier who tells him this also tells him, "Your emperor / Continues still a Jove" (IV, vi)], as if rewarding him for playing a part he has assigned to him, as if he is still serving Antony in betraying him; and by the swift death of Enobarbus from himself, feeling himself Judas [by now I hear this allusion in his prayer for death "That life . . . / May hang no longer on me" (IV, ix)] – caught so, one might think of Antony as a parody of Christ. Then that would mean thinking – taking the play's "history" as an interpretation of the "present" world – that the human race has become a parody of what we knew, might know, as the human; that human words will at any time parody human meaning. [But who are *we* to say so?] I make this explicit briefly, in closing, for two reasons. First, to call attention again to the moment, recalled near the close of *The Claim of Reason,* of Hegel's interpretation of Christianity as the new form of civilization that gives expression to the infinite right of subjective freedom, "the right of the subject's particularity, his right to be satisfied," recalled in order to release a fantasy of "the vanishing of the human," one that links the opposed fates of skepticism and romanticism. In these terms the speculation of *Antony and Cleopatra* is whether anything short of a new shift of civilization will "satisfy" our yet again increased subjectivity. I have said that the play's history is to be taken as of events within Christianity, as in effect stating that something now happening to Christianity, after its advent, is as momentous as that advent itself. One may of course take this as a reaction to the rise of Protestantism. But I am also taking it as the speculation that satisfaction is no longer imaginable within what we understand as religion, that the increasing velocity of the split between subjectivity and objectivity, or between the private and the presentable, no longer permits the common imagination of a significant conclusion. Second, I make explicit the figure of Antony as shadowing that of Christ in order to note that this relation in Shakespeare pertains to his method as well as to his matter; I mean pertains to his use of "sources," a use specified in his source Plutarch as recognizing lives from different cultures as "parallel." I seem to see Shakespeare's projection of Antony, as well as of Coriolanus, as saying: In Christendom there is really only one life which ours are fundamentally to be thought of as paralleling [or repeating, or imitating], or failing to, or, say, mocking; and then as questioning whether we can any longer bear up under the parallel of Christ, the consideration of our lives under the concepts of pride, ingratitude, suffering, betrayal, and redemption [from outside]. Being what we call Shakespeare's, his texts will at the same time consider what constitutes the "parallel" between [human] lives. Take, for example, the fact that the place at which Plutarch digresses in his life of Antony into an account of Timon of Athens, that is, into his account of Antony's taking upon himself the parallel to Timon – the expression of his sense of the world's ingratitude to his liberality and of the consequent invitation to misanthropy [an essential further link as well with Coriolanus] – this precise place is occupied instead in Shakespeare's recounting by the scene of Antony's heart-breaking, death-dealing magnificence in response to Enobarbus's leaving him. It is to be considered whether and how "occupied instead" makes sense. It is given sense if we take the Shakespearean corpus as the place in which each life may inflect any, all as perpetual others, each axiomatically at an unbreachable distance, constantly different; at any crossroads, say any transverse, inviting transfer of angle, transference of perspective.)

I said I imagine Cleopatra as managing to represent something like the recession of her peerlessness into the ordinariness or commonness of what has become of the human chance, to become created as "No more but e'en a woman" (IV, xv, 72). I put this together with her answering, I mean responding to, Antony's sense of the world's withdrawal, and her reinvention of marriage. I have already claimed this closing as a wedding. It is hallucinated, if you like; more than half mad. But if one thinks so it becomes the more urgent to think what this betokens about our presence at this scene of transfiguration, or transferred impersonation, that is, our attendance to this theater. I propose to do little more now than list certain elements of concentric, or, say, parallel, representations in play.

My guiding (in)tuition is that the invention of marriage *is* the (is Cleopatra's, whoever that is) response to Antony's abandonment; it is a return of the world through the gift of herself, by becoming, presenting herself as, whatever constitutes the world. She is herself her dowry, nothing less than a woman, one who will successively (and then simultaneously, as in fugue procedure; it may seem her infinite variety) present herself as a queen, a goddess, an actress, a lover, a mother, a nurse, a bride. So the ceremonies she invokes will move from, for example, coronation to religion to theater to marriage to revels to funeral, or from throne to altar to stage to bed to cradle to crypt. – Present herself to whom? Well, that is my present question. (Of new consents, new violations.)

It is my view that no one knows from outside whether a marriage exists (plighting a troth is not just making a promise), whether the gift is accepted, a legitimate bond conferred. No play could demonstrate this room for question with greater thoroughness or specificity than *Antony and Cleopatra*. No greater thoroughness, since each of the concluding ceremonies epitomizes the other; one is not in effect unless all are. No greater specificity, since our task is exactly to determine our relation to the events specifically before us (whether I am, for example, in relation to them as subject, suppliant, audience, lover, child, husband, or specifically not, specifically absent). It is definitive of the work of this theater to demonstrate that such specifications and doubts are our work (as parallel others, opposed to those that face us, stage us); that is to say, it is the work of this theater to present itself as an instance of the ceremonies and institutions toward which our relation is in doubt, exists in doubt, is unknowable from outside; one whose successful taking, or receiving, our lives, in some sense our immortality, depends upon, as Cleopatra's does.

Some might say of what I am calling unknowableness from outside that this marks a juncture that is undecidable. In this context such a description sounds Calvinistic, like making our election to heaven in fact, from our position, unfathomable. "Unknowable from outside" in my work is a form of words derivative of the skeptical threat. What skepticism threatens is precisely irretrievable outsideness, an uncrossable line, a position from which it is *obvious* (without argument) that the world is unknowable. What does "threaten" mean? Not that skepticism has in its possession a given place in which to confine and isolate us, but that it is a power that all who possess language possess and may desire: to dissociate oneself, excommunicate oneself from the community in whose agreement, mutual attunement, words exist. My work begins with philosophical defenses of the procedures of ordinary language philosophy, of appeals to the ordinariness of our attunements in words as responses to the skeptical threat; this is the burden of the first two parts of *The Claim of Reason*. In recent years I have identified what philosophy thus calls the ordinary or everyday with what in literature is thematized as the domestic, or marriage; and hence I look for the cloaking of skepticism in literature as what attacks the domestic, namely in what forms tragedy and melodrama. In the present introduction I have been hoping to glance back at that set of turns in order to follow them on, to suggest that the paradox of marriage (two becoming one) is the paradox of the ordinary (the union of public and private), in order to give a sense of why Cleopatra's designs on heaven, her quest for transcendence, takes the direction of a quest to become "no more but e'en a woman," which she specifically images as doing "the meanest chares," that is, as accepting the repetitiveness of the mundane, the ordinary. If one imagines that these routines must be subservient that is perhaps because one is not imagining what the routines are of an empress, a goddess, an actress, a lover. . .

So my use of the phrase "from outside," while it is produced in response to the skeptical threat in me, from me, so to my refusal of exemption from it (can one refuse what is in any case not at one's disposal?), is not meant to record my resignation to the skeptical conclusion, say that we are irretrievably barred outside (we may be irretrievably barred, period). Irretrievable outsideness and insideness give way to the acceptance of a repetition that includes endless specific succumbings to the conditions of skepticism and endless specific recoveries from it, endless as a circle, as a serpent swallowing itself. In Wittgenstein both the succumbing and the recovery are the work of what you might call philosophy. Until the passing of skepticism there is no *better* alternative for the mind, the human form of life, than procedures of philosophy that wish to end philosophy.

Since there is no living human position immune to the threat of outsideness, it must occur both in Antony and in Caesar. In Antony the threat is glamorized; in Caesar it is organized and denied. Caesar has violently occupied the world, but that is not the same as dwelling in it. So-called solutions to skepticism would be such occupations. I take Caesar's prophecy of the time of universal peace as the repetitive cry of peace that marks the false prophet. I do not blame him for this.

Now take, for a parting line of speculation, from among Cleopatra's self-presentations, her presenting of herself as an actress, an inhabitant of the realm (the empress of the empire, the child of the process) of theater, since *this* seems to be our literal business with the work I am calling Shakespeare's. (I say seems. Of course I share the temptation to idolatry of Shakespeare and would wish just to say something like: If this work does not work as theater it cannot work as anything else either, or as everything else. But here I am asking what "working as theater" means in this theater, what the conditions for it are [were]; asking it, needless to say, because I find that the play is asking it.) Cleopatra's specification of her consciousness of herself as actress shows Shakespeare at I imagine his most daring in his always daring us to become conscious of his theater: ". . . and I shall see / Some squeaking Cleopatra boy my greatness / In the posture of a whore" (V, ii, 218–20) – daring us to see the boy here and now squeaking *this* Cleopatra, in *that* line, to challenge us to ask and specify in what (other) position she is here and now presented, presents herself.

To see the theatricality of the boy in the woman would by now have become one of the tricks of self-reference that are the stock-in-trade of modernizers. Shakespeare's modernist temper uses that dare to show, and allows us to choose not to see, the theatricality of the woman, Cleopatra's theater; to show her sense that in playing her last in Egypt, in refusing to be cast as "an Egyptian puppet [to] be shown / In Rome" (V, ii, 207–8) she is not avoiding her theatricalization – her story will publicly be burlesqued and debased in Rome with or without her – but rather producing, as if in competition, her own theater, womaning herself, queening, divining, childing, mothering, nursing, enacting, creating herself. The return of the world after its abandonment of Antony (the "solution" to the skeptical state) has required the theatricalization of the world. It is to be *presented* to him.

How? How to Antony at any time, and how at all if he is gone? Now we have to ask what it is, as represented within their private passion for one another, he asks of Cleopatra and that she grants, of such a character that it represents the existence of a world for him and his existence in it, after all. (A path leads back from here to my description of Othello as wanting Desdemona to be the whole world to him. Neither of them understands him.) To this question an obvious answer is that he asks her satisfaction by him, the totality of it, and she, if she chooses, may convince him of it, endow him with it, show it, acknowledge it, consent. Here is the pertinence of Cleopatra's presentation of orgasm, staking the effect of her total theater, her transcendence, on that outcome ("Husband, I come" [V, ii, 286]).

Shakespeare can have given no more direct dare to us than this dare to bail out of the experience of one of his conclusions. The Clown in this same play is an equal dare and I suppose a more famous one; a sort of stage manager, with his props of a basket of figs and his worm and his prose; holding the span between the sublime and the ridiculous in a signature Shakespearean space, maintaining the common prose that falls from and rises to poetry. But we are, I believe, by now very sophisticated in accepting this span of theater. It is harder to stay in the experience when, as in

Cleopatra's declaring of orgasm (of its aspiration), the ridiculous and the sublime, or the common and the ecstatic, seem interfused, or rather interfering. But such, it seems to me, are the risks and stakes in this theater, for her and for us in attendance. Here is this woman (with a boy inside her that she might in another world be) who imagines herself, or is, a queen, a goddess, a world . . . (Or is it the other way around: a queen, a goddess . . . imagining themselves a woman?) And here we are, bystanders outside just now, drawn into a theater and then faced with theater, buying a book and then faced with a text, perhaps imagining ourselves in the presence of, or service of, a woman in the process of transcendence: If there is eternity it is here, now, before a stage, or a page, finite things and others. The interfusion or interference is an image of our tragical–comical–historical–romantical knowledge and risk of transcendence, preposterous challenges of our finitude, but without which, could we do without, we would not know necessity.

I believe I know two kinds of people on this subject: those who bear a tough contempt for the human race, for its pretensions to nobleness while it is trapped by nature; and those who achieve – I crave it – a tender mercy toward the common, poor material of which nobility, if it comes, has to be made, beckoned by freedom. And now I seem to recognize two further types: those who are certain they can always tell the difference between the first two types; and those who are certain there is no worthwhile difference. What is the difference between Cleopatra's anticipation or memory of Antony's "kiss / Which is my heaven to have" (V, ii, 301–2) and words that one imagines would be about the same in what are called drugstore novels; and, for that matter, what is the similarity of both of these with Jerome Kern and Dorothy Fields's "Heaven, I'm in heaven . . . when we're out together dancing cheek to cheek"? (Say the difference lies in the music. What causes the music?) Antony at the opening aspires to the nobleness of life against Rome; but at his close the pale criminal aspires to the Roman nobleness of death. He says he "will be / A bridegroom in my death, and run into't / As to a lover's bed" (IV, xiv, 98–100), but he proves an unsuccessful lover here. Cleopatra completes his aspiration, as elsewhere (to have inspired completion by her, in the face of his incapacity, is Antony's success as a lover) as, as it were, she takes death into her lover's bed; takes it not, I believe, to make death the totality and goal of love but on the contrary to let them live together, not removing death's sting or bite but transfiguring it into "a lover's pinch" (V, ii, 294), which makes it part of life, partner to it in the ordinary repetitions of ecstasy. Here is a further interpretation of orgasm as dying, the common nobleness, conceivably a redemption, of mortality.

Caesar demands to know the "manner" of Cleopatra's death, and is satisfied, or anyway calls it "probable," that she dies of an asp's bite, adding that "her physician tells me / She hath purused conclusions infinite / Of easy ways to die" (V, ii, 352–4). This takes the idea of her "manner" of death to be reducible to what we call the cause of death. But we need not (pretend to) be satisfied so to reduce the way of her death. Caesar and her physician will have their reasons for supposing her researches to have been into "easy ways" to die; but we can allow her capable of her own reasons, as surely Caesar also suspects she is. In particular capable of researching, and demanding, her own death. (I am appealing here to the difficult concept of one's own death as derived in Freud's *Beyond the Pleasure Principle* on the basis of the no less difficult idea of the death instinct. I say the idea of one's own death is derived but I think of it as the psychological basis from which Freud derived the need for or the place of the biological concept. Accordingly I understand Freud's intuition of a "beyond" called for by the Pleasure Principle not as something that would rebuke Cleopatra but as her very teaching, the instruction of her last enactments.)

That Cleopatra's death has a logic is expressed in her invitation:

> Come, thou mortal wretch,
> With thy sharp teeth this knot intrinsicate
> Of life at once untie . . .
>
> (V, ii, 303–5)

The logic is that it is intrinsic to (her, to human) life to be untied, to invite extrication, explication, to have a dénouement, like a story or a proof, and that her life can be told in terms of this "poor venomous fool," which is herself ("the serpent of old Nile" [I, v, 25]); and is Antony (whose kiss, as heaven, she imagines him to "spend" [V, ii, 301]); hence is their union, one she gives birth to and nurses, as well as individually to herself and to Antony, and is herself created by; and is us, invited by her, dared, to assess the form we take to deal her death (assess the "trail," the trace of our disappearance); this fool is all in all, as she is.

In the opening speech of the play, someone listed as "friend to Antony" prepares for Antony's appearance in these words:

> . . . you shall see in him
> The triple pillar of the world transform'd
> Into a strumpet's fool: behold and see.
> (I, i, 11–13)

It is alert to sense transformation in the idea of Antony. It would be casual not to sense transformation in the ideas of "the world," of "a strumpet," of "fool," of "see," and of "transformation." In imagining the scene in Rome in which her greatness is boyed and their "Alexandrian revels" "staged," "present[ed]," Cleopatra sees that "Antony / Shall be brought drunken forth" (V, ii, 217–18). To contest this staging, this beholding, she brings him forth as herself, her child, her lover, her husband, her death-spending life-dealing fool, her cause. The field of contest being her bed, her victory depends on revealing and concealing its victories, so that we have presented, that is represented, "One other gaudy night" (III, xiii, 182). Her death scene is thus an instance of that Shakespearean procedure of "deferred representation" that I characterize at the end of the *Hamlet* essay and that I find variously in the conclusions of *Othello* and *Coriolanus* and *The Winter's Tale*.

So we are forced after all to choose between Cleopatra's version of the relation of Antony and Cleopatra and Rome's version; between her theater, her seduction, and Rome's; between her cosmic narcissism and Caesar's worldly narcissism. "He words me, girls, he words me" (V, ii, 190); Caesar makes her up, to cast in his play. (Shakespeare does not spare himself this identification, as well.) But then again we have to ask why, in wording herself, to contest his word, she paints herself, presents the birth of her play, as in orgasm. (We must at some point even find the heart to figure the extent to which her narcissism, her self-involvement, is being expressed here autoerotically, that what we may academically have called a hallucinated marriage is an autoerotic fantasy.) What has this to do with returning, I mean representing, the lost world as her dowry?

The answer I have depends on taking the existence or occurrence of the woman's satisfaction (the satisfaction of our feminine side?)

as the essential object or event of the skeptical question: Is she satisfied and is the satisfaction directed to me? There is no satisfaction for me (my masculine side) apart from a favorable conclusion here; it is a conclusion that must be conferred, given, not one that I can cause or determine on the basis of my senses. My senses go out; satisfaction happens in my absence, only in it, by it. To elicit this gift, the extreme claim of male activeness, thus requires the man's acceptance of his absolute passiveness.

I have already indicated that Othello is destroyed by the requirement. It was within his play that this line of thought first began for me, specifically in suggesting that the pivot of *Othello's* interpretation of skepticism is Othello's placing of a finite woman in the place made and left by Descartes for God. The next step was the conviction that Leontes' jealousy is a cover for his doubt over whether his children are his, and that this is in turn a cover for doubt whether Hermione's satisfaction is of him, whether it proves or destroys his existence. The present step in this line of thought begins with my linking of the developments of cinema and of psychoanalysis as both originating in the sufferings of women, in particular in the form of a conviction in the woman's unknownness, hence in her existence, and that these developments may therefore be said to form a late stage in the progress of skepticism in the West, that history (assuming there is such thing, or one thing) that begins no later than Descartes and Shakespeare.[3] I assume that a

[3] The linking of psychoanalysis, cinema, and women in the history of skepticism is the principal business of a lecture I called "Psychoanalysis and Cinema: The Melodrama of the Unknown Woman" and delivered in 1985 as the Edith Weigert Lecture in Washington, D.C. It is to appear in a volume edited by Joseph Smith, M.D., under the title *The Images in Our Souls: Cavell, Psychoanalysis, Cinema*, to be published by the Johns Hopkins University Press. In seeking company for the claim of the woman's satisfaction as the final object in representing skepticism, skepticism as a masculine affair, that essay mentions, more hopefully than authoritatively, two texts by Jacques Lacan, "God and the *Jouissance* of the Woman" and "A Love Letter," quoting his remark "I believe in the *jouissance* of the woman in so far as it is something more" as what I call his Credo. The texts are included in a collection of Lacan's writings under the title *Female Sexuality*, translated and with introductions by Juliet Mitchell and Jacqueline Rose.

While I am underground I note a further matter of open speculation. I indicated in passing that certain yarns of the history of skepticism will be spun from the causes and effects of the new science, say in the motions from Copernicus to Newton. It is an inciting fact of our culture that Galileo was born the same year as Shakespeare. I do not claim that Shakespeare is alluding (as well as to Revelation 21:1) to Galileo when he has Antony say to Cleopatra, "Then must you needs find out new heaven, new earth," but I know that I sometimes imagine those words as among other

further stage of this progress might be the loss of the problem altogether, which, according to *The Claim of Reason,* will mean the loss of the idea of the human, hence of the human.

That Shakespeare's intuition of, let me say, the metaphysical importance of Cleopatra's satisfaction should find its tuition in Freud, or Freud's in Shakespeare, is one intimacy between them. I cite another in the essay on *Hamlet,* concerning the cost of the inheritance

things responding to the Galilean fact, so to speak, that there is no distinction between celestial and terrestrial laws of motion. It is a division Cleopatra is in her way also breaching. The double allusion would then give Antony's words to be claiming that for Cleopatra to set this bourn requires a vision of the end of the (old) world as promised in Christianity and as accomplished in science, so that their love interprets, succeeds, both religion and science. I do not claim that Shakespeare had read the major texts presenting the new science, nor knew more about it than he could have picked up in conversation, given his capacity to listen. When Cleopatra says in her initial lines: "I'll set a bourn how far to be belov'd" she is no doubt practicing her art of contention, or perverseness, to which she attributes, or by which she measures, her powers with men. In this spirit she would mean: I'll set a limit on how far you may go in loving me, or how far I'll believe your protestations, but keep them coming. Then Antony's response to her there, invoking new heaven, new earth, suggests an interpretation that her final scene carries further: I'll mark, or remark, the border between heaven and earth, so that it may be crossed, so that heaven and earth will become adjoining, communicating realms.

If there is an Elizabethan world picture, Shakespeare questions it, so shatters it, as surely as the new science did. No "source," no received conception, survives its incorporation into Shakespeare without sea-change. Thomas Kuhn in his lovely early book *The Copernican Revolution* traces the retheologizing of the Newtonian universe. *Antony and Cleopatra* reads to me like the eroticizing of what I just called the Galilean fact, the unity of heaven and earth. Respectable further theologizing of the world has, I gather, ceased. Eroticizing of it, respectable or disreputable, has not. Something like this is what Emerson and Thoreau would have meant in transcendentalizing the world, tracing the significance of things, deriving truth from fact. Then if, as I have claimed, *Antony and Cleopatra* proposes the overcoming of skepticism as a question of the theatricalization of the world, the further question opens as to the affinity of theater, so appropriated, with religion, and as to the competition of theater with science, when science is taken as the solution to (perhaps also as the cause of) skepticism. Here is space for unholy alliances, since then science would have, beyond its struggle with religion, its own cause to fear the revelations of theater. On the endless, and endlessly interesting, persistence of the distrust of theater, see Jonas Barish, *The Anti-Theatrical Prejudice* (University of California Press, 1981).

Speaking of unholy alliances, my sketch of the economy of masculine and feminine positions (as determined by the effort to overcome the skeptical abandonment of and by the world) of course invites the thought that this economy is itself one that women must seek to overcome. This thought raises three immediate questions as continuing from my sketch: (1) Is this overcoming to be seen as itself the end of the skeptical threat or to be seen as a task within the further working out of that threat? (2) Is the task assigned to women or assigned to the feminine, whether in women or in men? (3) Is this overcoming to be understood by continuing the line of Cleopatra's imagination, or by repudiating or circumventing this line?

between generations. Another goes this way. I say that Cleopatra's desire in her conclusion is to present the world, make a present of it, to Antony; to return or represent it by presenting, finding out new ways of representing, her satisfaction by him; and I find that this requires the theatricalization of the world, hence her enacting of it. Now the enacting, the theatricalization, of one's existence, in particular of one's erotic history, is what Freud and Breuer discovered in hysteria, the first of the forms in which the reality of the psychic was proven to them, by them. And in *The Interpretation of Dreams,* in at the last accounting for the origin of the dream work, Freud proposes to "[carry] over to dreams the conclusions we have been led to by hysteria." This means among other things that Freud's question about the work of dreaming concerning the limits of representation, the limits on manifesting a wish and its fulfillment, becomes a question about the limits on the expression of desire and its satisfaction, the limits on what can be presented, a question about the work of the theatricalization of human life. That Cleopatra, and one that words her, take this presentation as a task, as the theater work of communication, and take the stakes of this theater to be the proof of the continued existence of the human, of that form of life, that world, is the affinity I see in this play between Shakespeare and Freud.

I end by repeating that this theater is no surer to work, to take, than the marriage it presents is sure to work; that the risks of the ludicrous that Cleopatra runs with us are run by us in lending her sublimity; that Antony's subjection to mood is ours, this theater's. Then doesn't this just mean that to get the good of this work we must court seduction by it? And how can that compete with, interpret, philosophy? I guess the answer will begin in interpretations of seduction, of the fact that we are always already seduced, if we look and listen and want; interpretations of the seduction from seduction in psychoanalysis; of philosophy's own departure from, hence in, seduction – each interpretation no doubt in hopes of some more ennobling, more enabling, seduction, introduction, induction, education. What is the better way out of desire? What do we gain, say, by reduction, by making ourselves unseducible, minions of Caesar? What petty Rome to administer will be our reward? – Our moods, in words of Emerson's, do not believe in each other.

37

2

The Avoidance of Love
A Reading of *King Lear*

A COMMON way to remember the history of writing about Shakespeare is to say that until Bradley's *Shakespearean Tragedy* appeared in 1904, and culminating there, its main tradition had concentrated on Shakespeare's characters, whereas in recent generations emphasis has fallen on general patterns of meaning, systems of image or metaphor or symbol now taking the brunt of significance. Like most intellectual maps, this one is not only crude but fails worst in locating the figures one would like best to reach: Can Coleridge or Bradley really be understood as interested in characters *rather than* in the words of the play; or are the writings of Empson or G. Wilson Knight well used in saying that they are interested in what is happening in the words *rather than* what is happening in the speakers of the words? It is, however, equally easy and unhelpful to say that both ends of the tradition have been interested *both* in characters *and* in their words, first because this suggests that there are two things each end is interested in, whereas both would or should insist that they are interested only in one thing, the plays themselves; second, because there is clearly a shift in emphasis within that tradition, and a way of remarking that shift is to say that it moves away from studies of character into studies of words, and because such a shift raises problems of history and of criticism that ought not to be muffled in handy accommodations.

A full description, let alone explanation, of the history of Shakespearean criticism would be part of a full description of Western cultural history since the Renaissance. Failing that, one can still notice that the simply described shift from character to words is implicated in various more or less primitive theories whose hold on contemporary scholars is yet to be traced. For suppose we ask *why* such a shift has occurred. Immediately this becomes two questions: What has discouraged attention from investigations of character? What, apart from this, has specifically motivated an absorbing attention to words? I think that one reason a critic may shun direct contact with characters is that he or she has been made to believe or assume, by some philosophy or other, that characters are not people, that what can be known about people cannot be known about characters, and in particular that psychology is either not appropriate to the study of these fictional beings or that psychology is the province of psychologists and not to be ventured from the armchairs of literary studies. But is any of this more than the merest assumption; unexamined principles which are part of current academic fashion? For what is the relevant psychology? Of course, to account for the behavior of characters one is going to apply to them predicates like "is in pain," "is ironic," "is jealous," "is thinking of . . ." But does that require psychological expertise? No more than to apply these predicates to one's acquaintances. One reason a critic is drawn to words is, immediately, that attention to characters has often in fact been given apart from attention to the specific words granted them, so it looks as if attention to character is a distraction from the only, or the final, evidence there is for a reading of a literary work, namely the words themselves. But it is then unclear what the words are to be used as evidence for. For a correct interpretation? But what would an interpretation then be of? It often emerges that the evidence provided by the words is to support something called the symbolic structure or the pattern of something or other in the piece. But such concepts are bits of further theories which escape any support the mere presence of words can provide. Moreover, there is more than one procedure which could count as "attending to words themselves." (Just as there is more than one way of expressing "faithfulness to a text.") The New Critics encouraged attention to the ambiguities, patternings, tensions of words; the picture is of a (more or less hidden) structure of which the individual words are parts. Another mode of attention to the particular words themselves is directed to the voice which says them, and through that to the phenomenology of the straits of mind in which only those words said in that order will suffice; here the picture is of a spiritual instant or passage for which only these words discover release, in which they mean deeply not because they mean many things but because they mean one thing completely. This is not necessarily a matter of better or worse but of different modes or needs of poetry.

It seems reasonable to suppose that the success of the New Criticism in the academic study of literature is a function of the way it is *teachable:* You can train someone to read complex poems with sufficient complexity; there is always something to say about them. But it is not clear what would count as training someone to read a lyric. You will have to demonstrate how it rests in the voice, or hauls at it, and you perhaps will not be able to do that without undergoing the spiritual instant or passage for which it discovers release (that is, unable to say what it means without meaning it then and there); and you may or may not be able to do that during a given morning's class, and either eventuality is likely to be inopportune in that place.

The most curious feature of the shift and conflict between character criticism and verbal analysis is that it should have taken place at all. How could any serious critic ever have forgotten that to care about specific characters is to care about the utterly specific words they say when and as they say them; or that we care about the utterly specific words of a play because certain men and women are having to give voice to them? Yet apparently both frequently happen. Evidently what is to be remembered here is difficult to remember, or difficult to do – like attending with utter specificity to the person now before you, or to yourself. It has been common enough to complain of the overinterpretation a critic may be led to, or may have recourse to; the problem, however, is to show us where and why and how to bring an interpretation to a close. (This is no easier than, perhaps no different from, discovering when and how to stop philosophizing. Wittgenstein congratulated himself for having made this possible, saying tht in this discovery philosophy is given peace [*Investigations,* §133].)

My purpose here is not to urge that in reading Shakespeare's plays one put words back into the characters speaking them, and replace characters from our possession back into their words. The point is rather to learn something about what prevents these commendable activities from taking place. It is a matter of learning what it is one uses as data for one's assertions about such works, what kinds of appeal one in fact finds convincing. I should like to add that identical problems arise in considering the phenomenon of ordinary language philosophy: There the problem is also raised of determining the data from which philosophy proceeds and to which it appeals, and specifically the issue is one of placing the words and experiences with which philosophers have always begun in alignment with human beings in particular circumstances who can be imagined to be having those experiences and saying and meaning those words. This is all that "ordinary" in the phrase "ordinary language philosophy" means, or ought to mean. It does not refer to particular words of wide use, nor to particular sorts of people. It reminds us that whatever words are said and meant are said and meant by particular people, and that to understand what they (the words) mean you must understand what they (whoever is using them) mean, and that sometimes people do not see what they mean, that usually they cannot say what they mean, that for various reasons they may not know what they mean, and that when they are forced to recognize this they feel they do not, and perhaps cannot, mean anything, and they are struck dumb. (Here it is worth investigating the fact that the formula "He said . . ." can introduce either indirect discourse or direct quotation. One might feel: Indirect discourse doesn't literally report what someone *said,* it says what someone *meant.* Then why do we say "He said . . ." rather than "He meant . . .", an equally common formula, but used for other purposes? Perhaps the reason is that what is said *is* normally what is meant – if there is to be language. Not more than normally, however, because there are any number of [specific] ways in which and occasions on which one's words do not say what one means. Because the connection between using a word and meaning what it says is not inevitable or automatic, one may wish to call it a matter of convention. But then one must not suppose that it is a convention we would know how to forgo. It is not a matter of convenience or ritual, unless having language is a convenience or unless thinking and speaking are rituals.) If philosophy sometimes looks as if it wishes nothing more than to strike us dumb, then it should not be overlooked that philosophy also claims to know only what an ordinary human being can know, and that we are liable to silence so produced only because we have already spoken, hence thought, hence justified and excused, hence philosophized, and are hence always liable not merely to say more than we know (a favorite worry of modern philosophy) but to speak above the conscience at the back of our words, deaf to our meaning. A philosopher like Austin, it is true, concentrates on examples whose meaning can be brought out by appealing to widely shared, or easily imaginable, circumstances (once he has given directions for imagining them) – circumstances, roughly, that Wittgenstein refers to as one of "our language games." But Wittgenstein is also concerned with forms of words whose meaning cannot be elicited in this way – words we sometimes have it at heart to say but whose meaning is not secured by appealing to the way they are ordinarily (commonly) used, because there is no ordinary use of them, in that sense. It is not, therefore, that I mean something *other* than those words would ordinarily mean, but rather that what they mean, and whether they mean anything, depends solely upon whether I am using them so as to make my meaning. (An instance cited by Wittgenstein is Luther's remark that "faith resides under the left nipple.") In general, Part II of the *Philosophical Investigations* moves into this region of meaning. It is a region habitually occupied by poetry.

King Lear is particularly useful as a source for investigating the question of critical data and for assessing some causes of critical disagreement because there are a number of traditional cruxes in this play for which any critic is likely to feel compelled to provide a solution. Some important ones are these: How are we to understand Lear's motivation in his opening scene? How Cordelia's? Is Gloucester's blinding dramatically justified? What is the relation between the Lear plot and the Gloucester subplot? What happens to the Fool? Why does Edgar delay before revealing himself to his father? Why does Gloucester set out for Dover? Why does France not return with Cordelia? Why must Cordelia die?

In the first half of this essay I offer a reading of the play sticking as continuously to the text as I can – that is, avoiding theorizing about the data I provide for my assertions, appealing to any considerations which, in conscience, convince me of their correctness – in the course of which the traditional cruxes are either answered or altered. Then, in the second half, I ask why it is, if what I say is correct, that critics have failed to see it. This precipitates somewhat extended speculations about the difficulties in the perception of such drama as *King Lear* presents, and I do not expect, even if my reading were accepted, that these speculations will find very immediate assent, nor even very readily be found relevant. But since whatever critical discoveries I can claim to have made hardly result from unheard-of information, full conviction in them awaits a convincing account of what has kept them covered.

I

In a fine paper published a few years ago, Professor Paul Alpers notes the tendency of modern critics to treat metaphors or symbols rather than the characters and actions of Shakespeare's plays as primary data in understanding them, and undertakes to disconfirm a leading interpretation of the symbolic sort which exactly depends upon a neglect, even a denial, of the humanness of the play's characters.[1] If I begin by finding fault with his reading, I put him first to acknowledge my indebtedness to his work. His animus is polemical and in the end this animus betrays him. For he fails to account for the truth to which that leading interpretation is responding, and in his concern to insist that the characters of the play are human beings confronting one another, he fails to characterize them as specific persons. He begins by assembling quotations from several commentators which together compose the view he wishes to correct – the view of the "sight pattern":

> In *King Lear* an unusual amount of imagery drawn from vision and the eyes prompts us to apprehend a symbolism of sight and blindness having its culmination in Gloucester's tragedy. . . . The blinding of Gloucester might well be gratuitous melodrama but for its being imbedded in a field of meanings centered in the concept of *seeing*. This sight pattern relentlessly brings into the play the problem of seeing and what is always implied is that the problem is one of insight. . . . It is commonly recognized that just as Lear finds "reason in madness" so Gloucester learns to "see" in his blindness. . . . The whole play is built on this double paradox.[2]

But when Alpers looks to the text for evidence for this theory he discovers that there is none. Acts of vision and references to eyes are notably present, but their function is not to symbolize moral insight; rather, they insist upon the ordinary, literal uses of eyes:

[1] "*King Lear* and the Theory of the Sight Pattern," in R. Brower and R. Poirier, eds.. *In Defense of Reading* (New York: Dutton, 1963), pp. 133–52.
[2] Alpers gives the references for the elements of his quotation as follows: J. I. M. Stewart, *Character and Motive in Shakespeare* (New York: Longman, Green, 1949), pp. 20–1; R. B. Heilman, *This Great Stage* (Baton Rouge: Louisiana State University Press, 1948), p. 25; L. C. Knights, *Some Shakespearean Themes* (London: Chatto and Windus, 1959), p. 107; *King Lear*, ed. K. Muir (Cambridge: Harvard University Press, 1952, Arden edition), p. lx.

to express feeling, to weep, and to recognize others. Unquestionably there is truth in this. But the evidence for Alpers's view is not perfectly clear and his concepts are not accurately explored in terms of the events of the play. The acts of vision named in the lines he cites are those of giving *looks* and of *staring,* and the function of these acts is exactly *not* to express feeling, or else to express cruel feeling. Why? Because the power of the eyes to see is being used in isolation from their capacity to weep, which seems the most literal use of them to express feeling.

Alpers's dominant insistence upon the third ordinary use of the eyes, their role in recognizing others, counters common readings of the two moments of recognition central to the "sight pattern": Gloucester's recognition of Edgar's innocence and Lear's recognition of Cordelia. "The crucial issue is not insight, but recognition" (Alperts, p. 149): Gloucester is not enabled to "see" because he is blinded, the truth is heaped upon him from Regan's luxuriant cruelty; Cordelia need not be viewed symbolically, the infinite poignance of her reconciliation with Lear is sufficiently accounted for by his literal recognition of her. – But then it becomes incomprehensible why or how these children have *not* been recognized by these parents; they had not become literally invisible. They are in each case banished, disowned, sent out of sight. And the question remains: What makes it possible for them to be *received* again?

In each case, there is a condition necessary in order that the recognition take place: Gloucester and Lear must each first recognize himself, and allow himself to be recognized, revealed to another. In Gloucester, the recognition comes at once, on hearing Regan's news:

> O my follies! Then Edgar was abused.
> Kind Gods, forgive me that, and prosper him!
> > (III, vii, 90–1)

In each of these two lines he puts his recognition of himself first. Lear's self-revelation comes harder, but when it comes it has the same form:

> Do not laugh at me;
> For, as I am a man, I think this lady
> To be my child Cordelia.
> > (IV, vii, 68–70)

He refers to himself three times, then "my child" recognizes her simultaneously with revealing himself (as her father). Self-recognition is, phenomenologically, a form of insight; and it is because of its necessity in recognizing others that critics have felt its presence here.[3]

Lear does not attain his insight until the end of the fourth act, and when he does it is climactic. This suggests that Lear's dominating motivation to this point, from the time things go wrong in the opening scene, is to *avoid being recognized*. The isolation and avoidance of eyes is what the obsessive sight imagery of the play underlines. This is the clue I want to follow first in reading out the play.

If the blinding is unnecessary for Gloucester's true seeing of Edgar, why is Gloucester blinded? Alpers's suggestion, in line with his emphasis on the literal presence of eyes, is that because the eyes are physically the most precious and most vulnerable of human organs, the physical assault on them best dramatizes the human capacity for cruelty. But if the symbolic interpretation seems hysterical, this explanation seems overcasual, and in any case does not follow the words. Critics who have looked for a *meaning* in the blinding have been looking for the right thing. But they have been looking for an aesthetic meaning or justification; looking too high, as it were. It is aesthetically justified (it is "not an irrelevant horror" [Muir, p. lx]) just because it is morally, spiritually justified, in a way which directly relates the eyes to their power to see.

> GLOU. . . . but I shall see
> The winged vengeance overtake such
> children.
> CORN. See't shalt thou never.
>
> (III, vii, 64–6)

---

[3] This of course is not to say that such critics have correctly interpreted this feeling of insight, and it does not touch Alpers's claim that such critics have in particular interpreted "moral insight" as "the perception of moral truths"; nor, finally, does it weaken Alpers's view of such an interpretation as moralizing, hence evading, the significance of (this) tragedy. I am not, that is, regarding Alpers and the critics with whom, on this point, he is at odds, as providing alternative readings of the play, between which I am choosing or adjudicating. Their relation is more complex. Another way of seeing this is to recognize that Alpers does not deny the presence of a controlling "sight pattern" in *King Lear* but that he transforms the significance of this pattern.

And then Cornwall puts out one of Gloucester's eyes. A servant interposes, wounding Cornwall; then Regan stabs the servant from behind, and his dying words, meant to console or establish connection with Gloucester, ironically recall Cornwall to his interrupted work:

> FIRST SERV. O! I am slain. My Lord, you have one eye left
>   To see some mischief on him. Oh!   *Dies.*
> CORN. Lest it see more, prevent it. Out, vile jelly!
>   (III, vii, 80–2)

Of course the idea of punishment by plucking out eyes has been implanted earlier, by Lear and by Goneril and most recently by Gloucester himself, and their suggestions implicate all of them spiritually in Cornwall's deed. But Cornwall himself twice gives the immediate cause of his deed, once for each eye: to prevent Gloucester from seeing, and in particular to prevent him from seeing *him*. That this scene embodies the most open expression of cruelty is true enough; and true that it suggests the limitlessness of cruelty, once it is given its way – that it will find its way to the most precious objects. It is also true that the scene is symbolic, but what it symbolizes is a function of what it means. The physical cruelty symbolizes (or instances) the psychic cruelty which pervades the play; but what this particular act of cruelty means is that cruelty cannot bear to be seen. It literalizes evil's ancient love of darkness.

This relates the blinding to Cornwall's needs; but it is also related to necessities of Gloucester's character. It has an aptness which takes on symbolic value, the horrible aptness of retribution. (It is not merely literary critics who look for meaning in suffering, attempting to rationalize it. Civilizations have always done it, in their myths and laws; we do it in our dreams and fears of vengeance. They learned to do it from gods.) For Gloucester has a fault, not particularly egregious, in fact common as dirt, but in a tragic accumulation in which society disgorges itself upon itself, it shows clearly enough; and I cannot understand his immediate and complete acquiescence in the fate which has befallen him (his acknowledgment of his folly, his acceptance of Edgar's innocence, and his wish for forgiveness all take just twenty syllables) without supposing that it strikes him as a retribution, forcing him to an insight about his life as a whole. Not, however, necessarily a true insight. He has revealed his fault in the opening speeches of the play, in which he tells Kent of his *shame*. (That shame is the subject of those speeches is emphasized by Coleridge; but he concentrates, appropriately enough, on *Edmund's* shame.) He says that now he is "braz'd to it," that is, used to admitting that he has fathered a bastard, and also perhaps carrying the original sense of soldered fast to it. He recognizes the moral claim upon himself, as he says twice, to "acknowledge" his bastard; but all this means to him is that he acknowledge that he has a bastard for a son. He does not acknowledge *him*, as a son or a person, with *his* feelings of illegitimacy and being cast out. *That* is something Gloucester ought to be ashamed of; his shame is itself more shameful than his one piece of licentiousness. This is one of the inconveniences of shame, that it is generally inaccurate, attaches to the wrong thing.

In case these remarks should seem inappropriate in view of the moment at which Shakespeare wrote, and someone wishes at this stage to appeal to the conventions of Elizabethan theater according to which a bastard is an evil character, hence undeserving of the audience's sympathy, and thereby suggest that it is unthinkable that Gloucester should feel anything other than a locker-room embarrassment at what has sprung from him, then I should ask that two points be borne in mind: (1) It is a particular man, call him Shakespeare, we are dealing with, and while it is doubtless true that a knowledge of the conventions he inherited is indispensable to the full understanding of his work, the idea that these conventions supply him with solutions to his artistic purposes, rather than problems or media within which those purposes are worked out, is as sensible as supposing that one has explained why a particular couple have decided to divorce by saying that divorce is a social form. (There are, of course, proper occasions for explanations of that kind; for example, an explanation of why separation is not the same as divorce.) Shakespeare's plays are conventional in the way that their language is grammatical, in the way that a football game satisfies the rules of football: One has to know them to understand what is happening, but consulting them will not tell you who plays or speaks well and who mechanically, nor why a given remark or a particular play was made *here*, nor who won and who lost. You have to know something more for that, and you have to look. (2) At the moment at which *King Lear* was written, Sir Robert Filmer was an adolescent. It is hard not to suppose that when this eldest son and pillar of society wrote his defense of patriarchal society, and consequently of primogeniture, he was talking about something which had been problematic since his youth and something which needed his defense in 1630 because it was by then becoming openly questioned.[4] But this is perfectly clear from Edmund's opening soliloquy. The idea that Shakespeare favored primogeniture, or supposed that only a bastard would question it, is one which must come from a source beyond Shakespeare's words. In that soliloquy Edmund rails equally against his treatment as a bastard and as a younger son – as if to ask why a younger son should be treated like a bastard. Both social institutions seem to him arbitrary and unnatural. And nothing in the play shows him to be wrong – certainly not the behavior of Lear's legitimate older daughters, nor of Regan's lawful husband, nor of legitimate King Lear, who goes through an abdication without abdicating, and whose last legitimate act is to banish love and service from his realm. When Shakespeare writes a revenge tragedy, it is *Hamlet;* and when he presents us with a bastard, legitimacy as a whole is thrown into question.

That Gloucester still feels shame about his son is shown not just by his descriptions of himself, but also by the fact that Edmund "hath been out nine years, and away he shall again" (I, i, 32), and by the fact that Gloucester has to joke about him: Joking is a familiar specific for brazening out shame, calling enlarged attention to the thing you do not want naturally noticed. (Hence the comedian sports disfigurement.) But if the failure to recognize others is a failure to let others recognize you, a fear of what is revealed to them, an avoidance of their eyes, then it is exactly shame which is the cause of his withholding of recognition. (It is not simply his legal treatment that Edmund is railing against.) For shame is the specific discomfort produced by the sense of being looked at; the avoidance of the sight of others is the reflex it produces. Guilt is different; there the reflex is to avoid discovery. As long as no one *knows* what you have done, you are safe; or your conscience will press you to confess it and accept punishment. Under shame, what must be covered up is not your deed, but yourself. It is a more primitive emotion than guilt, as inescapable as the possession of a body, the first object of shame. – Gloucester suffers the same punishment he inflicts: In his respectability, he avoided eyes; when respectability falls away and the disreputable come into power, his eyes are avoided. In the

---

[4] See the introduction by Peter Laslett to his edition of Filmer's *Patriarcha* (Oxford: Blackwell Publisher, 1949).

fear of Gloucester's poor eyes there is the promise that cruelty can be overcome, and instruction about how it can be overcome. That is the content which justifies the scene of his blinding, aesthetically, psychologically, morally.

This raises again the question of the relation between the Gloucester subplot and the Lear plot. The traditional views seem on the whole to take one of two lines: Gloucester's fate parallels Lear's in order that it become more universal (because Gloucester is an ordinary man, not a distant king, or because in happening to more than one it may happen to any); or more concrete (since Gloucester suffers physically what Lear suffers psychically). Such suggestions are not wrong, but they leave out of account the specific climactic moment at which the subplot surfaces and Lear and Gloucester face one another.

> EDGAR. I would not take this from report; it is,
> And my heart breaks at it.
>
> (IV, vi, 142–3)

I have felt that, but more particularly I have felt an obscurer terror at this moment than at any other in the play. The considerations so far introduced begin, I think, to explain the source of that feeling.

Two questions immediately arise about that confrontation: (1) This is the scene in which Lear's madness is first broken through; in the next scene he is reassembling his sanity. Both the breaking through and the reassembling are manifested by his *recognizing* someone, and my first question is: Why is it Gloucester whom Lear is first able to recognize from his madness, and in recognizing whom his sanity begins to return? (2) *What* does Lear see when he recognizes Gloucester? What is he confronted by?

1. Given our notion that recognizing a person depends upon allowing oneself to be recognized by him, the question becomes: Why is it Gloucester whose recognition Lear is first able to bear? The obvious answer is: Because Gloucester is blind. Therefore one can be, can only be, *recognized by him without being seen,* without having to bear eyes upon oneself.

Leading up to Lear's acknowledgment ("I know thee well enough") there is that insane flight of exchanges about Gloucester's eyes; it is the only active cruelty given to Lear by Shakespeare, apart from his behavior in the abdication scene. But here it seems uncaused, deliberate cruelty inflicted for its own sake upon Gloucester's eyes.

> GLOU.   Dost thou know me?
> LEAR. I remember thine eyes well enough. Dost
>   thou squiny at me?
>   No, do thy worst, blind Cupid; I'll not love.
>   Read thou this challenge; mark but the penning of
>   it.
>   (IV,vi, 137–40)

(This last line, by the way, and Gloucester's response to it seem a clear enough reference to Gloucester's reading of Edmund's letter, carrying here the suggestion that he was blind then.)

> GLOU. Were all thy letters suns [sons?], I could not see.
> LEAR. Read.
> GLOU. What! with the case of eyes?
> LEAR. Oh, ho! are you there with me? No eyes in your head,
>   nor no money in your purse? Your eyes are in a heavy case,
>   your purse in a light: yet you see how this world goes.
> GLOU. I see it feelingly.
> LEAR. What! art mad? A man may see how this world goes with
>   no eyes. . . .
>
>   .   .   .   .
>   Get thee glass eyes;
>   And, like a scurvy politician, seem
>   To see the things thou dost not.
>   (IV, vi, 141–51, 172–4)

Lear is picking at Gloucester's eyes, as if to make sure they are really gone. When he is sure, he recognizes him:

> If thou wilt weep my fortunes, take my eyes;
> I know thee well enough; thy name is Gloucester.
>   (IV,vi, 178–9)

(Here "take my eyes" can be read as a crazy consolation: Your eyes wouldn't have done you any good anyway in this case; you would need to see what I have seen to weep my fortunes; I would give up my eyes not to have seen it.)

This picking spiritually relates Lear to Cornwall's and Regan's act in first blinding Gloucester, for Lear does what he does for the same reason they do – in order not to be seen by this man, whom he has brought harm. (Lear exits from this scene running. From what? From "A Gentleman, with Attendants." His first words to them are: "No rescue? What! A prisoner?" But those questions had interrupted the Gentleman's opening words to him, "Your most dear daughter——". Lear runs not because in his madness he cannot distinguish friends from enemies but because he knows that recognition of himself is imminent. Even madness is no rescue.)

2. This leads to the second question about the scene: What is Lear confronted by in acknowledging Gloucester? It is easy to say: Lear is confronted here with the direct consequences of his conduct, of his covering up in rage and madness, of his having given up authority and kingdom for the wrong motives, to the wrong people; and he is for the first time confronting himself. What is difficult is to show that this is not merely or vaguely symbolic, and that it is not merely an access of knowledge which Lear undergoes. Gloucester has by now become not just a figure "parallel" to Lear, but Lear's double; he does not merely represent Lear, but is psychically identical with him. So that what comes to the surface in this meeting is not a related story, but Lear's submerged mind. This, it seems to me, is what gives the scene its particular terror, and gives to the characters what neither could have alone. In this fusion of plots and identities, we have the great image, the double or mirror image, of everyman who has gone to every length to avoid himself, caught at the moment of coming upon himself face to face. (Against this, "take my eyes" strikes psychotic power.)

The identity is established at the end of the blinding scene, by Regan:

> Go thrust him out at gates, and let him smell
> His way to Dover.
>
> (III,vii, 92–3)

It is by now commonly appreciated that Gloucester had, when that scene began, no plans for going to Dover. Interpreters have accounted for this discrepancy by suggesting that Shakespeare simply wanted all his characters present at Dover for the climax, adding that the repeated question "Wherefore to Dover?" may have put that destination in Gloucester's mind, which has been kicked out of shape. But this interprets the wrong thing, for it overlooks the more obvious, anyway the first, discrepancy. The question is why *Regan* assumes that he is going to Dover. (Her husband, for example, does not: "Turn out that eyeless villain.") We may wish here to appeal to those drummed Dovers to explain her mind, and to suppose that she associates that name with the gathering of all her enemies. But the essential fact is that the name is primarily caught to the image of her father. In her mind, the man she is sending on his way to Dover is the man she *knows* is sent on his way to Dover: In her paroxysms of cruelty, she imagines that she has just participated in blinding her father.

And Gloucester apparently thinks so too, for he then, otherwise inexplicably, sets out for Dover. "Otherwise inexplicably": for it is *no* explanation to say that "the case-histories of suicides contain stranger obsessive characteristics than this" (Muir, xlix). There is no reason, at this stage – other than our cultural advantage in having read the play before – to assume that Gloucester is planning suicide. He sets out for Dover because he is *sent* there: by himself, in sending Lear, in whose identity he is now submerged; and by the thrust of Regan's evil and confusion. But he has no *reason* to go there, not even some inexplicable wish to commit suicide there. At the beginning of the plan to go to Dover he says, "I have no way" (IV, i, 18). It is only at the end of that scene that he mentions Dover *cliff* (73). One can, of course, explain that he had been thinking of the cliff all along. But what the text suggests is that, rather than taking a plan for suicide as our explanation for his insistence on using Dover cliff, we ought to see his thought of the cliff, and consequently of suicide, as *his* explanation of his otherwise mysterious mission to Dover. Better suicide than no reason at all.

When Shakespeare's lapses in plot construction are noticed, critics who know that he is nevertheless the greatest of the bards undertake to excuse him, or to justify the lapse by the great beauty of its surroundings. A familiar excuse is that the lapse will in any case not be noticed in performance. No doubt there are lapses of this kind, and no doubt they can sometimes be covered by such excuses. But it ought also to occur to us that what looks like a lapse is sometimes meant, and that our failure to notice the lapse is just that, our failure. This is what has happened to us in the present scene. We "do not notice" Regan's confusion of identity because we share it, and in failing to understand Gloucester's blanked condition (or rather, in insisting upon understanding it from our point of view) we are doing what the characters in the play are seen to do: We avoid him. And so we are implicated in the failures we are witnessing; we share the responsibility for tragedy.

This is further confirmed in another outstanding lapse, or crux – Gloucester's appearance, led by an old man, to Edgar–Tom. The question, as generally asked, is: Why does Edgar wait, on seeing his father blind, and hearing that his father knows his mistake, before revealing himself to him? The answers which suggest themselves to that question are sophisticated, not the thing itself. For example: Edgar wants to clear himself in the eyes of the world before revealing himself. (But he could still let his *father* know. Anyway, he does tell his father before he goes to challenge Edmund.) Edgar "wants to impose a penance on his father, and to guarantee the genuineness and permanence of the repentance" (Muir, 1). (This seems to me psychologically fantastic; it suggests that the first thing which occurs to Edgar on seeing his father blinded is to exact some further punishment. Or else it makes Edgar into a monster of righteousness; whereas he is merely self-righteous.) Edgar wants to cure his father of his desire to commit suicide. (But *revealing himself* would seem the surest and most immediate way to do that.) And so on. My dissatisfaction with these answers is not that they are psychological explanations, but that they are explanations of the wrong thing, produced by the wrong question: Why does Edgar *delay?* "Delay" implies he is going to later. But we do not *know* (at this stage) that he will; we do not so much as know that he intends to. In terms of our reading of the play so far, we are alerted to the fact that what Edgar does is most directly described as *avoiding recognition. That* is what we want an explanation for.

And first, this action bears the same meaning, or has the same consequences, it always has in this play: mutilating cruelty. This is explicit in one of Gloucester's first utterances after the blinding, led into Edgar's presence:

> Oh! dear son Edgar,
> The food of thy abused father's wrath;
> Might I but live to see thee in my touch,
> I'd say I had eyes again.
>
> (IV, i, 21–4)

So Edgar's avoidance of Gloucester's recognition precisely deprives Gloucester of his eyes again. This links him, as Lear was and will be linked, to Cornwall and the sphere of open evil.

This reading also has consequences for our experience of two subsequent events of the play.

1. In a play in which, as has often been said, each of the characters is either very good or very bad, this revelation of Edgar's capacity for cruelty – and the *same* cruelty as that of the evil characters – shows how radically implicated good is in evil; in a play of disguises, how often they are disguised. And Edgar is the ruler at the end of the play, Lear's successor, the man who must, in Albany's charge, "the gor'd state sustain." (A very equivocal charge, containing no assurance that its body may be nursed back to health; but simply nursed.) If good is to grow anywhere in this state, it must recognize, and face, its continuity with, its location within, a maze of evil. Edgar's is the most Christian sensibility in the play, as Edmund's is the most Machiavellian. If the Machiavellian fails in the end, he very nearly succeeds; and if the Christian succeeds, his success is deeply compromised.

2. To hold to the fact that Edgar is avoiding recognition makes better sense to me of that grotesque guiding of Gloucester up no hill to no cliff to no suicide than any other account I know. The special quality of this scene, with its purest outbreak of grotesquerie, has been recognized at least since Wilson Knight's essay of 1930.[5] But to regard it as *symbolic* of the play's emphasis on the grotesque misses what makes it so grotesque, and fails to account for the fact that Edgar and Gloucester find themselves in this condition. It is grotesque because it is so *literal* a consequence of avoiding the facts. It is not the emblem of the Lear universe, but an instance of what

---

[5] "*King Lear* and the Comedy of the Grotesque," one of the studies composing *The Wheel of Fire*, originally published by Oxford University Press, 1930; published in the fifth revised edition by Meridian Books, New York, 1957.

has led its minds to their present state: There are no lengths to which we may not go in order to avoid being revealed, even to those we love and are loved by. Or rather, especially to those we love and are loved by; to other people it is *easy* not to be known. That grotesque walk is not full of promise for our lives. It is not, for example, a picture of mankind making its way up Purgatory;[6] for Gloucester's character is not purified by it, but extirpated. It shows what people will *have* to say and try to mean to one another when they are incapable of acknowledging to one another what they have to acknowledge. To fill this scene with nourishing, profound meaning is to see it from Edgar's point of view; that is, to avoid what is there. Edgar is Ahab, trying to harpoon the meaning of his life into something external to it; and we believe him, and serve him. He is Hedda Gabler, with her ugly demand for beauty. In the fanciful, childish deceit of his plan, he is Tom Sawyer in the last chapters of *Huckleberry Finn,* enveloping Jim's prison with symbols of escape, instead of opening the door.

If one wishes a psychological explanation for Edgar's behavior, the question to be answered is: Why does Edgar avoid his father's recognition? Two answers suggest themselves. (1) He is himself ashamed and guilty. He was as gullible as his father was to Edmund's "invention." He failed to confront his father, to trust his love, exactly as his father had failed him. He is as responsible for his father's blinding as his father is. He wants to make it up to his father before asking for his recognition – to make it up instead of repenting, acknowledging; he wants to *do* something instead of stopping and seeing. So he goes on doing the very thing which needs making up for. (2) He cannot bear the fact that his father is incapable, impotent, maimed. He wants his father still to be a father, powerful, so that *he* can remain a child. For otherwise they are simply two human beings in need of one another, and it is not usual for parents and children to manage that transformation, becoming for one another nothing more, but nothing less, than unaccommodated men. That is what Lear took Edgar to be, but that was a mad, ironic compliment; to become natural again, human kind needs to do more than remove its clothes; for we can also cover up our embarrassment by nakedness. We have our inventions, our accommodations.

We learn in the course of Edgar's tale, after his successful duel

[6] Suggested by R. W. Chambers, *King Lear,* 1940; cited by Muir, p. l.

with Edmund, when it was that he brought himself to allow his father to recognize him:

> Never – O fault! – revealed myself unto him
> Until some half-hour past, when I was arm'd.
>   (V, iii, 192–3)

Armed, and with the old man all but seeped away, he feels safe enough to give his father vision again and bear his recognition. As sons fear, and half wish, it is fatal. Now he will never know whether, had he challenged recognition when recognition was denied, at home, both of them could have survived it. That Edgar is so close to the thing love demands contributes to the grotesque air of the late scenes with his father.[7] Love does maintain itself under betrayal; it does allow, and forward, its object's wish to find the edge of its own existence; it does not shrink from recognition that its object is headed for, or has survived, radical change, with its attendant destructions – which is the way love knows that a betrayal is ended, and is why it provides the context for new innocence. But Edgar does not know that love which has such power also has the power to kill, and, in going to the lengths he takes it, must be capable of absolute scrupulousness. It cannot lead, it can only accompany, past the point it has been, and it must feel that point. It is Edgar's self-assurance here which mocks his Christian thoroughness.

We now have elements with which to begin an analysis of the most controversial of the *Lear* problems, the nature of Lear's motivation in his opening (abdication) scene. The usual interpretations follow one of three main lines: Lear is senile; Lear is puerile; Lear is not to be understood in natural terms, for the whole scene has a fairy-tale or ritualistic character which simply must be accepted as the premise from which the tragedy is derived. Arguments ensue, in each case, about whether Shakespeare is justified in what he is asking his audience to accept. My hypothesis will be that Lear's behavior in this scene is explained by – the tragedy begins because of – the same motivation which manipulates the tragedy throughout its course, from the scene which precedes the abdication, through the storm, blinding, evaded reconciliations, to the final moments: by

---

[7] The passage from this sentence to the end of the paragraph was added as the result of a conversation with Rose Mary Harbison.

the attempt to avoid recognition, the shame of exposure, the threat of self-revelation.

Shame, first of all, is the right kind of candidate to serve as motive, because it is the emotion whose effect is most precipitate and out of proportion to its cause, which is just the rhythm of the *King Lear* plot as a whole. And with this hypothesis we need not assume that Lear is either incomprehensible or stupid or congenitally arbitrary and inflexible and extreme in his conduct. Shame itself is exactly arbitrary, inflexible, and extreme in its effect. It is familiar to find that what mortifies one person seems wholly unimportant to another: Think of being ashamed of one's origins, one's accent, one's ignorance, one's skin, one's clothes, one's legs or teeth. . . . It is the most isolating of feelings, the most comprehensible perhaps in idea, but the most incomprehensible or incommunicable in fact. Shame, I've said, is the most primitive, the most private, of emotions; but it is also the most primitive of *social* responses. With the discovery of the individual, whether in Paradise or in the Renaissance, there is the simultaneous discovery of the isolation of the individual; his presence to himself, but simultaneously to *others*. Moreover, shame is felt not only toward one's own actions and one's own being, but toward the actions and the being of those with whom one is identified – fathers, daughters, wives. . . , the beings whose self-revelations reveal oneself. Families, any objects of one's love and commitment, ought to be the places where shame is overcome (hence happy families are all alike); but they are also the place of its deepest manufacture, and one is then hostage to that power, or fugitive. – L. B. Campbell, in *Shakespeare's Tragic Heroes*,[8] collects valuable examples of Renaissance "doctrine," and sorts them perspicuously around Shakespeare's topics. But she follows a typical assumption of such investigations – that if Shakespeare's work is to be illuminated by these contemporary doctrines, he must illustrate them. For example:

> It must be evident, then, that there was in Shakespeare's day an old and firmly founded philosophy of anger, finding its sources in ancient medicine and ancient philosophy and in the mediaeval makings-over of those ancient sources as well. Ac-

[8] New York: Barnes and Noble, 1966; the quotation that follows is from pp. 181–2 of this edition. The book was first published in 1930 by Cambridge University Press.

cording to this philosophy, pride or self-esteem is the condition in which anger takes its rise, vengeance becomes its immediate object, and some slight, real or imagined, is its cause. Anger is folly; anger brings shame in its train. The sequence of passions is pride, anger, revenge, and unless madness clouds the reason altogether, shame.

But in *King Lear* shame comes first, and brings rage and folly in its train. Lear is not maddened because he had been wrathful, but because his shame brought his wrath upon the wrong object. It is not the fact of his anger but the irony of it, specifically and above all the *injustice* of it, which devours him.

That Lear is ashamed, or afraid of being shamed by a revelation, seems to be the Fool's understanding of his behavior. It is agreed that the Fool keeps the truth present to Lear's mind, but it should be stressed that the characteristic mode of the Fool's presentation is *ridicule* – the circumstance most specifically feared by shame (as accusation and discovery are most feared by guilt). Part of the exquisite pain of this Fool's comedy is that in riddling Lear with the truth of his condition he increases the very cause of that condition, as though shame should finally grow ashamed of itself, and stop. The other part of this pain is that it is the therapy prescribed by love itself. We know that since Cordelia's absence "the fool hath much pin'd away" (I, iv, 78), and it is generally assumed that this is due to his love for Cordelia. That need not be denied, but it should be obvious that it is directly due to his love for Lear; to his having to see the condition in Lear which his love is impotent to prevent, the condition moreover which his love has helped to cause, the precise condition therefore which his love is unable to comfort, since its touch wounds. This is why the Fool dies or disappears; from the terrible relevance, and the horrible irrelevance, of his only passion. This is the point of his connection with Cordelia, as will emerge.

I call Lear's shame a hypothesis, and what I have to say here will perhaps be hard to make convincing. But primarily it depends upon not imposing the traditional interpretations upon the opening events. Lear is puerile? Lear senile? But the man who speaks Lear's words is in possession, if not fully in command, of a powerful, ranging mind; and its eclipse into madness only confirms its intelligence, not just because what he says in his madness is the work of a marked intelligence, but because the nature of his madness, his melancholy and antic disposition, its incessant invention, is the sign, in fact and in Renaissance thought, of genius; an option of escape open only to minds of the highest reach. How then can we understand such a mind seriously to believe that what Goneril and Regan are offering in that opening scene is love, proof of his value to them; and to believe that Cordelia is withholding love? We cannot so understand it, and so all the critics are right to regard Lear in this scene as psychologically incomprehensible, or as requiring from them some special psychological makeup – if, that is, we assume that Lear believes in Goneril and Regan and not in Cordelia. But we needn't assume that he believes anything of the kind.

We imagine that Lear *must* be wildly abused (blind, puerile, and the rest) because the thing works out so badly. But it doesn't *begin* badly, and it is far from incomprehensible conduct. It is, in fact, quite ordinary. A parent is bribing love out of his children; two of them accept the bribe, and despise him for it; the third shrinks from the attempt, as though from violation. Only this is a king, this bribe is the last he will be able to offer; everything in his life, and in the life of his state, depends upon its success. We need not assume that he does not know his two older daughters, and that they are giving him false coin in return for his real bribes, though perhaps like most parents he is willing not to notice it. But more than this: There is reason to assume that the open possibility – or the open fact – that they are *not* offering true love is exactly what he wants. Trouble breaks out only with Cordelia's "Nothing," and her broken resolution to be silent. – What does he want, and what is the meaning of the trouble which then breaks out?

Go back to the confrontation scene with Gloucester:

If thou wilt weep my fortunes, take my eyes.

The obvious rhetoric of those words is that of an appeal, or a bargain. But it is also warning, and a command: If you weep for me, the same thing will happen to me that happened to you; do not let me see what you are weeping for. Given the whole scene, with its concentrated efforts at warding off Gloucester, that line says explicitly what it is Lear is warding off: Gloucester's sympathy, his love. And earlier:

GLOU. O! Let me kiss that hand.
LEAR. Let me wipe it first, it smells of mortality.
(IV, vi,134–5)

Mortality, the hand without rings of power on it, cannot be lovable. He feels unworthy of love when the reality of lost power comes over him. That is what his plan was to have avoided by exchanging his fortune for his love at one swap. He cannot bear love when he has no reason to be loved, perhaps because of the helplessness, the passiveness which that implies, which some take for impotence. And he wards it off for the reason for which people do ward off being loved, because it presents itself to them as a demand:

LEAR. No. Do thy worst, blind Cupid; I'll not love.
(IV, vi, 139)

Gloucester's presence strikes Lear as the demand for love; he knows he is being offered love; he tries to deny the offer by imagining that he has been solicited (this is the relevance of "blind Cupid" as the sign of a brothel); and he does not want to pay for it, for he may get it, and may not, and either is intolerable. Besides, he has recently done just that, paid his all for love. The long fantasy of his which precedes this line ("Let copulation thrive. . . . There is the sulphurous pit – burning, scalding, stench, consumption . . .") contains his most sustained expression of disgust with sexuality (ll. 116ff.) – as though furiously telling himself that what was wrong with his plan was not the debasement of love his bargain entailed, but the fact that love itself is inherently debased and so unworthy from the beginning of the bargain he had made for it. That is a maddening thought; but still more comforting than the truth. For some spirits, to be loved knowing you cannot return that love is the most radical of psychic tortures.

This is the way I understand that opening scene with the three daughters. Lear knows it is a bribe he offers, and – part of him anyway – wants exactly what a bribe can buy: (1) false love and (2) a public expression of love. That is, he wants something he does not have to return *in kind,* something which a division of his prop-

61

erty fully pays for. And he wants to *look* like a loved man – for the sake of the subjects, as it were. He is perfectly happy with his little plan, until Cordelia speaks. Happy not because he is blind, but because he is getting what he wants, his plan is working. Cordelia is alarming precisely because he *knows* she is offering the real thing, offering something a more opulent third of his kingdom cannot, must not, repay; putting a claim upon him he cannot face. She threatens to expose both his plan for returning false love with no love, and expose the necessity for that plan – his terror of being loved, of needing love.

Reacting to oversentimental or over-Christian interpretations of her character, interpreters have made efforts to implicate her in the tregedy's source, convincing her of a willfulness and hardness kin to that later shown by her sisters. But her complicity is both less and more than such an interpretation envisages. That interpretation depends, first of all, upon taking her later speeches in the scene (after the appearance of France and Burgundy) as simply uncovering what was in her mind and heart from the beginning. But why? Her first utterance is the aside:

> What shall Cordelia speak? Love, and be silent.

This, presumably, has been understood as indicating her decision to refuse her father's demand. But it needn't be. She asks herself what she can say; there is no necessity for taking the question to be rhetorical. She wants to obey her father's wishes (anyway, there is no reason to think otherwise at this stage, or at any other); but how? She sees from Goneril's speech and Lear's acceptance of it what it is he wants, and she would provide it if she could. But to pretend publicly to love, where you do not love, is easy; to pretend to love, where you really do love, is not obviously possible. She hits on the first solution to her dilemma: Love, and be silent. That is, love *by being* silent. That will do what he seems to want, it will avoid the expression of love, keep it secret. She is his joy; she knows it and he knows it. Surely that is enough? Then Regan speaks, and following that Cordelia's second utterance, again aside:

> Then poor Cordelia!
> And yet not so; since I am sure my love's
> More ponderous than my tongue.
> (I, i, 76–8)

Presumably, in line with the idea of a defiant Cordelia, this is to be interpreted as a reaffirmation of her decision not to speak. But again, it needn't be. After Lear's acceptance of Regan's characteristic outstripping (she has no ideas of her own; her special vileness is always to increase the measure of pain others are prepared to inflict; her mind is itself a lynch mob) Cordelia may realize that she will *have* to say something. "More ponderous than my tongue" suggests that she is going to move it, not that it is immovable – which would make it more ponderous than her love. And this produces her second groping for an exit from the dilemma: to speak, but making her love seem less than it is, out of love. Her tongue will move, and obediently, but against her condition – then poor Cordelia, making light of her love. And yet *she* knows the truth. Surely that is enough?

But when the moment comes, she is speechless: "Nothing, my lord." I do not deny that this can be read defiantly, as can the following "You have begot me, bred me, lov'd me" speech. She is outraged, violated, confused, so young; Lear is torturing her, claiming her devotion, which she wants to give, but forcing her to help him betray (or not to betray) it, to falsify it publicly. (Lear's ambiguity here, wanting at once to open and to close her mouth, further shows the ordinariness of the scene, its verisimilitude to common parental love, swinging between absorption and rejection of its offspring, between encouragement to a rebellion they failed to make and punishment for it.) It may be that with Lear's active violation, she snaps; her resentment provides her with words, and she levels her abdication of love at her traitorous, shameless father:

> Happily, when I shall wed,
> That lord whose hand must take my plight shall carry
> Half my love with him.
>
> (I,i, 100–2)

The trouble is, the words are too calm, too cold for the kind of sharp rage and hatred real love can produce. She is never in possession of her situation, "her voice was ever soft, gentle and low" (V, iii, 272–3); she is young, and "least" (I, i, 83). (This notation of her stature and of the quality of her voice is unique in the play. The idea of a defiant *small* girl seems grotesque, as an idea of Cordelia.) All her words are words of love; to love is all she knows how to do. That is her problem, and at the cause of the tragedy of King Lear.

I imagine the scene this way: The older daughters' speeches are public, set; they should not be said to Lear, but to the court, sparing themselves his eyes and him theirs. They are not monsters first, but ladies. He is content. Then Cordelia says to him, away from the court, in confused appeal to their accustomed intimacy, "Nothing" – don't force me, I don't know what you want, there is nothing I can say, to speak what you want I must not speak. But he is alarmed at the appeal and tries to cover it up, keeping up the front, and says, speaking to her and to the court, as if the ceremony is still in full effect: "Nothing will come of nothing; speak again." (*Hysterica passio* is already stirring.) Again she says to *him:* "Unhappy that I am, I cannot heave my heart into my mouth" – not the heart which loves him, that always has been present in her voice; but the heart which is shuddering with confusion, with wanting to do the impossible, the heart which is now in her throat. But to no avail. Then the next line would be her first attempt to obey him by speaking publicly: "I love your Majesty according to my bond; no more or less" – not stinting, not telling *him* the truth (what is the true *amount* of love this loving young girl knows to measure with her bond?), not refusing him, but still trying to conceal her love, to lighten its full measure. Then her father's brutally public, and perhaps still publicly considerate, "How, how, Cordelia! Mend your speech a little, lest you may mar your fortunes." So she tries again to divide her kingdom (". . . that lord whose hand must take my plight shall carry half my love with him"). Why should she wish to shame him publicly? He has shamed himself and everyone knows it. She is trying to conceal him; and to do that she cuts herself in two. (In the end, he faces what she has done here: "Upon such sacrifices, my Cordelia . . . " Lear cannot, at that late moment, be thinking of prison as a sacrifice. I imagined him there partly remembering this first scene, and the first of Cordelia's sacrifices – of love to convention.)

After this speech, said in suppression, confusion, abandonment, she is shattered, by her failure and by Lear's viciousness to her. Her sisters speak again only when they are left alone, to plan. Cordelia revives and speaks after France enters and has begun to speak *for* her:

> Sure, her offence
> Must be of such unnatural degree

That monsters it, or your fore-vouch'd affection
Fall into taint; which to believe of her,
Must be a faith that reason without miracle
Should never plant in me.

(I, i, 218–23)

France's love shows him the truth. Tainted love is the answer, love dyed – not decayed or corrupted exactly; Lear's love is still alive, but expressed as, colored over with, hate. Cordelia finds her voice again, protected in France's love, and she uses it to change the subject, still protecting Lear from discovery.

A reflection of what Cordelia now must feel is given by one's rush of gratitude toward France, one's almost wild relief as he speaks his beautiful trust. She does not ask her father to relent, but only to give France some explanation. Not the right explanation: What has "that glib and oily art" got to do with it? That is what her sisters needed, because their task was easy: to dissemble. Convention perfectly suits these ladies. But she lets it go at that – he hates me because I would not flatter him. The truth is, she *could* not flatter; not because she was too proud or too principled, though these might have been the reasons, for a different character; but because nothing she could have done would have *been* flattery – at best it would have been *dissembled flattery*. There is no convention for doing what Cordelia was asked to do. It is not that Goneril and Regan have taken the words out of her mouth, but that here she cannot say them, because for her they are true ("Dearer than eye-sight, space and liberty"). She is not disgusted by her sisters' flattery (it's nothing new); but heartbroken at hearing the words she wishes she were in a position to say. So she is sent, and taken, away. Or half of her leaves; the other half remains, in Lear's mind, in Kent's service, and in the Fool's love.

(I spoke just now of "one's" gratitude and relief toward France. I was remembering my feeling at a production given by students at Berkeley during 1946 in which France – a small part, singled out by Granville-Barker as particularly requiring an actor of authority and distinction – was given his full sensitivity and manliness, a combination notably otherwise absent from the play, as mature womanliness is. The validity of such feelings as touchstones of the accuracy of a reading of the play, and which feelings one is to trust and which not, ought to be discussed problems of criticism.)

It may be felt that I have forced this scene too far in order to fit it to my reading, that too many directions have to be provided to its acting in order to keep the motivation smooth. Certainly I have gone into more detail of this kind here than elsewhere, and I should perhaps say why. It is, first of all, the scene in which the problem of performance, or the performability, of this play comes to a head, or to its first head. Moreover, various interpretations offered of this scene are direct functions of attempts to *visualize* its progress; as though a critic's conviction about the greatness or weakness of the scene is a direct function of the success or unsuccess with which he or she has been able to imagine it concretely. Critics will invariably dwell on the motivations of Lear and Cordelia in this scene as a problem, even while taking their motivation later either as more or less obvious or for some other reason wanting no special description; and in particular, the motives or traits of character attributed to them here will typically be ones which have an immediate visual implication, ones in which, as it were, a psychological trait and its physical expression most nearly coalesce: At random, Lear is described as irascible (Schüking), arrogant, choleric, overbearing (Schlegel); Cordelia as shy, reluctant (Schüking), sullen, prideful (Coleridge), obstinate (Muir). This impulse seems to me correct, and honest: It is one thing to say that Cordelia's behavior in the opening scene is not inconsistent with her behavior when she reappears, but another to *show* its consistency. This is what I have wanted to test in visualizing her behavior in that scene. But it is merely a test, it proves nothing about my reading, except its actability; or rather, a performance on these lines would, or would not, prove that. And that is a further problem of aesthetics – to chart the relations between a text (or score), an analysis or interpretation of it, and a performance in terms of that analysis or interpretation.

The problem is not, as it is often put, that no performance is ideal, because this suggests we have some clear idea of what an ideal performance would be, perhaps an idea of it as embodying all true interpretations, every resonance of the text struck under analysis. But this is no more possible, or comprehensible, than an experiment which is to verify every implication of a theory. (Then what makes a theory convincing?) Performances are actions, and the imitations of actions. As with any action, performance cannot contain the totality of a human life – though one action can have a particularly summary or revelatory quality, and another will occur at a cross-

66

roads, and another will spin tangentially to the life and circumstances which call it out, or rub irrelevantly or mechanically against another. Some have no meaning for us at all, others have more resonance than they can express – as a resultant force answers to forces not visible in the one direction it selects. (Then what makes action bearable, or comprehensible?) I cannot at will give my past expression, though every gesture expresses it, and each elation and headache; my character is its epitome, as if the present were a pantomime of ghostly selections. What is necessary to a performance is what is necessary to action in the present, that it have its autonomy, and that it be in character, or out, and that it have a specific context and motive. Even if everything I have said about Cordelia is true, it needn't be registered explicitly in the way that first scene is played – there may, for example, be merit in stylizing it drastically. Only there will be no effort to present us with a sullen or prideful or defiant girl who reappears, with nothing intervening to change her, as the purest arch of love.

Nor, of course, has my rendering of the first scene been meant to bring out all the motivations or forces which cross there. For example, it might be argued that part of Lear's strategy is exactly to put Cordelia into the position of being denied her dowry, so that he will not lose her in marriage; if so, it half worked, and required the magnanimity of France to turn it aside. Again, nothing has been said of the theme of politics which begins here and pervades the action. Not just the familiar Shakespearean theme which opens the interplay between the public and private lives of the public creature, but the particularity of the theme in this play, which is about the interpenetration and confusion of politics with love; something which, in modern societies, is equally the fate of private creatures – whether in the form of divided loyalties, or of one's relation to the state, or, more pervasively, in the new forms love and patriotism themselves take: love wielding itself in gestures of power, power extending itself with claims of love. *Phèdre* is perhaps the greatest play concentrated to this theme of the body politic, and of the body, torn by the privacy of love; as it is closest to *King Lear* in its knowledge of shame as the experience of unacceptable love. And Machiavelli's knowledge of the world is present; not just in his attitudes of realism and cynicism, but in his experience of the condition to which these attitudes are appropriate – in which the inner and outer worlds have become totally disconnected, and man's life is all public, among strangers, seen only from outside. Luther saw the same thing at the same time, but from inside. For some, like Edmund, this is liberating knowledge, lending capacity for action. It is what Lear wants to abdicate from. For what Lear is doing in that first scene is trading power for love (pure power for mixed love); this is what his opening speech explicitly says. He imagines that this will prevent future strife now; but he is being counseled by his impotence, which is not the result of his bad decision, but produces it: He feels powerless to *appoint* his successor, recognized as the ultimate test of authority. The consequence is that politics becomes private, and so vanishes, with power left to serve hatred.

The final scene opens with Lear and Cordelia repeating or completing their actions in their opening scene; again Lear abdicates, and again Cordelia loves and is silent. Its readers have for centuries wanted to find consolation in this end: Heavy opinion sanctioned Tate's Hollywood ending throughout the eighteenth century, which resurrects Cordelia; and in our time, scorning such vulgarity, the same impulse fastidiously digs itself deeper and produces redemption for Lear in Cordelia's figuring of transcendent love. But Dr. Johnson is surely right, more honest and more responsive: Cordelia's death is so shocking that we would avoid it if we could – if we have responded to it. And so the question, since her death is restored to us, is forced upon us: Why does she die? And this is not answered by asking, What does her death mean? (cp. Christ died to save sinners); but by answering, What killed her? (cp. Christ was killed by us, because his news was unendurable).

Lear's opening speech of this final scene is not the correction but the repetition of his strategy in the first scene, or a new tactic designed to win the old game; and it is equally disastrous.

> CORD. Shall we not see these daughters and these sisters?
> LEAR. No, no, no, no!
>
> (V,iii, 7–8)

He cannot finally face the thing he has done; and this means what it always does, that he cannot bear being seen. He is anxious to go off to prison, with Cordelia; his love now is in the open – that much circumstance has done for him; but it remains imperative that it be confined, out of sight. (Neither Lear nor Cordelia, presumably, knows that the soldier in command is Gloucester's son; they feel unknown.) He is still ashamed, and the fantasy expressed in this speech ("We two alone will sing like birds i' the cage") is the same fantasy he brings on the stage with him in the first scene, the thwarting of which causes his maddened destructiveness. There Cordelia had offered him the marriage pledge ("Obey you, love you, and most honor you"), and she has shared his fantasy fully enough to wish to heal political strife with a kiss (or perhaps it is just the commonest fantasy of women):

> CORD.   Restoration hang
> Thy medicine on my lips.
> (IV, vii, 26–7)

(But after such abdication, what restoration? The next time we hear the words "hang" and "medicine," they announce death.) This gesture is as fabulous as anything in the opening scene. Now, at the end, Lear returns her pledge with his lover's song, his invitation to voyage (". . . so we'll live, and pray, and sing, and tell old tales, and laugh"). The fantasy of this speech is as full of detail as a daydream, and it is clearly a happy dream for Lear. He has found at the end a way to have what he has wanted from the beginning. His tone is not: We shall love *even though* we are in prison; but: Because we are hidden together we can love. He has come to accept his love, not by making room in the world for it, but by denying its relevance to the world. He does not renounce the world in going to prison, but flees from it, to earthly pleasure. The astonishing image of "God's spies" (V, iii, 17) stays beyond me, but in part it contains the final emphasis upon looking without being seen; and it cites an intimacy which requires no reciprocity with real men. Like Gloucester toward Dover, Lear anticipates God's call. He is not experiencing reconciliation with a daughter, but partnership in a mystic marriage.

If so, it cannot be, as is often suggested, that when he says,

> Upon such sacrifices, my Cordelia,
> The Gods themselves throw incense.
> (V, iii, 20–1)

he is thinking simply of going to prison with Cordelia as a sacrifice.

It seems rather that, the lines coming immediately after his love song, it is their love itself which has the meaning of sacrifice. As though the ideas of love and of death are interlocked in his mind – and in particular of death as a payment or placation for the granting of love. His own death, because acknowledging love still presents itself to him as an annihilation of himself. And her death, because now that he admits her love, he must admit, what he knew from the beginning, that he is impotent to sustain it. This is the other of Cordelia's sacrifices – of love to secrecy.

Edmund's death reinforces the juncture of these ideas, for it is death which releases his capacity for love. It is this release which permits his final act:

> . . . some good I mean to do
> Despite of mine own nature. Quickly send. . .
> (V, iii, 243–4)

What has released him? Partly, of course, the presence of his own death; but that in itself need not have worked this way. Primarily it is the fact that all who have loved him, or claimed love for him, are dead. He has eagerly prompted Edgar to tell the tale of their father's death; his reaction upon hearing of Goneril's and Regan's deaths is as to a solution to impossible, or illegitimate, love: "All three now marry in an instant"; and his immediate reaction upon seeing their dead bodies is: "Yet Edmund was belov'd." *That* is what he wanted to know, and he can acknowledge it now, when it cannot be returned, now that its claim is dead. In his following speech he means well for the first time.

It can be said that what Lear is ashamed of is not his need for love and his inability to return it, but of the *nature* of his love for Cordelia. It is too far from plain love of father for daughter. Even if we resist seeing in it the love of lovers, it is at least incompatible with the idea of her having any (other) lover. There is a moment, beyond the words, when this comes to the surface of the action. It is the moment Lear is waking from his madness, no longer incapable of seeing the world, but still not strong enough to protect his thoughts: "Methinks I should know you and know this man" (IV, vii, 64). I take it "this man" is generally felt to refer to Kent (disguised as Caius), for there is clearly no reason to suppose Lear knows the Doctor, the only other man present. Certainly this is plausible;

but in fact Lear never does acknowledge Kent, as he does his child Cordelia.[9] And after this recognition he goes on to ask, "Am I in France?" This question irresistibly (to me) suggests that the man he thinks he should know is the man he expects to be with his daughter, her husband. This would be unmistakable if he directs his "this man" to the Doctor, taking him for, but not able to make him out as, France. He finds out it is not, and the next time we see him he is pressing off to prison with his child, and there is no further thought of her husband. It is a standing complaint that Shakespeare's explanation of France's absence is perfunctory. It is more puzzling that Lear himself never refers to him, not even when he is depriving him of her forever. Either France has ceased to exist for Lear, or it is importantly from him that he wishes to reach the shelter of prison.

I do not wish to suggest that "avoidance of love" and "avoidance of a particular kind of love" are alternative hypotheses about this play. On the contrary, they seem to me to interpret one another.

---

[9] Professor Jonas Barish – to whom I am indebted for other suggestions about this essay as well as the present one – has pointed out to me that in my eagerness to solve all the *King Lear* problems I have neglected trying an account of Kent's plan in delaying making himself known ("Yet to be known shortens my made intent" [IV, vii, 9]). This omission is particularly important because Kent's is the one delay that causes no harm to others; hence it provides an internal measure of those harms. I do not understand his "dear cause" (IV, iii, 52), but I think the specialness of Kent's delay has to do with these facts: (1) It never prevents his perfect faithfulness to his duties of service; these do not require – Kent does not permit them to require – personal recognition in order to be performed. This sense of the finitude of the demands placed upon Kent, hence of the harm and of the good he can perform, is a function of his complete absorption into his social office, in turn a function of his being the only principal character in the play (apart from the Fool) who does not appear as a member of a *family*. (2) He does not delay revealing himself to Cordelia, only (presumably) to Lear. A reason for that would be that since the king has banished him it is up to the king to reinstate him; he will not presume on his old rank. (3) If his plan goes beyond finding some way, or just waiting, for Lear to recognize him first (not out of pride but out of right) then perhaps it is made irrelevant by finding Lear again only in his terminal state, or perhaps it always consisted only in doing what he tries to do there, find an opportunity to tell Lear about Caius and ask for pardon. It may be wondered that we do not feel Lear's fragmentary recognitions of Kent to leave something undone, nor Kent's hopeless attempts to hold Lear's attention to be crude intrusions, but rather to amplify a sadness already amplified past sensing. This may be accounted for partly by Kent's pure expression of the special poignance of the servant's office, requiring a life centered in another life, exhausted in loyalty and in silent witnessing (a silence Kent broke and Lear must mend); partly by the fact that Cordelia has fully recognized him: "To be acknowledg'd, Madam, is o'er-paid" (IV, vii, 4); partly by the fact that when his master Lear is dead, it is his master who calls him, and his last words are those of obedience.

Avoidance of love is always, or always begins as, an avoidance of a particular kind of love: Human beings do not just naturally not love, they learn not to. And our lives begin by having to accept under the name of love whatever closeness is offered, and by then having to forgo its object. And the avoidance of a particular love, or the acceptance of it, will spread to every other; every love, in acceptance or rejection, is mirrored in every other. It is part of the miracle of the vision in *King Lear* to bring this before us, so that we do not care whether the *kind* of love felt between these two is forbidden according to humanity's lights. We care whether love is or is not altogether forbidden to us, whether we may not altogether be incapable of it, of admitting it into our world. We wonder whether we may always go mad between the equal efforts and terrors at once of rejecting and of accepting love. The soul torn between them, the body feels torn (producing a set of images accepted since Caroline Spurgeon's *Shakespeare's Imagery* as central to *King Lear*), and the solution to this insoluble condition is to wish for the tearing apart of the world.

Lear wishes to escape into prison for another old reason – because he is unwilling to be seen to weep.

> The good years shall devour them, flesh and fell,
> Ere they shall make us weep: we'll see 'em starved first.
> (V, iii, 24–5)

See them shalt thou never. And in the end he still avoids Cordelia. He sees that she is weeping after his love song ("Wipe thine eyes"). But why is she in tears? Why does Lear think she is? Lear imagines that she is crying for the reasons that he is on the verge of tears – the old reasons, the sense of impotence, shame, loss. But *her* reasons for tears do not occur to him, that she sees him as he is, as he was, that he is unable to take his last chance; that he, at the farthest edge of life, must again sacrifice her, again abdicate his responsibilities; and that he cannot know what he asks. And yet, seeing that, it is for him that she is cast down. Upon such knowledge the gods themselves throw incense.

It is as though her response here is her knowledge of the end of the play; she alone has the capacity of compassion Lear will need when we next see him, with Cordelia dead in his arms: "Howl, howl, howl! O! you are men of stones." (Cp. the line and a half

Dante gives to Ugolino, facing his doomed sons, a fragment shored by Arnold: "I did not weep, I so turned to stone within. They wept.") Again he begins to speak by turning on those at hand: "A plague upon you, murderers, traitors all!" But then the tremendous knowledge is released: "I might have saved her." From the beginning, and through each moment until they are led to prison, he might have saved her, had he done what every love requires, put himself aside long enough to see through to her, and be seen through. I do not mean that it is clear that he could, at the end, have done what Edmund feared ("pluck the common bosom on his side, And turn our impress'd lances in our eyes"); but it is not clear that he could not. And even if he had not succeeded, her death would not be on his hands. In his last speech, "No, no, no, no" becomes "No, no, no life!" His need, or his interpretation of his need, becomes her sentence. This is what is unbearable. Or bearable only out of the capacity of Cordelia. If we are to weep her fortunes we must take her eyes.

Is this a Christian play? The question is very equivocal. When it is answered affirmatively, Cordelia is viewed as a Christ figure whose love redeems nature and transfigures Lear. So far as this is intelligible to me, I find it false both to the experience of the play and to the fact that it *is* a play. *King Lear* is not illustrated theology (anyway, which theology is thought to be illustrated, what understanding of atonement, redemption, etc., is thought to be figured?), and nature and Lear are not touched, but run out. If Cordelia exemplifies Christ, it is at the moment of crucifixion, not resurrection. But the moment of his death is the moment when Christ resembles us, finally takes the human condition fully into himself. (This is why every figure reaching the absolute point of rejection starts becoming a figure of Christ. And perhaps why it is so important to the Christ story that it begins with birth and infancy.) It is in his *acceptance* of this condition that we are to resemble him. If Cordelia resembles Christ, it is by having become fully human, by knowing her separateness, by knowing the deafness of miracles, by accepting the unacceptability of her love, and by nevertheless maintaining her love and the whole knowledge it brings. One can say she "redeems nature" (IV, vi, 207), but this means nothing miraculous, only that she shows nature not to be the cause of evil – there is no cause in nature which makes these hard hearts, and no cause outside either. The cause is the heart itself, the having of a heart, in a world made heartless. Lear is the cause. Murderers, traitors *all*.

Another way, the play can be said to be Christian – not because it shows us redemption (it does not) but because it throws our redemption into *question,* and leaves it up to us. But there is no suggestion that we can take it up only through Christ. On the contrary, there is reason to take this drama as an alternative to the Christian one. In the first place, Christianity, like every other vision of the play, is not opted for, but tested. Specifically, as was said earlier, in Edgar's conduct; more generally, in its suggestion that all appeals to gods are distractions or excuses, because the imagination uses them to wish for complete, for final solutions, when what is needed is at hand, or nowhere. But isn't this what Christ meant? And isn't this what Lear fails to see in wishing to be God's spy before he is God's subject? Cordelia is further proof of this: Her grace is shown by the absence in her of any unearthly experiences; she is the only good character whose attention is wholly on earth, on the person nearest her. It is during the storm that Lear's mind clouds most and floods with philosophy; when it clears, Cordelia is present.

These considerations take us back to the set of ideas which see Lear as having arrived, in the course of the storm, at the naked human condition – as if the storm was the granting of his prayer to "feel what wretches feel." It may seem that I have denied this in underlining Lear's cruelty to Gloucester and in placing him at the cause of Cordelia's death, because it may feel as if I am blaming Lear for his behavior here.[10] And what room is there for blame? Is he to blame for being human? For being subject to a cosmic anxiety and to fantasies which enclose him from perfect compassion? Certainly blame is inappropriate, for certainly I do not claim to know what *else* Lear might do. And yet I cannot deny that my pain at Lear's actions is not overcome by my knowledge of his own suffering. I might describe my experience of him here as one of unplaceable blame, blame no one can be asked to bear and no one is in a position to level – like blaming heaven. That does not seem to me inappropriate as an experience of tragedy, of what it is for

[10]In a detailed and very useful set of comments on an earlier draft of this essay, Professor Alpers mentions this as a possible response to what I had written; and it was his suggestion of Empson's appeal to the scapegoat idea as offering a truer response to Lear's condition that sent me back to Empson's essay (see note 11). It was as an effort to do justice to Alpers's reaction that I have included the ensuing discussion of scapegoats in *King Lear*. Beyond this, I have altered or expanded several other passages in the light of his comments, for all of which I am grateful.

which tragedy provides catharsis. (Neither Kent nor Cordelia requires tragedy for purification; the one preceding, the other transcending personal morality.) What I am denying is that to say Lear
becomes simply a man is to say that he achieves the unaccommodated human condition. The ambiguities here stand out in William Empson's suggestion of Lear as scapegoat and outcast.[11] This
cannot be wrong, but it can be made too much of, or the wrong
thing. We do not want the extremity of Lear's suffering to have
gone for nothing, or for too little, so we may imagine that it has
made him capable of envisioning ours. But as the storm is ending
he is merely humanly a scapegoat, as any man is on the wrong end
of injustice; and no more an outcast than any man out of favor.
Only at his finish does his suffering measure the worst that can
happen to a man, and there not because he is a scapegoat but because
he has made a scapegoat of his love. But that Cordelia is Lear's
scapegoat is compatible with Lear's being ours. And seeing him as
a scapegoat is not incompatible with seeing him as avoiding love
– on the contrary, it is this which shows what his connection with
us is, the act for which he bears total, sacrificial consequences. If
this play contains scapegoats, it is also about scapegoats, about what
it is which creates scapegoats and about the cost of creating them.
To insist upon Lear as scapegoat is apt to thin our sense of this
general condition in his world; and this again would put us in his
position – not *seeing* it from his point of view (maintaining ours),
but accepting his point of view, hence denying the other characters,
and using the occasion not to feel for him (and them) but to sym-
pathize with ourselves.

All the good characters are exiled, cast out – Cordelia and Kent
initially, Edgar at the beginning and Lear at the end of Act II,

---

[11]"Fool in Lear," in *The Structure of Complex Words* (Ann Arbor: University of
Michigan Press [Ann Arbor Paperback], 1967), pp. 145, 157. Because of Empson's
espousal of it, George Orwell's essay on Lear may be mentioned here ("Lear, Tolstoy
and the Fool," reprinted from *Shooting an Elephant and Other Essays*, in F. Kermode,
ed., *Four Centuries of Shakespearean Criticism* [New York: Avon Books, 1965], pp.
514–31). It is, perhaps, of the nature of Orwell's piece that one finds oneself remembering the feel of its moral passion and honesty and the clarity of its hold on
the idea of *renunciation* as the subject of the play, without being able oneself to produce
Orwell's, or one's own, evidence for the idea in the play – except that the meaning of the entire opening and the sense of its consequences assume, as it were, a
self-evidence within the light of that idea. It is probably as good a notation of the
subject as one word could give, and Orwell's writing, here as elsewhere, is exem-
plary of a correct way in which the moral sensibility, distrusting higher ambitions,
exercises its right to judge an imperfect world, never exempting itself from that
world.

Gloucester at the end of Act III. But there is from the opening lines a literal social outcast of another kind, the bastard, the central evil character. A play which has the power of transforming kings into fools equally has the power of overlapping kings and bastards – the naked human condition is more than any man bargains for. Empson finds Lear's "most distinct expression of the scapegoat idea" in the lines

> None does offend, none; I say none. I'll able 'em:
> Take that of me, my friend, who have the power
> To seal the accuser's lips.
>
> (IV, vi, 170–2)

Empson reads: "The royal prerogative has become the power of the outcast to deal directly on behalf of mankind." I do not question the presence of this feeling, but it is equivocal. For what is the nature of this new, direct power of sealing lips? The problem is not just that "None does offend, none; I say none" protests too much, as though Lear can't quite believe it. The problem is that Edmund also deals with men to seal their lips, and he can directly, even elatedly, use this human power because he is an outcast, because judgment has *already* been passed upon him. That is the justice of his position. And he could express himself in the words "None does offend." He would mean, as in his second soliloquy (I, ii, 124–40), that all are equally evil and evasive; hence no man is in a position from which to judge offense in others.

What would this prove, except that the Devil can quote scripture? But that is proof enough if it proves that the greatest truths are nothing, mean harm or help or nothing, apart from their application in the individual case. We see (do we see?) how Edmund's meaning repudiates the Gospels: He is not speaking on behalf of mankind, but on his own; and he is not forgoing judgment, but escaping it by making it indiscriminate, cynicizing it. Then do we see how Lear's mind, in its rage at injustice, is different from Edmund's? For Lear too has a private use for this indiscriminate condemnation of the world. Suppose we see in the progress of Lear's madness a recapitulation of the history of civilization or of consciousness: from the breaking up of familial bonds and the release of offenses which destroy the social cosmos (III, iv), through the fragile replacement of revenge by the institution of legal justice (III, vi), to the corruption

of justice itself and the breaking up of civil bonds (IV, vi). In raging
with each of these stages in turn, Lear's mind gusts to a calm as
the storm calms, drawing even with the world as it goes. (This is
why, adapting Empson's beautiful and compassionate perception,
Lear at this point removes his boots, at home again in the world.)
If he is an outcast, every man is, whose society is in rags about
him; if he is a scapegoat, every man is, under the general shiftings
of blame and in the inaccuracy of justice. Lear has not arrived at
the human condition he saw imaged in poor naked Tom (the sight
which tipped him from world-destroying rage into world-creating
madness); but one could say he now has this choice open to him.
He finds himself a man; so far he has abdicated. But he has not yet
chosen his mortality, to be one man among others; so far he is not
at one; atonement is not complete. He has come to terms with Goneril and Regan, with filial ingratitude; he has come back from the
way he *knew* madness lies. But he has not come to terms with parental insatiability (which he denounced in his "barbarous Scythian"
speech [I, i, 116], and which Gloucester renounces in "the food of
thy abused father's wrath" [IV, i, 22]). He has not come back to
Cordelia. And he does not.

Evidence for this in this scene is not solely that his "None does
offend" is said still stranded in madness (nor even in the possible
hint of power in the fact that he does not just take off his boots
but imagines them removed for him, as by a servant) but in the
content of his ensuing sermon ("I will preach to thee"):

> When we are born, we cry that we are come
> To this great stage of fools.
>
> (IV, vi, 184–5)

This is a sermon, presumably, because it interprets the well-known
text of tears with which each human life begins. But, as Empson
puts it, "the babies cannot be supposed to know all this about human
affairs." I think Lear is there feeling like a child, after the rebirth
of his senses (children do naturally "wawl and cry" at injustice);
and feeling that the world is an unnatural habitat for man; and feeling
it is unnatural because it is a stage. Perhaps it is a stage because its
actors are seen by heaven, perhaps because they are seen by one
another. Either way, it is Lear (not, for example, Gloucester, Lear's
congregation) who sees it there as a stage. But why a stage of fools?

There will be as many answers as there are meanings of "fool." But the point around which all the answers will turn is that it is when, and because, he sees the world as a stage that he sees it peopled with fools, with distortions of persons, with natural scapegoats, among whom human relationship does not arise. Then who is in a position to level this vision at the world? Not, of course, that it is invalid – no one could deny it. The catch is that there is no one to assert it – without asserting himself a fool. The world-accusing fool, like the world-accusing liar, suffers a paradox. Which is why "the praise of Folly" must mean "Folly's praise." (To say that the theatricalization of others makes them scapegoats is a way of putting the central idea of Part II of this essay.)

But if the sense in which, or way in which, Lear has become a scapegoat is not special about him, he can be said to be special there in his *feeling* that he is a scapegoat and in his universal casting of the world with scapegoats. This is an essential connection between him and Gloucester's family: Gloucester is in fact turned out of society, and while he is not left feeling that society has made a scapegoat of him, he has made scapegoats of his sons, deprived each of his birthright, the one by nature and custom, the other by decree. Each reciprocates by casting his father out, in each case by a stratagem, though the one apparently acts out of hatred, the other apparently out of love; and each of the brothers makes a scapegoat of the other, the one by nature and custom, the other by design. Like Edgar, Lear casts himself in the role of scapegoat, and then others suffer for it; like Edmund, he finds himself the natural fool of Fortune, a customary scapegoat, and then kill, kill, kill, kill, kill, kill (cf. IV, vi, 189) – the mind clawing at itself for a hold. These nests of doublings (and in no play is Shakespeare's familiar doubling of themes so relentless, becoming something like the medium of the drama itself, or its vision of the world) suggest that the dramatic point of Shakespeare's doublings is not so much to amplify or universalize a theme as to focus or individuate it, and in particular to show the freedom under each character's possession of his character. Each way of responding to one's foolishness is tested by every other; each way of accepting one's having been cast out is tested by every other; that Gloucester is not driven mad by filial ingratitude (though he is no stranger to the possibility: His very openness in looking at it ["I'll tell thee, friend, I am almost mad myself" (III, iv, 169–70)] makes him a sensitive touchstone of normalcy in this) means that there is no necessary route Lear's spirit has followed. One will want to object that from the fact that a route is not necessary to Gloucester it does not follow that it is not necessary to Lear. But that is the point. To find out why it is necessary one has to discover who Lear is, what *he* finds necessary, his specific spins of need and choice. His tragedy is that he has to find out too, and that he cannot rest with less than an answer. "Who is it that can tell me who I am?" (I, iv, 238). At the first rebuff in his new condition, Lear is forced to the old tragic question. And the Fool lets out his astonishing knowledge: "Lear's shadow." At this point Lear either does not hear, or he thinks the Fool has *told* him who he is, and takes it, as it seems easy to take it, to mean roughly that he is in reduced circumstances. It would be somewhat harder to take if he heard the suggestion of *shade* under "shadow." But the truth may still be harder to be told, harder than anything that can just be told.

Suppose the Fool has precisely answered Lear's question, which is only characteristic of him. Then his reply means: Lear's shadow can tell you who you are. If this is heard, it will mean that the answer to Lear's question is held in the inescapable Lear which is now obscure and obscuring, and in the inescapable Lear which is projected upon the world, and that Lear is double and has a double. And then this play reflects another long curve of feeling about doubling, describing an emphasis other than my recent suggestion that it haunts the characters with their freedom. In the present guise it taunts the characters with their lack of wholeness, their separation from themselves, by loss or denial or opposition. (In Montaigne: "We are, I know not how, double in ourselves, so that what we believe we disbelieve, and cannot rid ourselves of what we condemn."[12] By the time of Heine's *Doppelgänger* ["Still ist die Nacht . . ."], the self is split from its past and from its own feeling, however intimately present both may be.) But in either way, either by putting freedom or by putting integrity into question, doubling sets a task, of discovery, of acknowledgment. And both ways are supported in the moment Lear faces Gloucester and confuses identities with him.

If on a given experience of the play one is caught by the reference to adultery and then to "Gloucester's bastard son" which launches Lear's long tirade against the foulness of nature and of man's justice,

[12]Auden uses this as the epigraph to *The Double Man;* I have not yet found its context.

one may find that absent member of the Gloucester family presiding over Lear's mind here. For Lear's disgust with sexual nature is not far from Edmund's early manic praise of it, especially in their joint sense of the world as alive in its pursuit; and Edmund's stinging sensitivity to the illegitimacy of society's "legitimacy" prefigures Lear's knowledge of the injustice of society's "justice." If, therefore, we are to see in this play, in Miss Welsford's fine phrase, the investing of the king with motley, then in this scene we may see the king standing up for bastards – an illegitimate king in an unlawful world. (Edmund had tossed off a prayer for bastards, and perhaps there is a suggestion that the problem with prayers is not that few are answered but that *all* are, one way or another.) As the doublings reflect one another, each character projecting some more or less eccentric angle to a common theme, one glimpses the possibility of a common human nature which each, in his or her own way, fails to achieve; or perhaps glimpses the idea that its gradual achievement is the admission of reflection in oneself of every human theme. As Christ receives reflection in every form of human scapegoat, every way in which one man bears the brunt of another's distortion and rejection. For us the reflection is brightest in Cordelia, because of her acceptance, perhaps because she is hanged; it is present, on familiar grounds, in the mysteries of the Fool. I cannot help feeling it, if grossly, in the figure of the bastard son. I do not press this. Yet it makes us reflect that evil is not wrong when it thinks of itself as good, for at those times it recaptures a craving for goodness, an experience of its own innocence which the world rejects.

There is hope in this play, and it is not in heaven. It lies in the significance of its two most hideous moments: Gloucester's blinding and Cordelia's death. In Gloucester's history we found hope, because while his weakness has left him open to the uses of evil, evil *has* to turn upon him because it cannot bear him to witness. As long as that is true, evil does not have *free* sway over the world. In Cordelia's death there is hope, because it shows the gods more just – more than we had hoped or wished: Lear's prayer is answered again in this. The gods are, in Edgar's wonderful idea, clear. Cordelia's death means that *every* falsehood, every refusal of acknowledgment, will be tracked down. In the realm of the spirit, Kierkegaard says, there is absolute justice. Fortunately, because if all we had to go on were the way the world goes, we would lose the concept of justice altogether; and then human life would become unbearable. Kant banked the immortality of the soul on the fact that in *this* world goodness and happiness are unaligned – a condition which, if never righted, is incompatible with moral sanity, and hence with the existence of God. But immortality is not necessary for the soul's satisfaction. What is necessary is its own coherence, its ability to judge a world in which evil is successful and the good are doomed; and in particular its knowledge that while injustice may flourish, it cannot rest content. This, I take it, is what Plato's *Republic* is about. And it is an old theme of tragedy.

Its companion theme is that our actions have consequences which outrun our best, and worst, intentions. The drama of *King Lear* not merely embodies this theme, it comments on it, even deepens it. For what it shows is that the *reason* consequences furiously hunt us down is not merely that we are half blind, and unfortunate, but that we go on doing the thing which produced these consequences in the first place. What we need is not rebirth, or salvation, but the courage, or plain prudence, to see and to stop. To abdicate. But what do we need in order to do that? It would be salvation.

II

These last remarks come from a response not so much to the content of the play as to its form. It is a drama not about the given condition in which the soul finds itself (in relation to gods or to earth) but about the soul, as Schopenhauer puts the vision of Kant, as the provider of the given, of the conditions under which gods and earth can appear. It is an enactment not of fate but of responsibility, including the responsibility for fate. However this is finally to be put, its reception demands a particular kind of perception.

What I have in mind can best be brought out in the following way. Suppose that what I have said about why Gloucester is blinded, why he goes to Dover, why he tries suicide, why Edgar avoids his recognition, why he reveals himself when he does, what produces Edmund's attempt to undo his sentence upon Lear and Cordelia, why Gloucester is the first person Lear recognizes, why Cordelia weeps after Lear's imprisoned fantasy, etc. etc. – suppose my answers are true. The problem is then unavoidable: How can critics not have seen them? For it is not that the answers I take to be correct are *recherché;* one needn't have the learning of Bradley or Chambers, or the secrets of Empson, or the discrimination of Johnson, or the passion of Coleridge or Keats, to arrive at them. Their difficulty is of a different kind, an opposite kind.

It is the difficulty of seeing the obvious, something which for some reason is always underestimated, habitually perhaps but not solely by critics, even when the art which hosts them is devoted to that seeing, and the artist set against that underestimation. What *seems* obvious is traced out by the invisible powers of fashion, which offers us reasons whose convenience is almost irresistible. (If this is something we know, it is also something we equally underestimate.) The examples which emerge as most pressing are these: When the well-made play shows us what drama is we say that Shakespeare is poor at plotting, and since we know he is great we excuse him, and then we cross our minds and say that the defects will not be noticed in the heat of performance. When scruples and exercises of New Criticism tell us what poems are, we say that Shakespeare's plays are poems and therefore structures of meaning, and in this way account for their densities, assuring ourselves that even if we do not or cannot perceive them in a given moment they nevertheless have their effect. When we are made to know that Shakespeare lived in Shakespeare's age and so dealt in his age's understandings and conventions, we can forget that it is Shakespeare demanding of us; and so *his* bastard slumps back into "the" bastard of his age, from which he had pointedly lifted it. In some cases (typically in the first kind of example) psychology is invoked to take up the moral or aesthetic slack, in other cases (typically in the last kind of example), and doubtless in response to its earlier misuse, psychology is said to be irrelevant. And in all cases the drama is missed, our perception of it blanked.

I pause here to indicate why I am not trying unduly to blur the immodest or melodramatic quality of the claims I have made: that quality will itself be serviceable if it provides further data for investigating the act of criticism.[13] I am assuming, that is, that criticism is inherently immodest and melodramatic – not merely from its

---

[13]The facts of intolerance, expressed as part of an examination of their causes and reasons, particularly of the starkness of their appearance in the criticism of modern arts, is the content of Michael Fried's contribution to *Art Criticism in the Sixties* (New York: October House, 1967), four papers that composed a symposium held at Brandeis University in May 1966.

temptations to uninstructive superiority and to presumptuous fellow feeling (with audience or artist) but from the logic of its claims, in particular from two of its elements: (1) A critical position will finally rest upon calling a claim *obvious;* (2) a critical discovery will present itself as the *whole* truth of a work, a provision of its total meaning. Taken in familiar ways, these claims seem easily disconfirmable. How can a claim be obvious if not everyone finds it obvious? (And there is always someone who does not – maybe the critic himself won't tomorrow.) And how can a claim to total meaning be correct when so much is left out? (And there is always something.) But if critical judgments are felt to be refuted on *such* grounds, they are not merely intolerant but a little idiotic. (That is the implied claim of such refutations. I don't say it is never justified.) But suppose we hold on to the intolerance and hold off the idiocy for a moment. Then we must ask: How can serious people habitually make such *vulnerable* claims? (Meaning, perhaps, claims so *obviously* false?) But suppose there is another way of taking them; that is, suppose our familiar ways of taking them are what make them seem a bit simple. What are these ways? They take a claim to obviousness as a claim to certainty, and they take the claim to totality as a claim to exhaustiveness. The first of these ways is deeply implicated in the history of modern epistemology, and its effect has been to distrust conviction rather than to investigate the concept of the obvious. (Wittgenstein's later philosophy can be thought of as investigations of obviousness.) The second of these ways expresses the exclusiveness of a lived world, instanced by the mutual offense and the interminable and glancing criticisms of opposed philosophies, and its effect has been to distrust exclusiveness or to attempt exhaustiveness rather than to investigate the concept of totality. It is in the nature of both of these sources of intolerance to appear to be private; because in both one at best has nothing to go on but oneself. (A fashionable liberalism has difficulty telling the difference between seriousness and bigotry. A suggestion of the difference is that the bigot is never isolated. A more ambitious connoisseur will number the differences between seriousness and madness.) This is why a critical discovery is often accompanied by a peculiar exhilaration and why recognition of a critical lapse is accompanied by its peculiar chagrin. One will want to know how (and whether) these emotions differ from the general relish of victory and the general anguish at defeat – say, in science. I do not say that in every case there are differences, but I point to the different ways in which concepts such as "discovery," "advance," "talent," "professional," "insight," "depth," "competition," "influence," etc. are, or may be, applied in criticism and in science – the different shapes of the arenas in which victory and defeat are determined. It seems difference enough that one imagines a major scientific insight occurring to a person with an impulse to race into the streets with it, out of relief and out of the happy knowledge that it is of relevance to his fellow townsmen; whereas the joy in a major critical insight may be unsharable if one lacks the friends, and even not need to be spoken (while perhaps hoping that another will find it on his or her own). This must go with the fact that the topics of criticism are not objects but works, things which are *already* spoken. And if arrogance is inherent in criticism (and therefore where not in the humanities?), then humility is no less painful a task there than anywhere else. Nor is it surprising that the specific elements of arrogance afflict both criticism and philosophy: If philosophy can be thought of as the world of a particular culture brought to consciousness of itself, then one mode of criticism (call it philosophical criticism) can be thought of as the world of a particular work brought to consciousness of itself.

That the perceptions of an age are formed and disturbed by ghostly fashions is scarcely news. And the difficulties of maturing past them are not the difficulties I am primarily interested in here; they are not peculiar to our failure to confront such drama as *King Lear* unearths. This failure has to do with the mode of this drama itself. Indeed, if my reading of it is correct, the drama is exactly about this difficulty. The difficulty lies in a refusal, a refusal expressed as a failure to acknowledge. (That this is a refusal, something each character is *doing* and is going on doing, is what makes these events add up to tragedy rather than to melodrama – in which what you fail to see is simply something out of sight; or to a scene of natural catastrophe – in which what you fail to prevent is simply beyond prediction or reach.) But isn't this at most the difficulty of the characters in the play? What has this got to do with our difficulties in "appreciating this mode of drama," whatever that turns out to mean?

I have more than once suggested that in failing to see what the true position of a character is, in a given moment, we are exactly put in his condition, and thereby implicated in the tragedy. How? Obviously we are not, as Edgar is, standing in Gloucester's presence; we can neither delay nor not delay, avoid nor not avoid, revealing ourselves to him. If, therefore, my suggestion makes sense, there must be an answer to the question: *What* connects us with Edgar when we accept his conduct in the scenes with his father? What is the point or mechanism of this identification? And the answer to this question is the answer to the question: What is the medium of this drama, how does it do its work upon us? My reading of *King Lear* will have fully served its purpose if it provides data from which an unprejudicial description of its "work" can be composed. One such description would be this: The medium is one which keeps all significance continuously before our senses, so that when it comes over us that we have missed it, this discovery will reveal our ignorance to have been willful, complicitous, a refusal to see. This is a fact of my experience in reading the play (it is not a fact of my experience in seeing the play, which may say something either about its performability or about the performances I have seen of it, or about the nature of performance generally). It is different from the experience of comprehending meanings in a complex poem or the experience of finding the sense of a lyric. These are associated with a thrill of recognition, an access of intimacy, not with a particular sense of exposure. The progress from ignorance to exposure, I mean the treatment of an ignorance which is not to be cured by information (because it is not caused by a lack of information), outlines one motive to philosophy; this is a reason for calling Shakespeare's theater one of philosophical drama. (A test of this would be to consider that the experience of these discoveries – or their proper organ – is as of memory. What precedes certain discoveries is a necessity to *return* to a work, in fact or in memory, as to unfinished business. And this may be neutral as between rereading and reseeing. Then one recalls that one sense of philosophy takes memory as its organ of knowledge. An outstanding question is then: What sends us back to a piece or a passage? – as though it is not finished with us. In the opening pages of *Biographia Literaria,* Coleridge takes as his first measure of the worth of a poem the fact that we return to it. Knowing that not just any way of returning will constitute such a measure [say, one in order to prepare for tomorrow's lesson, or to look up an illustration for a thing one already knows], he adds that the return is to be made "with the greatest pleasure." But he is not there concerned to characterize the nature of this pleasure, nor our need of it. The trouble with speaking of this returning as a *remembering* is that it provides access to something we haven't first known and then *forgotten*. Suppose we say that the experience is one of *having to remember*. Then one thinks of Wordsworth's rehearsal [in Book VIII of the *Prelude*] of the motive, and resolution, to know of good and evil, "not as for the mind's delight but for her safety" – the feminine cast registering the mind's need for protection, but the masculine drift showing knowledge that such safety is not achieved through protection, but in action. Evidently Wordsworth is not speaking merely of his past, but of the motive, and resolution, to write – write poetry of such ambitions as the poem he is now writing, and thus give to action the body of the past joined with the soul of the present. And why should the need that sends us back to art be disconnected from the necessity upon which the artist goes for it?)

A structural strategy in *King Lear* brings this out another way. The abdication scene has always been known to be extraordinary, and a familiar justification of it has been that we, as spectators, simply must accept it as the initial condition of the dramatic events and then attend to its consequences. Of course we can do this, or something like it: In a certain context someone says, "Once upon a time there was an old king who had three daughters. Two were very cruel, but the youngest, who was very good and beautiful, was her father's favorite. . . ." So people sometimes say that *King Lear* opens as a fairy tale opens. But it doesn't. It is not narrated, and the first characters we see are two old courtiers discussing the event of the day. The element of fairy tale then appears, centered in other characters, against whose mode of reality the opening figures we have met stand as measures and witnesses, here and hereafter, thus at once heightening and confining the unreal or unseen power we may respond to as a "fairy-tale character," focusing it upon the figure of Lear and suggesting it to be something whose sudden changes befall ordinary human beings. If the drama is taken to show the tragic consequences of this initial condition, it should simultaneously be taken to show, what fairy tales have always known, the lengths there are to go in order to remove a spell; the purity, above all the faithfulness, it requires. In Shakespeare's world this was still visible only in extraordinary events. By the time of the worlds of Ibsen and Chekhov, after fairy tales had been collected and shelved, the spell finds its life in our ordinary lives: Nothing can break the one without breaking the other. I have pointed to other explicit moments of magic in the play, Cordelia's kiss and Lear's song to her. The moral of such moments extends back to the abdication scene: There is no problem of *accepting* them; on the contrary, they are – well, magical.

The idea that the abdication scene strains belief suggests a careful ignorance of the quick routes taken in one's own rages and jealousies and brutalities. Obviously what makes it believable is not an overwhelming tenderness (*that* temptation is yet to come); what is apparently irresistible is recourse to some interpretation which deadens awareness of the ordinary, the civilized violence escaping from it (recourses such as "ritualistic," "fairy tale," "an old crochety tyrant," "an archaic setting"). This uncovers what I meant by the structural strategy of the play's opening scene: We *do* accept its events as they come to light; anyway we sit through them, and we accommodate ourselves to them one way or another; after which, as a consequence of which, we have to accept less obviously extraordinary events as unquestionable workings out of a bad beginning. To speak of this as a strategy may suggest that Shakespeare intended it to have this effect; and do I want to make such a claim? But why not? A critic who strains at this claim will allow himself to swallow the notion that Shakespeare counted on the fact that he was only using an old story whose initial improbabilities he needn't be responsible for. Maybe. Only this raises, and makes unwelcome, urgent questions: Why does he use *this* story? What does he see in it? Why *show* the abdication rather than begin with various accounts of it? Whereas all I need as evidence for saying that Shakespeare intended the strategy of our accepting it (that is, all the claim comes to) is that he put it there and we do accept it, if in confusion. If further explanation is required, then I have equally clear facts to appeal to: What we witness is simultaneously confirmed by the rest of the audience, if the work is successful (this cognitive function of audience is, so far as I know, unremarked, but it seems to me as evident as the contagion and power of laughter an audience can generate, or the enthusiasm it inspires in a public utterance); again, we are helped by the initial verisimilitude in the characters of Kent and Gloucester; and helped further in seeing that no one present on the stage *accepts* Lear's behavior – all who speak (save one) find it extraordinary. So should we. But also ordinary. And a strategy whose point is to break up our sense of the ordinary (which is not the same as a strategy whose point is to present us with spectacularly extraordinary events) also has claim to be called philosophical: This is perhaps why an essential response in both philosophy and tragedy is that of wonder. (Later versions of this strategy are Marxian and Kierkegaardian dialectic, which dramatize both the historical contingency in states we had hitherto accepted as inevitable and the necessity in states we had hitherto thought passing.)

Having lost the power to distinguish the acceptable from the questionable, do we nevertheless still know right from wrong? Whatever the gaudy distractions of Christianizing in reading Shakespeare's plays, it serves him better than the stinting distractions of moralizing. Many critics seem to know quite well what is good for Lear and what he ought not to have done.[14] But suppose we are merely scrupulous and compassionate enough to recognize that any of this is what we do not know, or anyway that the characters themselves know every bit as much in that line as we do. (If not, then again it is not tragedy which has been revealed.) The form of problem we face is: Why *can't* they do or see something? What power has taken them over? For the *content* of Lear's conflict is not tragic; I mean the public conflict – he need not, for example, choose to sacrifice either his daughter or the lives of his subjects. Here the well-known experience of *inevitability* in a tragic sequence comes to attention. But to what shall we attribute it? Not, in all conscience, and after Bradley, to Fate or character or some overriding classical passion – not merely because we can no longer attach old weight to these words, but because, immediately, they do not account for the particular lie of events in the plots Shakespeare selects for tragedy. And more important, they are directly false to our experience, which is, for all their hidden manipulation, by circumstance or passion, that these figures are radically and continuously *free,* operating under their own power, at every moment choosing their destruction. Kant tells us that man lives in two worlds, in one of which he is free and in the other determined. It is as if in a theater these two worlds are faced off against one another, in their intimacy and their mutual inaccessibility. The audience is free – of the circumstance and passion of the characters, but that freedom cannot reach

---

[14] This is the attitude that Alpers's study is meant most directly to discourage.

the arena in which it could become effective. The actors are determined – not because their words and actions are dictated and their
future sealed, but because, if the dramatist has really peopled a
world, the characters are exercising all the freedom at their command, and specifically failing to. Specifically; not exercising or ced-
ing it once for all. They are, in a word, men and women; and our
liabilities in responding to them are nothing other than our liabilities
in responding to any person – rejection, brutality, sentimentality,
indifference, the relief and the terror in finding courage, the ironies
of human wishes.

It was not wrong to read the sense of inevitability in terms of a
chain of cause and effect; what was wrong, what became insufficient
to explain our lives, was to read this chain as if its first link lay in
the past, and hence as if the present were the scene of its ineluctable
effects, in the face of which we must learn suffering. With Kant
(because with Luther) and then Hegel and Nietzsche, not to say
Freud, we became responsible for the meaning of the suffering itself,
indeed for the very fact that the world is to be comprehended under
the rule of causation at all. What has become inevitable is the fact
of endless causation itself, together with the fact of incessant freedom. And what has become the tragic fact is that we cannot or will
not tell which is which. When tragedy leapt from inevitability, we
had been taken into the confidence of the tale; hints of the characters'
ignorance of their fate were laid ("dramatic irony"). The awe in
experiencing it was like the awe in suddenly falling into the force
of nature or of crowds or in watching a building collapse. We are
not in Shakespeare's confidence. Now tragedy grows from the fortunes we choose to interpret, to accept, as inevitable, and we have
no more hints of ignorance than the characters have. Edmund sees
something like this (in his early soliloquy, ". . . we make guilty of
our disasters the sun, the moon, and stars"), but, being Edmund,
he finds it comic. And no play can show more instances and ranges
than *King Lear* in which God's name and motive are taken in vain.
The past cannot now be clarified as Teiresias clarified it (that would
now be a relief, however terrible its terms), for the present is not
clear or strong enough to believe such predictions. It is only about
others that prophecy commands our attention. (Hence, for example,
the vogue of game theory, and the fashion of looking for the "cause"
of historical events.) But the seer is not needed. Nothing we can
know or need to know is unknown.

"Surely," it will be said, "whatever all this is supposed to mean, it is not relevant to our relation with those figures up there, it applies at best to their relations with one another, or to ours with one another. You forget this is theater; that they are characters up there, not persons; that their existence is fictional; that it is not up to us to confront them morally, actually enter their lives." How might I forget this? By becoming like the child who screams at Red Riding Hood the truth of her situation? But I don't scream out, any longer; that is just a matter of getting older and learning how to behave. (Though of course "just a matter" does not mean that it is not profound learning. It is as profound as learning not to wet the bed, and I can do that in my sleep. If I couldn't, the learning wouldn't yet have amounted to much.) What am I to remember, and what good would it do if I did? I know people are annoyed by what seems feigned innocence, and with a final mustering of patience they tell me that I am to remember that I am in a theater. And how do I do that? How do I remember something there is no obvious way for me to forget? ("Don't forget where you are" is not meant to inform me of the place I am in, but calls to my attention a more or less distracted or obsessive piece of behavior which I immediately know to be unacceptable there – like smoking in church.) Am I to remember to be entertained? But suppose I am not; why should I be? Am I to remember that I am not responsible for those people up there? Presumably this is not a way of saying that they are none of my business or that they have not been made real for me by their creator. But what else is it a way of saying? Am I to remember that I do not have to confront them, give them my warnings or advice or compassion? But I am confronting them (unless my head or heart is lowered, in fear or boredom) and I *have* this advice or warning or compassion or anxiety; if you haven't, you don't see what I see. But I cannot *offer* it to them or *share* it with them. That is true; they cannot hear my screams. But that is something else; that is something I do not have to remember, something I know as I know that I cannot choose the content of my dreams or suffer my daughter's pain or alter my father's childhood.

So the question arises: Why do I choose to subject myself to this suffering? Why do I deliberately confront a situation which fills me with a pity and terror I know are ineffective? Two familiar lines of answer have been drawn to such a question. One of them looks to the use to be made of these feelings in the aesthetic context, their (cathartic) effect upon *me;* the other denies that it is real pity and terror that I feel, but rather some aesthetic (more or less distant) counterpart of them. Whatever their respective merits and obscurities, both answers pass the sense of the question which is troubling me, which is brought out by asking: How do I know I am to *do* nothing, confronted by such events? The answer "Because it is an aesthetic context" is no answer, partly because no one knows what an aesthetic context is, partly because, if it means anything, a factor of its meaning is "a context in which I am to do nothing"; which is the trouble.

But my object here is not a theory of tragedy. It is simply to suggest, staying within the evidence of the reading I have given of one play, how this mode of drama works upon us and what mode of perception it asks of us. For I feel confident not only that this play works upon us differently from other modes of theater, but that it is dramatic in a way, or at a depth, foreign to what we have come to expect in a theater, even that it is essentially dramatic in a way our theater and perception do not fathom. These are scarcely new thoughts, but no statement of them I know has seemed to me to get out clearly enough what this sense of drama is. Doubtless only someone who shares this sense will credit or consider the few suggestions I can make about it here.

Clearly, as we are always told, its particular dramatic effect is a function of the fact that its words are poetry. Sometimes Shakespeare's plays are said to be poems, but obviously they are not poems; they are made in a medium which knows how to use poetry dramatically. It is an accomplishment of the same magnitude, even of the same kind, as the discovery of perspective in painting and of tonality in music – and, apparently, just as irretrievable, for artistic purposes now. The question is: How does the medium function which uses poetry in this way?

It is not uncommon to find Shakespeare's plays compared to music, but in the instances I have seen, this comparison rests upon more or less superficial features of music, for example, on its balance of themes, its recurrences, shifts of mood, climaxes – in a word, on its theatrical properties. But music is, or was, dramatic in a more fundamental sense, or it became so when it no longer expanded festivals or enabled dancing or accompanied songs, but achieved its own dramatic autonomy, worked out its progress in its own terms. Perhaps this begins with Monteverdi (born three years after Shakespeare), but in any case it is secured only with the establishment of tonality and has its climax in the development of sonata form. The essence of the quality I have in mind has to do with the notion of *development:* not, as in early sonata forms, merely with an isolated section in which fragments of earlier material are recolored and reassembled, but with the process, preeminent in late Beethoven and Brahms, in which the earlier is metamorphosed into new stabilities, culminating in a work like the "Hammerklavier" Sonata, in which *all* later material can be said to be "contained" in the rising and falling interval of a third in the opening two bars. The question I wish to raise here is: How is music made this way to be perceived? *What* are we to perceive in order to understand and respond to what is said? Obviously not, in the example alluded to, merely or primarily the rising and falling thirds. I will say that the quality we are to perceive is one of *directed motion,* controlled by relations of keys, by rate of alteration, and by length and articulation of phrases. We do not know where this motion can stop and we do not understand why it has begun here, so we do not know where we stand nor why we are there. The drama consists in following this out and in finding out what it takes to follow this out.

The specific comparison with Shakespeare's drama has to do with the two most obvious facts about what is required in following this music: first, that one hears its directedness; second, that one hears only what is happening now.

The critical element appears to be that of directedness, because obviously all music, and all language and all conduct, shares the property that not everything of significance is perceptible now. And yet there is the decisive difference between waiting for a sentence in prose or conversation to end and attending to a line of poetry or a tonal phrase, a difference suggested by such facts as these: In conversation, a remark which begins a certain way can normally have only one of a definite set of endings; we know why a remark has begun as it has or we can find out why in obvious ways; and the remark will come to an end of its own accord, what counts as an end being given in the language; so if, for example, we *hang* on these words, that is not because of something happening in these words before us now. It is as if dramatic poetry and tonal music, forgoing these givens, are made to imitate the simplest facts of life:

that life is lived in time, that there is a now at which everything that happens happens, and a now at which for each man and each woman everything stops happening, and that what has happened is not here and now, and that what might have happened then and there will never happen then and there, and that what will happen is not here and now and yet may be settled by what is happening here and now in a way we cannot know or will not see here and now. The perception or attitude demanded in following this drama is one which demands a continuous attention to what is happening at each here and now, as if everything of significance is happening at this moment, while each thing that happens turns a leaf of time. I think of it as an experience of *continuous presentness*. Its demands are as rigorous as those of any spiritual exercise – to let the past go and to let the future take its time; so that we not allow the past to determine the meaning of what is now happening (something else may have come of it) and that we not anticipate what will come of what has come. Not that anything is possible (though it is) but that we do not know what is, and is not, next.

Epistemology will demonstrate that we cannot know, cannot be certain of, the future; but we don't believe it. We anticipate, and so we are always wrong. Even when what we anticipate comes to pass we get the wrong idea of our powers and of what our safety depends upon, for we imagine that we *knew* this would happen, and take it either as an occasion for congratulations or for punishments, of ourselves or others. Instead of acting as we can and remaining equal to the consequences. (Here one might consider the implication of the fact that you say, "I knew it!" with sharp relief or sudden anguish, and that of course it does not mean that in fact you were fully apprized of a particular outcome. It means, roughly, that "something told you," something you wish you had harkened to. And while that is no doubt true, the frame of mind in which you express it, by saying in that particular way that you *knew,* assures that you will not harken. Because it reveals a frame of mind in which you had tried, and are going on trying now, to alchemize a guess or a hope or a suspicion into a certainty, a *pry* into the future rather than an intimation of conscience.)

Nietzsche thought the metaphysical consolation of tragedy was lost when Socrates set *knowing* as the crown of human activity. And it is a little alarming, from within the conviction that the medium of drama which Shakespeare perfected also ended with him, to think again that Bacon and Galileo and Descartes were contemporary with those events. We will hardly say that it was *because* of the development of the new science and the establishing of epistemology as the monitor of philosophical inquiry that Shakespeare's mode of tragedy disappeared. But it may be that the loss of presentness – which is what the disappearance of that mode of tragedy means – is what works us into the idea that we can save our lives by knowing them. This seems to be the message both of the new epistemology and of Shakespeare's tragedy themselves.

In the unbroken tradition of epistemology since Descartes and Locke (radically questioned from within itself only in our period), the concept of knowledge (of the world) disengages from its connections with matters of information and skill and learning, and becomes fixed to the concept of certainty alone, and in particular to a certainty provided by the (by my) senses. At some early point in epistemological investigations, the world normally present to us (the world in whose existence, as it is typically put, we "believe") is brought into question and vanishes, whereupon all connection with a world is found to hang upon what can be said to be "present to the senses"; and that turns out, shockingly, not to be the world. It is at this point that the doubter finds himself cast into skepticism, turning the existence of the external world into a problem. Kant called it a scandal to philosophy and committed his genius to putting a stop to it, but it remains active in the conflicts between traditional philosophers and their ordinary language critics, and it inhabits the void of comprehension between Continental ontology and Anglo-American analysis as a whole. Its relevance to us at the moment is only this: The skeptic does not gleefully and mindlessly forgo the world we share, or thought we shared; he is neither the knave Austin took him to be, nor the fool the pragmatists took him for, nor the simpleton he seems to men of culture and of the world. He forgoes the world for just the reason that the world is important, that it is the scene and stage of connection with the present: He finds that it vanishes exactly with the effort to *make* it present. If this makes him unsuccessful, that is because the presentness achieved by certainty of the senses cannot compensate for the presentness which had been elaborated through our old absorption in the world. But the wish for genuine connection is there, and there was a time when the effort, however hysterical, to assure epistemological presentness was the best expression of seriousness about our relation to the world, the expression of an awareness that presentness was threatened, gone. If epistemology wished to make knowing a substitute for that fact, that is scarcely foolish or knavish, and scarcely some simple mistake. It is, in fact, one way to describe the tragedy *King Lear* records.

For its characters, having for whatever reason to forgo presentness to their worlds, extend that disruption in their knowing of it (Lear and Edmund knowing they cannot be loved, Regan knowing the destination of Gloucester, Edgar knowing he is contemned and has to win acceptance). But how do we stop? How do we learn that what we need is not more knowledge but the willingness to forgo knowing? For this sounds to us as though we are being asked to abandon reason for irrationality (for we know what these are and we know these are alternatives), or to trade knowledge for superstition (for we know when conviction is the one and when it is the other – the thing the superstitious always take for granted). This is why we think skepticism must mean that we cannot know the world exists, and hence that perhaps there isn't one (a conclusion some profess to admire and others to fear). Whereas what skepticism suggests is that since we cannot know the world exists, its presentness to us cannot be a function of knowing. The world is to be *accepted;* as the presentness of other minds is not to be known, but acknowledged. But what is this "acceptance," which caves in at a doubt? And where do we get the idea that there is something we cannot do (e.g., prove that the world exists)? For this is why we take Kant to have said that there are things we cannot know; whereas what he said is that something cannot be known – *and* cannot coherently be doubted either, for example, that there is a world and that we are free. When Luther said we cannot know God but must have faith, it is clear enough that the inability he speaks of is a logical one: There is not some comprehensible activity we cannot perform, and equally not some incomprehensible activity we cannot perform. Our relation to God is that of parties to a testament (or refusers of it); and Luther's logical point is that you do not accept a promise by knowing something about the promisor. How, if this is the case, we become confused about it clearly requires explanation, and the cure will be sufficiently drastic – crucifying the intellect. But perhaps no less explanation is required to understand why we have the idea that knowing the world exists is to be understood as an instance of knowing that a particular object exists (only, so to speak, an enormously large one, the largest). Yet this idea is shared by all traditional epistemologists.[15] (Its methodological expression is the investigation of our knowledge of the external world by an investigation of a claim that a particular object exists.) Nor is it surprising that it is the intellect which, still bloody from its victories, remains to be humbled if the truth here is to emerge. Reason seems able to overthrow the deification of everything but itself. To imagine that what is therefore required of us is a new rage of irrationality would be about as intelligent as to imagine that because heaven rejects the prideful man what it craves is a monkey. For the point of forgoing knowledge is, of course, to know.

To overcome knowing is a task Lear shares with Othello and Macbeth and Hamlet, one crazed by knowledge he can neither test nor reject, one haunted by knowledge whose authority he cannot impeach, one cursed by knowledge he cannot share. Lear abdicates sanity for the usual reason: It is his way not to know what he knows, or to know only what he knows. At the end, recovered to the world, he still cannot give up knowledge, the knowledge that he is captured, lost, receiving just punishment, and so he does again the thing for

---

[15]A particularly brilliant occurrence of it runs through Hume's *Dialogues on Natural Religion:* It is the essential assumption of Cleanthes (the new believer) which Philo (the new skeptic) does not question, and I suppose that one or other of them, or both together, pretty well exhaust Hume's discoveries in this region. Freed from this assumption, the *experience* of design or purpose in the world (which Cleanthes always begins with and comes back to, and which Philo confirms) has a completely different force. It is no longer a modest surmise about a particular object, for which there is no good evidence (none against, but none for); but rather, being a natural and *inescapable* response, it has, in terms of Hume's own philosophizing, the same claim to reveal the world as our experience of causation (or of objecthood) has. – This is essentially the view of Hume's *Dialogues* that I have presented in my classes over a number of years. In the spring of 1967 I began studying and teaching the writings of Heidegger, and the discussion of the concepts of *world* and *worldhood* near the beginning of *Being and Time* seem to me not only intuitively clear against this background, but to represent the beginnings of a formidable phenomenological investigation of a phase of empiricism, indeed of traditional epistemology altogether. Part II of this essay bears marks of that reading, notably in the transition from the concept of being in someone's *presence* to that of being in his *present;* but the ideas do not derive from that reading, and my understanding of Heidegger's work is still too raw for me to wish to claim support from it.

I am not unaware of the desperate obscurity of these remarks about traditional epistemology, both in this note and in the section of this essay from which it is suspended. That is the point at which my reliance on my doctoral thesis ("The Claim to Rationality," Harvard University, 1961) is most sustained. This is now superseded by *The Claim of Reason.*

which he will now irrecoverably be punished. It is the thing we do
not know that can save us. (This is what fairy tales told, when third
sons collected or comforted abandoned things and hags. It is what
theology knew as grace. Ignorance of it is the damnation of Faust,
the one piece of knowledge he could not bargain for.)

In addition to the notions of continuous presentness and of the
attempt to overcome knowledge, I have sometimes wanted to speak
of the *reality of time* as a way of hitting off the experience of this
mode of drama. At each moment, until their last, the future of each
character in *King Lear* is open; and in the end each closes it, except
for Cordelia, who chooses, out of love, to let it close. This is not
the way time is conceived in other dramaturgy. In *Phédre,* time is
frozen, as place is; the action is transfixed by the lucidity which
arrays itself against the truth, absorbing its brilliance, and the lucidity
which supervenes as truth breaks through. In Ibsen, time is molded
to fit the moments at which drama, carefully prepared, explodes
into the action. It depends for its effect not on the fact of time but
upon the feats of timing, upon something's happening at the right,
or the wrong, time. One slip and it is melodrama; but then one
slip and Racine is oratory. In *Phédre* we are placed unprotected under
heaven, examined by an unblinking light. In *Hedda Gabler,* we watch
and wait, unable to avert our eyes, as if from an accident or an
argument rising at the next table in a restaurant, or a figure standing
on the ledge of a skyscraper. In *King Lear* we are differently implicated, placed into a world not obviously unlike ours (as Racine's
is, whose terrain we could not occupy) nor obviously like ours (as
Ibsen's is, in whose rooms and rhythms we are, or recently were,
at home), and somehow participating in the proceedings – not listening, not watching, not overhearing, almost as if dreaming it,
with words and gestures carrying significance of that power and
privacy and obscurity; and yet participating, as at a funeral or marriage or inauguration, confirming something; it could not happen
without us. It is not a dispute or a story, but history happening,
and we are living through it; later we may discover what it means,
when we discover what a life means.

In each case the first task of the dramatist is to gather us and then
to silence and immobilize us. Or say that it is the poster which has
gathered us and the dimming house lights which silence us. Then
the first task of the dramatist is to reward this disruption, to show

that this very extraordinary behavior, sitting in a crowd in the dark, is very sane. It is here that we step past the carry of Dr. Johnson's words. He is right in dismissing – anyway, in denying – the idea that we need to have what happens in a theater made credible, and right to find that such a demand proceeds from a false idea that otherwise what happens in a theater is incredible, and right to say that our response to the events on a stage is neither to credit nor to discredit them: We know we are in a theater. But then he does not stop to ask, What is it that we then know? What is a theater? Why are we there? – anyway, not for longer than it takes to answer, ". . . the spectators . . . come to hear a certain number of lines recited with just gesture and elegant modulation." It is not clear to me how seriously this straight-faced remark is meant. Its rhetoric may be that of the academic's put-down of the enthusiast. (Listeners come to an opera to hear a certain number of tunes sung with just pitch and elegant phrasing. Spectators at a football game go to see a certain number of gigantic men attack one another for the possession of a bag of air.) Or it may be that *Garrick's* gestures and modulations were worth assembling for. Or it may be that the London theaters of that time typically provided an experience of expert recitation. What seems clear enough is that the theater was not important to Johnson; that a certain provision of inside entertainment was sufficient to justify the expense of an evening there. But if the point is entertainment, then his difficult acquaintance Hume had reraised a question which needs attention: Why should such matters provide entertainment? Hume's even more difficult acquaintance Rousseau, for whom the theater was important, reraised the next question: What is the good of such entertainment?

What is the state of mind in which we find the events in a theater neither credible nor incredible? The usual joke is about the Southern yokel who rushes to the stage to save Desdemona from the black man. What is the joke? That he doesn't know how to behave in a theater? That would be plausible here, in a way it would not be plausible in accounting for, or dealing with, the child screaming at Red Riding Hood, or the man lighting a cigarette in church. It treats him like the visitor who drinks from the finger bowl. That fun depends upon the anxious giggle at seeing our customs from a distance, letting them show for a moment in their arbitrariness. We have no trouble understanding what his mistake has been, and the glimpse of arbitrariness is beneficial because the custom justifies itself again: We see the point of having the finger bowl and so (apart from threats to symbol and caste) it doesn't matter that there are other ways of keeping clean; it is enough that this is our way. But what mistake has the yokel in the theater made, and what is *our* way? He thinks someone is strangling someone. – But that is true; Othello is strangling Desdemona. – Come on, come on; you know, he thinks that very man is putting out the light of that very woman right now. – Yes, and that is exactly what is happening. – You're not amusing. The point is that he thinks something is really happening, whereas nothing is really happening. It's playacting. The woman will rise again to die another night. – That is what I thought was meant, what I was impatiently being asked to accede to. The trouble is that I really do not understand what I am being asked, and of course I am suggesting that you do not know either. You tell me that that woman will rise again, but I know that she will not, that she is dead and has died and will again die, die dead, die with a lie on her lips, damned with love. You can say there are two women, Mrs. Siddons and Desdemona, both of whom are mortal, but only one of whom is dying in front of our eyes. But what you have produced is two names. Not all the pointing in the world to *that* woman will distinguish the one woman from the other. The trouble can be put two ways; or there are two troubles and they pull opposite ways; you can't point to one without pointing to the other; and you can't point to both at the same time. Which just means that *pointing* here has become an incoherent activity. Do you wish to say that Mrs. Siddons has not died, or does not die? These are not incomprehensible remarks, but the first implies that she had been in danger and the second suggests that she is not scheduled for death. At least our positions would then be distinguishable, if incomprehensible. I mean, the intentions with which we go to the theater are equally incomprehensible. You go, according to what has so far come out, in order to find that Mrs. Siddons is not dead; I go to watch Desdemona die. I don't particularly enjoy the comparison, for while I do not share your tastes they seem harmless enough, where mine are very suspect.

The case of the yokel has its anxieties. How do we imagine we might correct him? – that is, *what* mistake do we suppose him to have made? If we grant him the concept of playacting, then we will tell him that this is an instance of it: "They are only acting; it isn't real." But we may not be perfectly happy to have had to say that.

Not that we doubt that it is true. If the thing *were* real. . . . But somehow we had *accepted* its nonfactuality; it made it possible for there to have been a play. When we say it, in assurance, it comes out as an empirical assertion. Doubtless it has a very high degree of probability; anyway there is no reason to think that Mrs. Siddons is in danger, though of course it is not logically absurd to suppose otherwise. – But now our philosophical repressions are getting out of control. This isn't at all what we meant to be saying. Beforehand, her danger was absolutely out of the question; we did not have to rule it out in order to go on enjoying the proceedings. We do not *have* to now either, and yet the empirical and the transcendental are not as clearly separate as, so to speak, we thought they were. "They are only pretending" is something we typically say to children, in reassurance; and it is no happier a thing to say in that context, and no truer. The point of saying it there is not to focus them on the play, but to help bring them out of it. It is not an instructive remark, but an emergency measure. If the child cannot be brought out of the play by working through the content of the play itself, he should not have been subjected to it in the first place.

Neither credible nor incredible: That ought to mean that the concept of credibility is inappropriate altogether. The trouble is, it is inappropriate to real conduct as well, most of the time. That couple over there, drinking coffee, talking, laughing. Do I believe they are just passing the time of day, or testing out the field for a flirtation, or something else? In usual cases, not one thing or another; I neither believe nor disbelieve. Suppose the man suddenly puts his hands to the throat of the woman. Do I believe or disbelieve that he is going to throttle her? The time for that question, as soon as it comes to the point, is already passed. The question is: What, if anything, do I do? What I believe hangs on what I do or do not do and on how I react to what I do or do not do. And whether something or nothing, there will be consequences. At the opening of the play it is fully true that I neither believe nor disbelieve. But I am something, perplexed, anxious. . . . Much later, the warrior asks his wife if she has said her prayers. Do I believe he will go through with it? I know he will; it is a certainty fixed forever; but I hope against hope he will come to his senses; I appeal to him, in silent shouts. Then he puts his hands on her throat. The question is: What, if anything, do I do? I do nothing; that is a certainty fixed forever. And it has its consequences. *Why* do I do nothing? Because they are only pretending? That would be a reason not to do anything if it were true of the couple over there, who just a moment ago were drinking coffee, laughing. There it is a reason because it tells me something I did not know. Here, in the theater, what does it tell me? It is an excuse, whistling in the dark; and it is false. Othello is not pretending. Garrick is not pretending, any more than a puppet in that part would be pretending. I know everything, and yet the question arises: Why do I sit there? And the honest answer has to be: There is nothing I can do. Why not?

If the yokel is not granted the concept of playacting, you will not be able to correct him, and that has its own anxiety; not just that of recognizing that people may be wholly different from oneself, but in making us question the inevitability of our own concept of acting, its lucidity to ourselves. You may then have to restrain him and remove him from the theater; you may even have to go so far as to stop the play. *That* is something we can do; and its very extremity shows how little is in our power. For that farthest extremity has not touched Othello; he has vanished. It has merely interrupted an evening's work. Quiet the house, pick up the thread again, and Othello will reappear, as near and as deaf to us as ever. – The transcendental and the empirical crossing; possibilities shudder from it.

The little joke on the yokel is familiar enough of its kind. The big joke, and not just on the yokel, is his idea that *if* the thing were in fact happening he would be able to stop it, be equal to his chivalry. It is fun to contemplate his choices. Will he reason with Othello? (After Iago has destroyed his reason.) Tell him the truth? (Which the person who loves him has been doing over and over.) Threaten him, cross swords with him? (That, one would like to see.) – There is nothing and we know there is nothing we can do. Tragedy is meant to make sense of that condition.

It is said by Dr. Johnson, and felt by Tom Jones's friend Partridge, that what we credit in a tragedy is a possibility, a recognition that if we were in such circumstances we would feel and act as those characters do. But I do not consider it a very live possibility that I will find myself an exotic warrior, having won the heart of a young high-born girl by the power of my past and my capacity for poetry, then learning that she is faithless. And if I did find myself in that position I haven't any idea what I would feel or do. – That is not what is meant? Then what is? That I sense the possibility that I shall feel impotent to prevent the object I have set my soul on,

and won, from breaking it; that it is possible that I shall trust someone who wishes me harm; that I can become murderous with jealousy and know chaos when my imagination has been fired and then
gutted and the sense of all possibility has come to an end? But I
know, more or less, these things now; and if I did not, I would
not know what possibility I am to envision as presented by this
play.

It may seem perverse or superficial or plain false to insist that we
confront the figures on a stage. It may seem perverse: because it is
so obvious what is meant in saying we do *not* confront them, namely, that they are characters in a play. The trouble with this objection
is its assumption that it is obvious what kind of existence characters
in a play have, and obvious what our relation to them is, obvious
why we are present. Either what I have been saying makes these
assumptions less comfortable, or I have failed to do what I wished
to do. It may seem superficial: because saying that we "confront"
them seems just a fancy way of saying that we *see* them, and nobody
would care to deny that. The trouble is that we no more merely
see these characters than we merely see people involved elsewhere
in our lives – or, if we do merely see them that shows a specific
response to the claim they make upon us, a specific form of acknowledgment; for example, rejection. It may seem plain false: because we can no more confront a character in a play than we can
confront any fictitious being.

The trouble is, there they are. The plain fact, the only plain fact,
is that we do not *go up* to them, even that we cannot. – "Obviously
not. Their existence is fictional." – Meaning what? That they are
not real? Meaning what? That they are not to be met with in space
and time? This means they are not in nature. (That is, as Leibniz
puts it, they are not objects to which one of *every* pair of opposite
predicates truly applies – e.g., that one or the other of them has
children or has not, ate breakfast or did not. But no such pair can
be ruled out in advance of coming to know a character; and more
is true of him than we take in at a glance, or in a generation of
glances. And more that we are responsible for knowing. Call him
our creation, but then say that creation is an exhausting business.
It would not be creation from nothing, but from everything – that
is, from a totality, the world of the words.) And neither is God in
nature, neither are square roots, neither is the spirit of the age or

the correct tempo of the "Great Fugue." But if these things do not exist, that is not because they are not in nature. And there have so far always been certain people who have known how to find each of them. Calling the existence of Lear and others "fictional" is incoherent (if understandable) when used as an explanation of their existence, or as a denial of their existence. It is, rather, the name of a problem: *What* is the existence of a character on the stage, what kind of (grammatical) entity is this? We know several of its features:

1. A character is not, and cannot become, aware of us. Darkened, indoor theaters dramatize the fact that the audience is invisible. A theater whose house lights were left on (a possibility suggested, for other reasons, by Brecht) might dramatize the equally significant fact that we are also inaudible to them, and immovable (that is, at a *fixed* distance from them). I will say: We are not in their presence.

2. They are in our presence. This means, again, not simply that we are seeing and hearing them, but that we are acknowledging them (or specifically failing to). Whether or not we acknowledge others is not a matter of choice, any more than accepting the presence of the world is a matter of choosing to see or not to see it. Some persons sometimes are capable of certain blindnesses or deafnesses toward others; but, for example, avoidance of the presence of others is not blindness or deafness to their claim upon us; it is as conclusive an acknowledgment that they are present as murdering them would be. Tragedy shows that we are responsible for the death of others even when we have not murdered them, and even when we have not manslaughtered them innocently. As though what we have come to regard as our normal existence is itself poisoning.

But doesn't the fact that we do not or cannot go up to them just mean that we do not or cannot acknowledge them? One may feel like saying here: The acknowledgment cannot be *completed*. But this does not mean that acknowledging is impossible in a theater. Rather it shows what acknowledging, in a theater, is. And acknowledging in a theater shows what acknowledgment in actuality is. For what is the difference between tragedy in a theater and tragedy in actuality? In both, people in pain are in our presence. But in actuality acknowledgment *is* incomplete; in actuality there is no acknowledgment, unless we put ourselves in their presence, reveal ourselves to them. We may find that the point of tragedy in a theater is exactly relief from this necessity, a respite within which to prepare for this necessity, to clean out the pity and terror which stand in the way of acknowledgment outside. ("Outside of here it is death" – maybe Hamm the actor has the theater in mind.)

3. It is a question how acknowledgment is to be expressed, that is, how we are to put ourselves in another's presence. In terms which have so far come out, we can say: We must learn to reveal ourselves, to allow ourselves to be seen. When we do not, when we keep ourselves in the dark, the consequence is that we convert the other into a character and make the world a stage for him. There is fictional existence with a vengeance, and there is the theatricality which theater such as *King Lear* must overcome, is meant to overcome, shows the tragedy in failing to overcome.[16] The conditions of theater literalize the conditions we exact for existence outside – hiddenness, silence, isolation – hence make that existence plain. Theater does not expect us simply to stop theatricalizing; it knows that we can theatricalize its conditions as we can theatricalize any others. But in giving us a place within which our hiddenness and silence and separation are accounted for, it gives us a chance to stop.

[16]That the place of art is not pervasively threatened by the production of objects whose hold upon us is theatrical, and that serious modernist art survives only in its ability to defeat theater, are companion subjects of Michael Fried's "Art and Objecthood" (*Artforum*, no. 10 [June 1967], pp. 12–23). It is, among other things, the most useful and enlightening explanation of the tastes and ambitions of the fashionable modern sensibility I know of. Its conjunction with what I am saying in this essay (even to the point of specific concepts, most notably that of "presentness") is more exact than can be made clear in a summary, and will be obvious to anyone reading it. I take this opportunity to list other of Fried's recent writings which develop the notions and connections of modernism and seriousness and theatricality, but which I have not had occasion to cite specifically: "Shape as Form: Frank Stella's New Paintings," *Artforum*, 5, no. 3 (November, 1966), pp. 18–27; "The Achievement of Morris Louis," *Artforum*, 5, no. 6 (February 1967), pp. 34–40 (the material of this essay is incorporated in Fried's *Morris Louis* (Abrams, 1970); "New Work by Anthony Caro," *Artforum*, 5, no. 6 (February 1967), pp. 46–7; "Jules Olitski," introductory essay to the catalogue of an exhibition of Olitski's work at the Corcoran Gallery, Washington, D.C., April–June 1967; "Two Sculptures by Anthony Caro," *Artforum*, 6, no. 6 (February 1968), pp. 24–5. Because Fried's work is an instance of what I called "philosophical criticism" above, let me make explicit the fact that this title is not confined to such pieces as "Art and Objecthood" nor to those on Stella and on Olitski, all of which are intensely theoretical or speculative; it applies equally to the two short pieces on Caro, each of which just consists of uninterrupted descriptions (in the first case of four, in the second case of two) of Caro's sculptures. Moreover, this writing would not be "philosophical" in the relevant sense if it did not essentially contain, or imply, descriptions of that sort. Not, of course, that I suppose my having spoken of bringing "the world of a particular work . . . to consciousness of itself" will convey what sorts of descriptions these are, to anyone who has not felt them. To characterize them further would involve investigations of such phenomena as "attending to the words themselves" and "faithfulness to a text."

When we had the idea that acknowledgment must be incomplete in a theater, it was as if we felt *prevented* from approaching the figures to whom we respond. But we are not prevented; we merely in fact, or in convention, do not approach them. Acknowledgment is complete without that; that is the beauty of theater. It is right to think that in a theater *something* is omitted which must be made good outside. But what is omitted is not the claim upon us, and what would make good the omission is not necessarily approaching the other. For approaching the other outside does not satisfy the claim, apart from making ourselves present. (Works without faith.) Then what expresses acknowledgment in a theater? What plays the role there that revealing ourselves plays outside? That is, what counts as putting ourselves into a character's presence? I take this to be the same as the question I asked at the beginning of this discussion: What is the mechanism of our identification with a character? We know we cannot approach him, and not because it is not done but because nothing would count as doing it. Put another way, they and we do not occupy the same space; there is no path from my location to his. (We could also say: There is no distance between us, as there is none between me and a figure in my dream, and none, or no one, between me and my image in a mirror.) We do, however, occupy the same time.

And the time is always now; time is measured solely by what is now happening to them, for what they are doing now is all that is happening. The time is of course not necessarily *the* present – that is up to the playwright. But the time presented, whether the present or the past, is this moment, at which an arrival is awaited, in which a decision is made or left unmade, at which the past erupts into the present, in which reason or emotion fail. . . . The novel also comprises these moments, but only as having happened – not necessarily *in* the past; that is up to the novelist. – But doesn't this amount only to saying that novels are narrated and that the natural sound of narration is the past tense? Whereas plays have no narrator. – What does it mean to say they have no narrator, as though having one is the normal state of affairs? One may feel: The lack of a narrator means that we confront the characters more directly, without interposed descriptions or explanations. But then couldn't it equally be said that, free of the necessity to describe or explain, the dramatist is free to leave his characters more opaque?

Here I want to emphasize that no character in a play *could* (is, logically, in a position from which to) narrate its events. This can be seen various ways:

1. No mere character, no mere human being, commands the absolute credibility of a narrator. When he (who?) writes: "He lay flat on the brown, pine-needled floor of the forest, his chin on his folded arms, and high overhead the wind blew in the tops of the pine trees," there is no doubt possible that there is a forest here and that its floor is pine-needled and brown, and that a man is lying flat on it. No character commands this credibility of assertion, not because he may not be as honest as a man can be, but because he is an actor; that is, what he is doing or suffering is part of what is happening; he is fixed in the present. The problem is not so much that he cannot, so to speak, see *over* the present, but that he cannot insert a break in it; if he narrates, then *that* is what he is doing, that has become what is now happening. But a narrator cannot, I feel like saying, make anything happen; that is one source of his credibility. (The use of so-called first-person narrative cedes absolute credibility, but then *this* narrator is not so much a character of the events he describes as he is the antagonist of the reader. We shall have to return to this.)

2. This comes out if we notice the two points in *King Lear* at which Shakespeare provides a character with a narration: the Gentleman's account to Kent concerning Cordelia's reception of his letters (IV, iii, 12–33) and Edgar's late account of his father's death (V, iii, 181–218). As one would expect of any narration by one character to another, these speeches have the effect of interrupting the action, but the difference is that the Gentleman speaks when Shakespeare has interrupted the action for him (or when the events are themselves paused, as for breath); whereas Edgar takes it upon himself to interrupt the action, and as with every other action in this play, Shakespeare tallies its cost. This act of narration occurs within the same continuity of causation and freedom and responsibility as every other act of the play. For it emerges that this long tale has provided the time within which Edmund's writ on the life of Lear and on Cordelia could be executed. Edgar's choice to narrate then and there is as significant as the content of his narration, and his responsibility for this choice is expressed by the fact that his narration (unlike the Gentleman's) is first person. This further suggests why one may feel that a "first-person narrative" is not a nar-

rative; or rather, why the more a first-person account takes on the formal properties of a narrative, a tale, the more suspicious the account becomes. For a first-person account is, after all, a confession; and the one who has something to confess has something to conceal. And the one who has the word "I" at his or her disposal has the quickest device for concealing himself. And the one who makes a tale with this word is either distracted from the necessity of authenticating his use of it, or he is admitting that he cannot provide its authentication by himself, and so appealing for relief. We have had occasion to notice moments in Edgar's narration which show that he remains concealed to himself throughout his revelations. The third-person narrator, being deprived of self-reference, cannot conceal himself; that is to say, he or she has no self, and therefore nothing, to conceal. This is another source of his credibility. Then what is the motive for telling us these things? Which really means: What is ours in listening to it?

Philosophy which proceeds from ordinary language is proceeding from the fact *that* a thing is said; that it is (or can be) said (in certain circumstances) is as significant as what it says; its being said then and there is as determinative of what it says as the meanings of its individual words are. This thought can sometimes bring to attention the extraordinary *look* of philosophical writing. The form of, say, Descartes's *Meditations* is that of a first-person narrative; "Nevertheless, I must remember that I am a man, and that consequently I am accustomed to sleep and in my dreams to imagine the same things that lunatics imagine when awake, or sometimes things which are even less plausible." But one realizes that there is no particular person the narrative is about (if, that is, one had realized that it looks as if there were some particular person it is about and that if there is not there ought to be some good reason why it sets out to look as if there were), and that its motive, like the motive of a lyric poem, is absolute veracity. And someone whose motive is absolute veracity is likely to be very hard to understand.

3. Accounts which are simultaneous with the events they describe – which are written or spoken in the present tense – are, for instance, reports or announcements; reporters and announcers are people who tell you what *is* happening. There is room, so to speak, for their activity because they are in a position to know something *we* do not know. But here, in a theater, there is no such position. We are present at what is happening.

I will say: We are not in, and cannot put ourselves in, the presence of the characters; but we are in, or can put ourselves in, their *present*. It is in making their present ours, their moments as they occur, that we complete our acknowledgment of them. But this requires making their present *theirs*. And that requires us to face not only the porousness of our knowledge (of, for example, the motives of their actions and the consequences they care about) but the repudiation of our perception altogether. This is what a historian has to face in knowing the past: The epistemology of other minds is the same as the metaphysics of other times and places. Those who have felt that the past has to be *made* relevant to the present fall into the typical error of parents and children – taking difference from each other to threaten, or promise, severance from one another. But we are severed; in denying that, one gives up not only knowledge of the position of others but the means of locating one's own. In failing to find the character's present we fail to make *him* present. Then he is indeed a fictitious creature, a figment of my imagination, like all the other people in my life whom I find I have failed to know, have known wrong. How terribly difficult this is to stop doing is indexed by the all but inescapable temptation to think of the past in terms of theater. (For a while I kept a list of the times I read that some past war or revolution was a great drama or that some historical figure was a tragic character on the stage of history. But the list got too long.) As if we were spectators of the past. But from what position are we imagining that we can see it? One there, or one here? The problem is sometimes said to be that we have our own perspective, and hence that we see only from an angle. But that is the same impulse to theatricality, now speaking with a scientific accent. (If bias or prejudice is the issue, then each has an ordinary moral obligation to get over it.) For there is no *place* from which we can see the past. Our position is to be discovered, and this is done in the painful way it is always done, in piecing it out totally. That the self, to be known truly, must be known in its totality, and that this is practical, if interminable, is the teaching, in their various ways, of Hegel, of Nietzsche, and of Freud.

If the suggestion is right that the "completion of acknowledgment" requires self-revelation, then making the characters present must be a form of, or require, self-revelation. Then what is revealed? Not something about me personally. Who my Gloucester is, and where my Dover is, what my shame attaches to, and what love I

have exiled in order to remain in control of my shrinking kingdom
– these are still my secrets. But perhaps I am better prepared for
the necessity to give them up, freed of pity for myself and terror
at myself. What I reveal is what I share with everyone else present
with me at what is happening: that I am hidden and silent and fixed.
In a word, that there is a point at which I am helpless before the
acting and the suffering of others. But I know the true point of my
helplessness only if I have acknowledged totally the fact and the
true cause of their suffering. Otherwise I am not emptied of help,
but withholding it. Tragedy arises from the confusion of these states.
Catharsis, if that is the question, is a matter of purging attachment
from everything but the present, from pity for the past and terror
of the future. My immobility, my transfixing, rightly attained, is
expressed by that sense of awe, always recognized as the response
to tragedy.[17] In another word, what is revealed is my separateness
from what is happening to them; that I am I, and here. It is only
in this perception of them as separate from me that I make them
present. That I make them *other,* and face them.

And the point of my presence at these events is to join in confirming this separateness. Confirming it as neither a blessing nor a
curse, but a fact, the fact of having one life – not one rather than
two, but this one rather than any other. I cannot confirm it alone.
Rather, it is the nature of this tragedy that its actors have to confirm
their separateness alone, through isolation, the denial of others. What
is purged is my difference from others, in everything but separateness.

Their fate, up there, out there, is that they must act, they are in
the arena in which action is ineluctable. My freedom is that I am
not now in the arena. Everything which can be done is being done.
The present in which action is alone possible is fully occupied. It
is not that my space is different from theirs but that I have no space
within which I can move. It is not that my time is different from
theirs but that I have no present apart from theirs. The time in
which that hint is laid, in which that knowledge is fixed, in which
those fingers grip that throat, is all the time I have. There is no

---

[17] Here I may mention J. V. Cunningham's *Woe or Wonder: The Emotional Effect
of Shakespearean Tragedy* (Denver: University of Denver Press, 1951), a work I have
more than once had on my mind in thinking of these topics, less for particular detail
than for its continuous sense that the effect of tragedy is specific to it, hence part
of its logic.

time in which to stop it. At his play, Claudius knows this; which makes him an ideal auditor of serious drama. Only, he was unlucky enough to have seen the play after he had actually acted out the consequences of its, and of his, condition: so it caught his conscience instead of scouring it.

Now I can give one answer to the question: Why do I do nothing, faced with tragic events? If I do nothing because I am distracted by the pleasures of witnessing this folly, or out of my knowledge of the proprieties of the place I am in, or because I think there will be some more appropriate time in which to act, or because I feel helpless to undo events of such proportion, then I continue my sponsorship of evil in the world, its sway waiting upon these forms of inaction. I exit running. But if I do nothing because there is nothing to do, where that means that I have given over the time and space in which action is mine and consequently that I am in awe before the fact that I cannot do and suffer what it is another's to do and suffer, then I confirm the final fact of our separateness. And that is the unity of our condition.

The only essential difference between them and me is that they are there and I am not. And to empty ourselves of all other difference can be confirmed in the presence of an audience, of the community, because every difference established between us, other than separateness, is established by the community – that is, by us, in obedience to the community. It is by responding to this knowledge that the community keeps itself in touch with nature. (With Being, I would say, if I knew how.) If C. L. Barber is right (in *Shakespeare's Festive Comedy*) in finding that the point of comedy is to put society back in touch with nature, then this is one ground on which comedy and tragedy stand together. Comedy is fun because it can purge us of the unnatural and of the merely natural by laughing at us and singing to us and dancing for us, and by making us laugh and sing and dance. The tragedy is that comedy has its limits. This is part of the sadness within comedy; the emptiness after a long laugh. Join hands here as we may, one of the hands is mine and the other is yours.

Fortune, in this light, is an instrument of tragedy not because it turns, and turns outside of us. (This is about what Kent thinks of it – "Fortune, good night; smile once more; turn thy wheel" [II, ii, 173]; and Edgar – "made tame to Fortune's blows" [IV, vi, 222].) This idea can prompt caution, or feed the wish for vengeance, or inspire a pretty and noble renunciation. Noble Kent is sincere, but Edgar is not; as he is voicing his view of fortune he is waiting for his chance. That he has altered himself in disguising himself becomes revelatory of his character; as it is revelatory of Kent that his disguise does not alter him; he remains the faithful servant through all. Fortune, in the light of this play, is tragic because it is *mine;* not because it wheels but because each man takes his place upon its wheel. This is what I take Edmund and Lear to discover. Edmund, as he is fallen, and with his life over, is waiting his chance to do some good; and he says, "The wheel is come full circle; I am here" (V, iii, 174). That "I am here" – imitating Abraham's response when God calls his name (Genesis 22:1) – is the natural expression of the knowledge that my life is mine, the ultimate piece of fortune. That is what I understand Lear's huge lines of revelation to mean: "I am bound upon a wheel of fire" (IV, vii, 46–7). His tears scald not because his fortunes are low but because he feels them to be his; all the isolated thrusts of rejection, the arbitrary cuts of ingratitude, the loyalties which shamed and the loves which flayed, the curses flung vile and infinite and sterile against the breaking of his state, these all now make sense, they make the sense his life makes, fortune no longer comes from outside, his life is whole, like a wheel which turns. It is here he takes his life wholly upon himself. So his succeeding lines show his sense of rebirth. That one has to die in order to become reborn is one tragic fact; that one's wholeness deprives others of their life is another; that one's love becomes incompatible with one's life and kills the thing it loves is another. Lear is reborn, but into his old self. That is no longer just tragic, it suggests that tragedy itself has become ineffective, outworn, because now even death does not overcome our difference. Here again, Gloucester's life amplifies Lear's. For it is one thing, and tragic, that we can learn only through suffering. It is something else that we have nothing to learn from it.

Tragedy is not about the fact that all men are mortal (though perhaps it is about the fact that mortals go to any lengths to avoid that knowledge). Every death is about that fact, and attendance at a tragedy is not a substitute for attendance at a funeral. (We need one another's presence for more than one reason.) A tragedy is about a *particular* death, or set of deaths, and specifically about a death which is neither natural nor accidental. The death is *inflicted* (as in suicide or homicide) and it is a punishment or an expiation (like an execution or a sacrifice). But if the death is inflicted, it *need* not have happened. So a radical contingency haunts every story of tragedy. Yet no one *knows* that it could have been prevented because no one knows what would have prevented it. By the time we see these events, or any others whose tragedy shows, the maze of character and circumstance is unchartable. Of course if Othello had not met Iago, if Lear had not developed his plan of division, if Macbeth had not listened to his wife. . . . But could these contingencies have been prevented? If one is assured they could have been, one is forgetting who these characters are. For if, for example, Othello hadn't met Iago he would have created another, his magnetism would have selected him, and the magic of his union would have inspired him. So a radical necessity haunts every story of tragedy. It is the enveloping of contingency and necessity by one another, the entropy of their mixture, which produces events we call tragic. Or rather, it is why the death which ends a tragedy strikes one as *inexplicable:* necessary, but we do not know why; avoidable, but we do not know how; wrapped in meaning, but the meaning has not come out, and so wrapped in mystery. This is clearest in the case of Lear, where critics differ over whether he dies from grief or (illusory) joy. But it is equally true of Shakespeare's other tragic heroes: We know from the witches well before Macbeth dies that his death will be mysterious, satisfying (in its efforts to evade) a prophecy; Hamlet knows that his death will remain mysterious, because now that it is time he has not time to tell his story, and he knows that Horatio, whom out of friendship he commissions to tell it, does not understand it; Othello dies upon a kiss, and it is as though he dies *from* it. Of course we may in each case determine upon a cause of death; but the cause does not explain *why* they die. And the question is raised.

It is not then answered. There is no answer, of the kind we think there is. No answer outside of us. Edgar's closing lines have tempted some into looking there for a summary of the play's meaning: "Speak what we feel, not what we ought to say." But at the beginning Lear and Cordelia spoke what they felt, anyway certainly not what they ought to have said. And so it began. These plays begin as mysteriously as they end, with a crazy ritual, some witches, a ghost, an incomprehensible petulant accusation and denial. And they begin and end this way for the same reason, to maintain us in a present.

At the beginning there is no reason why things have come to this pass, nothing an exposition could clarify. It is a crossroads, they are there. There is danger in the truth that everything which happens is "contained" in these openings. For this postulate of "organic form," the dominant postulate of modern analysis both in poetry and in music, may suggest that what succeeds the presence of the opening is all that *could* have succeeded it. Whereas what succeeds it is one working out of its content. – This is still misleading, for what does "its content" mean? What succeeds the opening is . . . a succession from it. What goes on to happen is not inevitable; but anything that goes on to happen inevitably bears marks of what has gone before. What has gone before was not inevitable, but when it has happened its marks are inevitable. What the idea of "organic structure" omits is the necessity of action, the fact of succession. "The content" of the opening means *nothing* until it is brought out; we could say there is no content until it is brought out. And when it all comes out and is brought to a close its content is not exhausted. We could say it has infinite content: but what this comes to is that we have stopped pursuing it (or it us), that we have been shown that a stop can be *made*. Of course the artist sees more deeply into the possibilities of succession than we do – so we often praise his faculty of invention; but he also sees more poignantly what does not succeed – and we do not often enough sense his power of silence; and he must also bring whatever happens to a close – but we are rarely grateful enough for his mastery of form, as if we took this mastery to be the observation of formalities (in order that we may anticipate) rather than the formation of the observable (in order that we may see).

At the close of these successions we are still in a present; it is another crossroads. *King Lear, Othello,* and *Hamlet* close with promises of words and understanding to come; as if to say, what has happened has stopped but it has not come to an end; we have yet to come to terms with what has happened; we do not know where it will end. *Macbeth* closes not with promises of further words, but just with promises, a hurried string of them, as if to get out of the range of Macbeth's eyes, there in his head; as if those present know, but do not care now to linger over the knowledge, that there are still witches unaccounted for. It is at such inopportune moments that we are cast into the arena of action again, crossroads again beneath our feet. Because the actors have stopped, we are freed to act again; but also compelled to. Our hiddenness, our silence, and our placement are now our choices.

One last word, in this light, about a pair of familiar topics in discussions of tragedy. Why are princes (or the high born) the subjects of tragedy? Why is high tragedy no longer, apparently, an available artistic option? Everything said, in my hearing, about the appropriateness of the high born is right enough: They show most dramatically a downfall, which tragedy comments upon; the life of an entire community is staked in their fortunes; they rationalize the use of elevated style, in particular, of poetry. To this list I would add two simple, or geometrical, features of the prince: (1) The state of which he is head, as befits the medieval universe, is closed. The extremest consequences attending on his life and death, however extensive and however high their cost, are finite, run a certain course – so long, that is, as the state survives. However far his life and death have entered his subjects, each has a position from which to assess its effects, and pay for them. (2) His life and death are the largest in his state, hence easiest to see matched or lost to one another; and since his legitimate succession is the only promise of continued life to his state, his death has to be accounted for. When the closed world burst into the infinite universe, consequences became fully unlimited and untraceable. (Lear suffers even this. His bursting is the sign that the play itself, and tragedy as a whole, has burst its bounds. I have had occasion to notice that when the king confuses abdication, not only does he drain himself of authority, he saps his institutions of authority altogether. Then ceremony is mere ceremony. So at the end no convention has the force to oppose force, of arms or of feeling; no shared form of life controls vengeance or shapes passion. Tragedy was the price of justice, in a disordered world. In a world without the hope of justice, no price is right.)

Now we are surrounded by inexplicable pain and death; no death is more mysterious or portentous than others; because every death which is not the fruit of a long life is now unaccounted for, since we cannot or will not account for it: not just because, taking local examples, we no longer know why a society may put its own people to death for breaking its rules, nor when it may intervene with death in a foreign place, nor because highway deaths need not happen, nor because the pollution of our air and water has become deliberate, nor because poverty has become inflicted – but because we do not know our position with respect to such things. We are present at these events, and no one is present without making something happen; everything which is happening is happening to me, and I do not know what is happening. I do not know that my helplessness is limited only by my separateness, because I do not know which fortune is mine and which is yours. The world did not become sad; it was always sad. Tragedy has moved into the world, and with it the world becomes theatrical.

Classical tragedies were always national, so perhaps it is not surprising that nations have become tragic. And of the great modern nations which have undergone tragedy, through inexplicable loss of past or loss of future or self-defeat of promise, in none is tragedy so intertwined with its history and its identity as in America. It is cast with uncanny perfection for its role, partly because its power is so awe-inspiring, partly because its self-destruction is so heart-breaking. It had a mythical beginning, still visible, if ambiguous, to itself and to its audience: before there was Russia, there was Russia; before there were France and England, there were France and England; but before there was America there was no America. America was *discovered,* and what was discovered was not a place, one among others, but a setting, the backdrop of a destiny. It began as theater. Its Revolution, unlike the English and French and Russian revolutions, was not a civil war; it was fought against outsiders, its point was not reform but independence. And its Civil War was not a revolution; the oppressed did not rise, and the point was not the overthrow of a form of government but secession and union; the point was its identity. And neither of these points was settled, nor has either been lost, through defeat or through loss of empire or change of political constitution. So its knowledge is of indefeasible power and constancy. But its fantasies are those of impotence, because it remains at the mercy of its past, because its present is continuously ridiculed by the fantastic promise of its origin and its possibility, and because it has never been assured that it will survive. Since it had a birth, it may die. It feels mortal. And it wishes proof not merely of its continuance but of its existence, a fact it has never been able to take for granted. Therefore its need for love is insatiable. It has surely been given more love than any other nation: Its history, until yesterday, is one in which outsiders have been drawn to it and in which insiders are hoarse from their expressions of devotion to it. Those who voice politically radical wishes for this country may forget the radical hopes it holds for itself, and not know that the hatred of America by its intellectuals is only their own version of patriotism. It is the need for love as proof of its existence which makes it so frighteningly destructive, enraged by ingratitude and by attention to its promises rather than to its promise, and which makes it incapable of seeing that it is destructive and frightening. It imagines its evils to come from outside. So it feels watched, isolated in its mounting of waters, denying its shame with mechanical lungs of pride, calling its wrath upon the wrong objects.

It has gone on for a long time, it is maddened now, the love it has had it has squandered too often, its young no longer naturally feel it; its past is in its streets, ungrateful for the fact that a hundred years ago it tore itself apart in order not to be divided; half of it believes the war it is now fighting is taking place twenty-five years ago, when it was still young and it was right that it was opposing tyranny. People say it is isolationist, but so obviously it is not isolationist: Since it asserted its existence in a war of secession and asserted its identity in a war against secession it has never been able to bear its separateness. *Union* is what it wanted. And it has never felt that union has been achieved. Hence its terror of dissent, which does not threaten its power but its integrity. So it is killing itself and killing another country in order not to admit its helplessness in the face of suffering, in order not to acknowledge its separateness. So it does not know what its true helplessness is. People say it is imperialist and colonialist, but it knows that it wants nothing more. It was told, as if in a prophecy, that no country is evil which is not imperialist or colonialist. So it turns toward tyranny, to prove its virtue. It is *the* anti-Marxist country, in which production and possession are unreal and consciousness of appreciation and of its promise is the only value. The Yankee is as unpractical as the Cavalier, his action as metaphysical as his greatest literature. Yet what needs doing, could he see his and his world's true need, he could do, no one else so capable of it or so ready for it. He *could*. It's a free country. But it will take a change of consciousness. So phenomenology becomes politics.

Since we are ineluctably actors in what is happening, nothing can be present to us to which we are not present. Of course we can still know, more than ever, what is going on. But then we always could, more or less. What we do not now know is what there is to acknowledge, what it is I am to make present, what I am to make myself present to. I know there is inexplicable pain and death everywhere, and now if I ask myself why I do nothing the answer must be, I choose not to. That is, doing nothing is no longer something which has a place insured by ceremony; it is the thing I am doing. And it requires the same energy, the same expense of cunning and avoidance, that tragic activity used to have to itself. Tragedy, could it now be written, would not show us that we *are* helpless – it never did, and we are not. It would show us, what it always did, *why* we (as audience) are helpless. Classically, the reason was that pain and death were in our presence when we were not in theirs. Now the reason is that we absent ourselves from them. Earlier, the members of the audience revealed only their common difference from the actors. Now each man is revealed privately, for there is no audience, apart from each man's making himself an audience; what is revealed is that there is no community, no identity of condition, but that each man has his reasons, good or bad, for choosing not to act. After a tragedy now, should one be written, the members of the audience would not see one another measured against nature again, but ranged against it, as if nature has been wiped out and the circle of social and historical arbitrariness is now complete. The point of reason, the thing that made it seem worth deifying, was not simply that it provided godlike power, but that it could serve to rationalize and hence to minimize distress. But the consequences of its uses, since no one is responsible for them – that is, no one more than anyone else – is that it has made everything require an answer, and only I have the answer; that is, no one has it if I have not. And if I have not, I am guilty; and if I have, and do not act upon it, I am guilty. What we forgot, when we deified reason, was not that reason is incompatible with feeling, but that knowledge requires acknowledgment. (The withdrawals and approaches of God can be looked upon as tracing the history of our attempts to overtake and absorb acknowledgment by knowledge; God would be the name of that impossibility.) Either you have to be *very* careful what you know – keep it superficial or keep it away from the self and one's society and history and away from art and from heaven – or else in order not to acknowledge what you have learned you will have to stifle or baffle feeling, stunt the self. This is why, in the visions of Marx and of Kierkegaard, reason and philosophy must be made to end.

In such circumstances, a purpose of tragedy remains unchanged: to make us practical, capable of acting. It used to do that by showing us the natural limitations of action. Now its work is not to purge us of pity and terror, but to make us capable of feeling them again, and this means showing us that there is a place to act upon them. This does not mean that tragedy now must become political. Because first, it was always political, always about the incompatibility between a particular love and a particular social arrangement for love. Because second, and more specifically, we no longer know what is and is not a political act, what may or may not have recognizable political consequences. That, for example, editorials and public denunciations of a government now have consequences which are accommodated by that government is something we have grown accustomed to. And we have known since Agamemnon that the child of a king may be sacrificed by its parent for the success of the state. But we had hardly expected, what now is apparently coming to be the case, that the ordinary citizen's ordinary faithfulness to his children may become a radical political act. We have known, anyway since eighteenth-century France and nineteenth-century America and Russia, that high art can be motivated by a thirst for social change. But in an age in which the organs of news, in the very totality and talent of their coverage, become distractions from what is happening, presenting everything happening as overwhelmingly present, like events in old theater – in such an age the intention to serious art can itself become a political act: not because it can label the poison in public words, purify the dialect of the tribe – perhaps it can't, for all words now are public and there is no known tribe – but because it is the intention to make an object which bears one's conviction and which might bring another to himself; it is an attestation of faith that action remains mine to perform or withhold, of knowledge that the world of fashion and loss and joylessness is not all there is and is powerless if I do not give it power; it provides, apart from good people, what evidence there is of things unseen, and is the region in which absolute virtue is, and is all that is, rewarded. Such knowledge is good for the soul. It is also good for the society which still likes to see virtue rewarded; it is destructive to the society which has lost the habit of virtue. We could also say: We no longer know what is and is not news, what is and is not a significant fact of our present history, what is and is not relevant to one's life. The newspaper tells me that everything is relevant, but I cannot really accept that because it would mean that I do not have one life, to which some things are relevant and some not. I cannot really deny it either because I do not know why things happen as they do and why I am not responsible for any or all of it. And so to the extent that I still have feeling to contend with, it is a generalized guilt, which only confirms my paralysis; or else I convert the disasters and sensations reported to me into topics of conversation, for mutual entertainment, which in turn irritates the guilt.

One function of tragedy would be to show me that this view of the world is itself chosen, and theatrical. It would show that events are still specific, that guilt will alter itself or puff itself out of shape, in order to deny debt for the specific deed for which one is responsible, that the stakes of action and inaction are what they always were, that monsters of evil are only men, that the good in the world is what good men do, that at every moment there is a present passing me by and that the reason it passes me by is the old reason, that I am not present to it. In *King Lear,* we miss presentness through anticipation, we miss the present moment by sweet knowledge of moments to come or bitter knowledge of moments past. Now we miss presentness through blindness to the fact that the space and time we are in are specific, supposing our space to be infinite and our time void, losing ourselves in space, avoided by time.

If a tragedy would not know how to look, which could bring presentness back, still it knows something: It knows that this ignorance is shared by all modernist arts, each driving into itself to maintain the conviction it has always inspired, to reaffirm the value which men have always placed upon it. It knows that, to make us practical, our status as audience will have to be defeated, because the theater no longer provides a respite from action, but one more deed of inaction; hence it knows that theater must be defeated, inside and out. It knows that we do not have to be goaded into action, but, being actors, to be given occasion to stop – in our case, to stop choosing silence and hiddenness and paralysis, or else to choose them in favor of ourselves. It knows that this requires that we reveal ourselves and that, as always, this is not occasioned by showing me that something happening is relevant to me – that is inescapably the case – but by showing me something to which I am relevant, or irrelevant. Oedipus and Lear could learn this by learning what, within the wheeling of events, they are affected by and what they are causing. Their tragic fact was that they could find who they were only by finding themselves at the cause of tragedy. They are heroic because they care completely who they are; they are tragic because what they find is incompatible with their existence. Our tragic fact is that we find ourselves at the cause of tragedy, but without finding ourselves.

We have, as tragic figures do, to go back to beginnings, either to undo or to be undone, or to do again the thing which has caused tragedy, as though at some point in the past history is stuck, and time marks time there waiting to be released. Lear causes tragedy when his fast intent to shake all cares pushes his final care into the open. In normal periods, tragic acts are skirted by one's cares remaining superficial enough or mutually compatible enough for them not to suffer naked exposure. In the typical situation of tragic heroes, time and space converge to a point at which an ultimate care is exposed and action must be taken which impales one's life upon the founding care of that life – that in the loss of which chaos is come, in the loss of which all is but toys, in the loss of which there is nothing and nothing to come, and disgust with the self, natural enough at any time, becomes overwhelming. Death, so caused, may be mysterious, but what founds these lives is clear enough: the capacity to love, the strength to found a life upon a love. That the love becomes incompatible with that life is tragic, but that it is maintained until the end is heroic. People capable of such love could have removed mountains; instead it has caved in upon them. One moral of such events is obvious: If you would avoid tragedy, avoid love; if you cannot avoid love, avoid integrity; if you cannot avoid integrity, avoid the world; if you cannot avoid the world, destroy it. Our tragedy differs from this classical chain not in its conclusion but in the fact that the conclusion has been reached without passing through love, in the fact that no love seems worth founding one's life upon, or that society – and therefore I myself – can allow no context in which love, for anything but itself, can be expressed. In such a situation it can look as if the state is the villain and all its men and women merely victims. But that picture is only a further extension of the theatricality which causes it. Our problem is that society can no longer hear its own screams. Our problem, in getting back to beginnings, will not be to find the thing we have always cared about, but to discover whether we have it in us always to care about something.

The classical environment of tragedy was the extraordinary and the unnatural, and it is tempting, now that things have changed, to say that the environment of tragedy has become the ordinary and the natural. Except that we no longer know what is ordinary and natural, and hence no longer know what is tragic and what is not (so it is not surprising that tragedies are not written). We could say that just this amnesia is our tragedy. Except that it is not amnesia and it is not necessarily bad — for it is not as if we knew or could remember a state of society in which the ordinary was the natural state of affairs. All we know is at one time a state of affairs was *accepted* by those trained to it as natural. (From which it does not follow that all such states of affairs are good, nor even that those born to the manner found it good.) That itself may seem cause enough for envy. Yet we know no less about our own state of affairs. Except that we also know our reversals of fortune can come about through *any* change: It no longer requires the killing of kings; the heaving of past into present; a forest of enemies advancing. Our ghostly commissions are unnoticeable; perhaps they are only the halfhearted among our parents' wishes, which they would have been half proud to see us decline and which we only half know have been executed. Reversal can also come with a shift in what we accept as natural, as in those odd moments throughout which, as in successful prayer, we really know, say, that a black man is a man like any other; that our child or parent is a person like any other, entitled to and cursed by the same separateness as any other; that the good opinion of people we do not care about is humiliating to care about and that the bad opinion of people we do care about may be humiliating to care about too much. At such moments the way we live appears unnatural, the world we have chosen becomes extraordinary and unnecessary, the death lingering for us seems unnatural, as though we have chosen to die as we have chosen to live, for nothing. If that is theatrical, it is equally theatrical to *look for something* for which to live or die. There are only the old things, and they are at hand, or nowhere. Then how, in space and out of time, shall we make ourselves present to them?

Hamlet dies before an audience, harping on the audience present to him, and his consciousness of himself is immortalized by his consciousness of it. That is not an option for us, not merely because we cannot command an audience, since no one's position is relevantly different from mine; but because, since no one's position is relevantly different from mine, to convert others into an audience is to further the very sense of isolation which makes us wish for an audience. Its treatment of this fact is what makes *King Lear* so threatening, together with its consequent questioning of what we accept as natural and legitimate and necessary. The cost of an ordinary life and death, of insisting upon one's one life, and avoiding one's own cares, has become the same as the cost of the old large lives and deaths, requires the same lucidity and exacts the same obscurity and suffering. This is what Lear knows for the moment before his madness; it is the edge Gloucester's blinding has led him to. Immediately after Lear's prayer (III, iv, 28–36), he gives himself up to the tempest in his mind and to the storm which is to destroy the world; Gloucester's thoughts, just after his prayer (IV, i, 66–71), turn to Dover and its cliff. That is, successful prayer is prayer for the strength to change, it is the beginning of change, and change presents itself as the dying of the self and hence the ending of the world. The cause of tragedy is that we would rather murder the world than permit it to expose us to change. Our threat is that this has become a common option; our tragedy is that it does not seem to us that we are taking it. We think *others* are taking it, though they are not relevantly different from ourselves. Lear and Gloucester are not tragic because they are isolated, singled out for suffering, but because they had covered their true isolation (the identity of their condition with the condition of other men) within hiddenness, silence, and position; the ways people do. It is the enormity of this plain fact which accompanies the overthrow of Lear's mind, and we honor him for it.

But we will not abdicate. As though this was *his* answer, while ours will come later, on another occasion, from outside. And it does look, after the death of kings and out of the ironies of revolutions and in the putrefactions of God, as if our trouble is that there used to be answers and now there are not. The case is rather that there used not to be an unlimited question and now there is. "Human reason has this peculiar fate that in one species of its knowledge it is burdened by questions which, as prescribed by the very nature of reason itself, it is not able to ignore, but which, as transcending all its powers, it is not able to answer" (preface to the first edition of the *Critique of Pure Reason,* opening sentence). Hegel and Marx, as we know, found this fate not in human reason but in human history. Hegel then denied the distinction between them,

Marx thought they could at last be distinguished. Hegel thought both were finished, Marx thought both could now begin. The world whistles over them. We cannot hear them.

If it is right to relate the drama in *King Lear* to the drama in music, then it should not surprise us that this source of drama disappeared from theater, for it has more recently disappeared from music as well – anyway, disappeared as something that can be taken for granted. The comparison between Shakespearean theater and tonal music is not a mere analogy, but it is not an explanation either. For it is not as if we know so well how we listen to this music that we can apply our knowledge there to the theater. On the contrary, it seems to me equally illuminating, and perhaps even closer to an explanation, to say that, when we understand, we listen to the music most familiar to us in the way we follow lines and actions in that medium which makes poetry drama. In my experience, this kind of listening is no longer fully possible with the disappearance of tonality – perhaps it is this continuous presentness which we miss most in the difficulties of posttonal music, more than its lack of tunes and harmony and pulse rhythm. It would, I believe, be possible to study the work of serious composers of the past two generations or so, and certainly those now at work, in terms of the ways in which they avoid, and attempt to reclaim, its history of drama. This suggests that faithfulness now to the art of music is not expressed by an effort, as it may be put, to find modes or organization based upon sound itself (a form of words which may describe all music, or none at all) but to discover what it is about sounds in succession which at any time has allowed them to be heard as presentness.

Nietzsche began writing by calling for the rebirth of tragedy from the spirit of music. But that had already happened, as drama lost the use of poetry and turned to music. What Nietzsche heard in Wagner was something else – the death, and the call for the death, of music and of drama and hence of society as they had been known.

3

Othello and the Stake of the Other

To study the imagination of the body's fate under skepticism, I ask how it is that we are to understand, at the height of *The Winter's Tale,* Hermione's reappearance as a statue. Specifically I ask how it is that we are to understand Leontes' acceptance of the "magic" that returns her to flesh and blood, and hence to him. This is a most specific form of resurrection. Accepting it means accepting the idea that she had been turned to stone; that that was the right fate for her disappearance from life. So I am asking for the source of Leontes' conviction in the rightness of that fate. Giving the question that form, the form of my answer is by now predictable: For her to return to him is for him to recognize her; and for him to recognize her is for him to recognize his relation to her; in particular to recognize what his denial of her has done to her, hence to him. So Leontes recognizes the fate of stone to be the consequence of his particular skepticism. One can see this as the projection of his own sense of numbness, of living death. But then why was this *his* fate? It is a most specific form of remorse or of (self-)punishment.

Its environment is a tale of harrowing by jealousy, and a consequent accusation of adultery, an accusation known by every outsider, everyone but the accuser, to be insanely false. Hence Leontes is inevitably paired with Othello. I call attention to two further ways in which *The Winter's Tale* is a commentary upon *Othello,* and therefore contrariwise. First, both plays involve a harrowing of the power of knowing the existence of another (as chaste, intact, as what the knower knows his other to be). Leontes refuses to believe a true oracle, Othello insists upon believing a false one. Second, in both plays the consequence for the man's refusal of knowledge of his other is an imagination of stone. It is not merely an appetite for beauty that produces Othello's most famous image of his victim, as a piece of cold and carved marble (". . . whiter skin of hers than snow, / And smooth, as monumental alabaster" [V, ii, 4–5]). Where does his image come from?

To introduce what I have to say about *Othello,* I want to give a final source for thinking of tragedy as a kind of epistemological problem, or as the outcome of the problem of knowledge – of the dominance of modern philosophical thought by it. When I said toward the end of the introduction to this book, recalling how the beginning of a line of thought began for me, that "the pivot of Othello's interpretation of skepticism is Othello's placing of a finite woman in the place of God," I was recalling a claim of mine to have given a certain derivation for the problem of the other. But I was also echoing one formulation Descartes gives his motive in wanting to secure God beyond doubt, viz., to know beyond doubt that he is not alone in the world (third Meditation). Now I ask, in passing but explicitly, why it is Descartes does not try to defeat that possibility of isolation in what would seem (to whom?) the most direct and the surest way, by locating the existence of one other *finite* being.

He says simply that he can easily imagine that ideas "which represent men similar to myself" could be "formed by the combination of my other ideas, of myself, of corporeal objects, and of God, even though outside of me there were no other men in the world." He is setting up, of course, a powerful move toward God. And we can gather from this, something that seems borne out in the sequel of his *Meditations,* that the problem of others (other finite beings) is not discovered, or derived, by Descartes to be a special problem of knowledge; this is surely one reason it would not have been discovered to be such in subsequent epistemology. But the more one meditates upon the unique place Descartes makes for his relation to his own body, the less clear and distinct it is that he has available to himself the formulation of the idea of another body as having a unique relation to its mind in that special quasi-substantial way that he asserts is not like the way a ship is related to its pilot. But without such an idea, what is the content of the idea of "men similar to myself"? I do not conceive of Descartes's appealing to the route of analogy here, since he must be far surer that other human bodies go with minds than any sureness he can extract by inferring from another body's behavior alone. After all, the body has essentially nothing to do with the soul! I might express his difficulty as follows.

His sense of himself as composed of his contrary natures (of what he means by mind and body, the one characterized in opposition to the other, each essentially what the other is not) is the idea of a double nature, symbolized centrally in the culture we share with him (but perhaps now only in literature) as the figure of Christ. So the thing of incarnation, the mysterious meeting of heaven and earth, occurs in Descartes's thought not alone in the inspirer of Christianity but in each individual human being. From here you may conclude that the human problem in recognizing other human beings is the problem of recognizing another to be Christ for oneself. (What is the significance of the charge that Descartes proves the existence at best of a philosopher's God?)

In the light of this passing of the question of the other, a change is noticeable in the coda Descartes supplies his argument at the end of this third Meditation:

> The whole force of the argument I have here used to prove the existence of God consists in the fact that I recognize that it would not be possible for my nature to be what it is, possessing the idea of a God, unless God really existed – the same God, I say, the idea of whom I possess, the God who possesses all these high perfections . . . [who] cannot be a deceiver.

The main point of summary is that I could not have produced the idea I have of God, for it can have come from nothing less than God himself. But a new note of necessity is also struck, that without the presence of this idea in myself, and (hence) the presence of the fact of which it is the imprint, my own nature would necessarily not be what it is. (Nietzsche's idea of the death of God can be understood to begin by saying roughly or generally as much: The idea of God is part of (the idea of) human nature. If that idea dies, the idea of human nature equally dies.) So not only the fact, as it were, of my existence, but the integrity of it, depends upon this idea. And so these meditations are about the finding of self-knowledge after all; of the knowledge of a human self by a human self.

That the integrity of my (human, finite) existence may depend on the fact and on the idea of another being's existence, and on the possibility of *proving* that existence, an existence conceived from my very dependence and incompleteness, hence conceived as perfect, and conceived as producing me "in some sense, in [its] own image" – these are thoughts that take me to a study of *Othello*.

Briefly, to begin with, we have the logic, the emotion, and the scene of skepticism epitomized. The logic: "My life upon her faith" (I, iii, 294) and ". . . when I love thee not / Chaos is come again" (III, iii, 91–2) set up the stake necessary to best cases; the sense I expressed by the imaginary major premise "If I know anything, I know this." One standing issue about the rhythm of *Othello*'s plot is that the progress from the completeness of Othello's love to the perfection of his doubt is too precipitous for the fictional time of the play. But such precipitousness is just the rhythm of skepticism; all that is necessary is the stake. The emotion: Here I mean not Othello's emotion toward Desdemona, call it jealousy; but the structure of his emotion as he is hauled back and forth across the keel of his love. Othello's enactment, or sufferance, of that torture is the most extraordinary representation known to me of the "astonishment" in skeptical doubt. In Descartes's first Meditation: "I realize so clearly that there are no conclusive indications by which waking life can be distinguished from sleep that I am quite astonished, and my bewilderment is such that it is almost able to convince me that I am sleeping." (It does not follow that one is *convinced* that one is awake.) When Othello loses consciousness ("Is't possible? – Confess? – Handkerchief? – O devil!" [IV, i, 42–3]), it is not from conviction in a piece of knowledge but in an effort to stave the knowledge off. The scene: Here I have in mind the pervasive air of the language and the action of this play as one in which Othello's mind continuously outstrips reality, dissolves it in trance or dream or in the beauty or ugliness of his incantatory imagination; in which he visualizes possibilities that reason, unaided, cannot rule out. Why is he beyond aid? Why are the ear and the eye in him disjoined? We know that by the time he formulates his condition this way:

> By the world,
> I think my wife be honest, and think she is not,
> I think that thou are just, and think thou are not;
> I'll have some proof . . .
>
> (III, iii, 389–92)

he is lost. Two dozen lines earlier he had demanded of Iago "the ocular proof," a demand that was no purer a threat than it was a command, as if he does indeed wish for this outcome, as if he has a use for Iago's suspicions, hence a use for Iago that reciprocates Iago's use of him. Nothing I claim about the play here will depend on an understanding of the relation between Iago and Othello, so I will simply assert what is suggested by what I have just said, that such a question as "Why does Othello believe Iago?" is badly formed. It is not conceivable that Othello believes Iago and *not* Desdemona. Iago, we might say, offers Othello an opportunity to believe something, something to oppose to something else he knows. What does he know? Why does it require opposition? – What do we know?

We have known (say, since G. Wilson Knight's "The *Othello* Music") that Othello's language, call it his imagination, is at once his, and the play's, glory, and his shame, the source of his power and of his impotence; or we should have known (since Bradley's *Shakespearean Tragedy*) that Othello is the most romantic of Shakespeare's heroes, which may be a way of summarizing the same facts. And we ought to attend to the perception that Othello is the most Christian of the tragic heros (expressed in Norman Rabkin's *Shakespeare and the Common Understanding*). Nor is there any longer any argument against our knowledge that Othello is black; and there can be no argument with the fact that he has just married, nor with the description, compared with the cases of Shakespeare's other tragedies, that this one is not political but domestic.

We know more specifically, I take it, that Othello's blackness means something. But what specifically does it mean? Mean, I mean, to him – for otherwise it is not Othello's color that we are interested in but some generalized blackness, meaning perhaps "sooty" or "filthy," as elsewhere in the play. This difference may show in the way one takes Desdemona's early statement: "I saw Othello's visage in his mind" (I, iii, 252). I think it is commonly felt that she means she overlooked his blackness in favor of his inner brilliance; and perhaps further felt that this is a piece of deception, at least of herself. But what the line more naturally says is that she saw his visage as he sees it, that she understands his blackness as he understands it, as the expression (or in his word, his manifestation) of his mind – which is not overlooking it. Then how does he understand it?

As the color of a romantic hero. For he, as he was and is, manifested by his parts, his title, and his "perfect soul" (I, ii, 31), is the hero of the tales of romance he tells, some ones of which he wooed and won Desdemona with, others of which he will die upon. It is accordingly the color of one of enchanted powers and of magical protection, but above all it is the color of one of purity, of a perfect soul. Desdemona, in entering his life, hence in entering his story of his life, enters as a fit companion for such a hero; his perfection is now opened toward hers. His absolute stake in his purity, and its confirmation in hers, is shown in what he feels he has lost in losing Desdemona's confirmation:

> . . . my name, that was as fresh
> As Dian's visage, is now begrim'd, and black
> As mine own face.
>
> (III, iii, 392–4)

Diana's is a name for the visage Desdemona saw to be in Othello's mind. He loses its application to his own name, his charmed self, when he no longer sees his visage in Desdemona's mind but in Iago's, say in the world's capacity for rumor. To say he loses Desdemona's power to confirm his image of himself is to say that he loses his old power of imagination. And this is to say that he loses his grasp of his own nature; he no longer has the same voice in his history. So then the question becomes: How has he come to displace Desdemona's imagination by Iago's? However terrible the exchange, it must be less terrible than some other. Then we need to ask not so much how Iago gained his power as how Desdemona lost hers.

We know – do we not? – that Desdemona has lost her virginity, the protection of Diana, by the time she appears to us. And surely Othello knows this! But this change in her condition, while a big enough fact to hatch millennia of plots, is not what Othello accuses her of. (Though would that accusation have been much more unfair than the unfaithfulness he does accuse her of?) I emphasize that I am assuming in Othello's mind the theme and condition of virginity to carry their full weight within a romantic universe. Here is some recent Northrop Frye on the subject: "Deep within the stock convention of virgin-baiting is a vision of human integrity imprisoned in a world it is in but not of, often forced by weakness into all kinds of ruses and stratagems, yet always managing to avoid the one fate which really is worse than death, the annihilation of one's identity. . . . What is symbolized as a virgin is actually a human

conviction, however expressed, that there is something at the core
of one's infinitely fragile being which is not only immortal but has
discovered the secret of invulnerability that eludes the tragic hero"
(*The Secular Scripture*, [Harvard University Press, 1976], p. 86).

Now let us consolidate what we know on this sketch so far. We
have to think in this play not merely about marriage but about the
marriage of a romantic hero and of a Christian man; one whose
imagination has to incorporate the idea of two becoming one in
marriage and the idea that it is better to marry than to burn. It is
a play, though it is thought of as domestic, in which not a marriage
but an idea of marriage, or let us say an imagination of marriage,
is worked out. "Why did I marry?" is the first question Othello
asks himself to express his first raid of suspicion (III, iii, 246). The
question has never been from his mind. Iago's first question to him
is "Are you fast married?" and Othello's first set speech ends with
something less than an answer: "But that I love the gentle Desdemona, / I would not my unhoused free condition / Put into cir-
cumscription and confine / For the sea's worth." Love is at most
a necessary not a sufficient condition for marrying. And for some
minds, a certain idea of love may compromise as much as validate
the idea of marriage. It may be better, but it is not perfect to marry,
as St Paul implies.

We have, further, to think in this play not merely generally of
marriage but specifically of the wedding night. It is with this that
the play opens. The central of the facts we know is that the whole
beginning scene takes place while Othello and Desdemona are in
their bridal bed. The simultaneity is marked: "Even now, now,
very now, an old black ram / Is tupping your white ewe" (I, i, 88–
9). And the scene is one of treachery, alarms, of shouts, of armed
men running through a sleeping city. The conjunction of the bridal
chamber with a scene of emergency is again insisted on by Othello's
reappearance from his bedroom to stop a brawl with his single
presence; a reappearance repeated the first night in Cyprus. As
though an appearance from his place of sex and dreams is what
gives him the power to stop an armed fight with a word and a
gesture. – Or is this more than we know? Perhaps the conjunction
is to imply that their "hour of love" (I, iii, 298–9), or their two
hours, have each been interrupted. There is reason to believe that
the marriage has not been consummated, anyway reason to believe
that Othello does not know whether it has. What is Iago's "Are

you fast married?" asking? Whether a public, legal ceremony has taken place or whether a private act; or whether the public and the private have ratified one another? Othello answers by speaking of his nobility and his love. But apart from anything else this seems to assume that Iago's "you" was singular, not plural. And what does Othello mean in Cyprus by these apparently public words?

> . . . come, my dear love,
> The purchase made, the fruits are to ensue,
> The profit's yet to come 'twixt me and you.
> (II, iii, 8–10)

What is the purchase and what the fruits or profit? Othello has just had proclaimed a general celebration at once of the perdition of the Turkish fleet and of his nuptials (II, ii). If the fruits and profit are the resumption of their privacy then the purchase was the successful discharge of his public office and his entry into Cyprus. But this success was not his doing; it was provided by a tempest. Is the purchase their (public) marriage? Then the fruits and profit are their conjugal love. Then he is saying that this is yet to come. It seems to me possible that the purchase, or price, was her virginity, and the fruits or profit their pleasure. There could hardly be greater emphasis on their having had just one shortened night together, isolated from this second night by a tempest (always in these matters symbolic, perhaps here of a memory, perhaps of an anticipation). Or is it, quite simply, that this is something he wishes to *say* publicly, whatever the truth between them? (How we imagine Desdemona's reaction to this would then become all-important.)

I do not think that we must, nor that we can, choose among these possibilities in Othello's mind. On the contrary, I think Othello cannot choose among them. My guiding hypothesis about the structure of the play is that the thing *denied our sight* throughout the opening scene – the thing, the scene, that Iago takes Othello back to again and again, retouching it for Othello's enchafed imagination – is what we are shown in the final scene, the scene of murder. This becomes our ocular proof of Othello's understanding of his two nights of married love. (It has been felt from Thomas Rymer to G. B. Shaw that the play obeys the rhythm of farce, not of tragedy. One might say that in beginning with a sexual scene denied our sight, this play opens exactly as a normal comedy closes, as if turning comedy inside out.) I shall follow out this hypothesis here only to the extent of commenting on that final scene.

However one seeks to interpret the meaning of the great entering speech of the scene ("It is the cause, it is the cause, my soul. . . . Put out the light, and then put out the light"), I cannot take its mysteries, its privacies, its magniloquence, as separate from some massive denial to which these must be in service. Othello must mean that he is acting impersonally, but the words are those of a man in a trance, in a dream state, fighting not to awaken; willing for anything but light. By "denial" I do not initially mean something requiring psychoanalytical, or any other, theory. I mean merely to ask that we not, conventionally but insufferably, assume that we know this woman better than this man knows her – making Othello some kind of exotic, gorgeous, superstitious lunkhead; which is about what Iago thinks. However much Othello deserves each of these titles, however far he believes Iago's tidings, he cannot just believe them; somewhere he also *knows* them to be false. This is registered in the rapidity with which he is brought to the truth, with no further real evidence, with only a counterstory (about the handkerchief) that bursts over him, or from him, as the truth. Shall we say he recognizes the truth too late? The fact is, he recognizes it when he is ready to, as one alone can; in this case, when its burden is dead. I am not claiming that he is trying not to believe Iago, or wants not to believe what Iago has told him. (This might describe someone who, say, had a good opinion of Desdemona, not someone whose life is staked upon hers.) I am claiming that we must understand Othello, on the contrary, to want to believe Iago, to be trying, against his knowledge, to believe him. Othello's eager insistence on Iago's honesty, his eager slaking of his thirst for knowledge with that poison, is not a sign of his stupidity in the presence of poison but of his devouring need of it. I do not quite say that he could not have accepted slander about Desdemona so quickly, to the quick, unless he already believed it; but rather that it is a thing he would rather believe than something yet more terrible to his mind; that the idea of Desdemona as an adulterous whore is more convenient to him than the idea of her as chaste. But what could be more terrible than Desdemona's faithlessness? Evidently her faithfulness. But how?

Note that in taking Othello's entering speech as part of a ritual of denial, in the context of taking the murder scene as a whole to be a dream enactment of the invisible opening of the play, we have an answer implied to our original question about this play, concerning Othello's turning of Desdemona to stone. His image denies that he scarred her and shed her blood. It is a denial at once that he has taken her virginity and that she has died of him. (But it is at the same time evidence that in suffering the replacement of the problem of God by the problem of the other this man has turned both objects into stone, so that we might at this moment understand his self-interpretation to be that of an idolater, hence religiously as well as socially to be cast out.) The whole scene of murder is built on the concept of sexual intercourse or orgasm as a dying. There is a dangerously explicit quibble to this effect in the exchange

> OTH. Thou art on thy death bed.
> DES. Ay, but not yet to die.
> (V, ii, 51–2)

The possible quibble only heightens the already heartbreaking poignance of the wish to die in her marriage bed after a long life.

Though Desdemona no more understands Othello's accusation of her than, in his darkness to himself, he does, she obediently shares his sense that this is their final night and that it is to be some dream-like recapitulation of their former two nights. This shows in her premonitions of death (the Willow Song, and the request that one of the wedding sheets be her shroud) and in her mysterious request to Emilia, ". . . tonight / Lay on my bed our wedding sheets" (IV, ii, 106–7), as if knowing, and faithful to, Othello's private dream of her, herself preparing the scene of her death as Othello, utilizing Iago's stage directions, imagines it must happen ("Do it not with poison, strangle her in her bed, even the bed she hath contaminated." "Good, good, the justice of it pleases, very good" [IV, i, 203–5]); as if knowing that only with these sheets on their bed can his dream of her be contested. The dream is of contamination. The fact the dream works upon is the act of deflowering. Othello is reasonably literal about this, as reasonable as a man in a trance can be:

> When I have pluck'd the rose,
> I cannot give it vital growth again,

It must needs wither; I'll smell it on the tree,
A balmy breath, that doth almost persuade
Justice herself to break her sword: once more:
Be thus, when thou art dead, and I will kill thee,
And love thee after.

(V, ii, 13–19)

(Necrophilia is an apt fate for a mind whose reason is suffocating in its sumptuous capacity for figuration, and which takes the dying into love literally to entail killing. "That death's unnatural, that kills for loving" [V, ii, 41]; or that turns its object to live stone. It is apt as well that Desdemona sense death, or the figure of death, as the impending cause of death. And at the very end, facing himself, he will not recover from this. "I kissed thee ere I killed thee." And after too. And not just now when you died from me, but on our previous nights as well.)

The exhibition of wedding sheets in this romantic, superstitious, conventional environment can only refer to the practice of proving purity by staining. – I mention in passing that this provides a satisfactory weight for the importance Othello attaches to his charmed (or farcical) handkerchief, the fact that it is spotted, spotted with strawberries.

Well, were the sheets stained or not? Was she a virgin or not? The answers seem as ambiguous as to our earlier question whether they are fast married. Is the final, fatal reenactment of their wedding night a clear denial of what really happened, so that we can just read off, by negation, what really happened? Or is it a straight reenactment, without negation, and the flower was still on the tree, as far as he knew? In that case, who was reluctant to see it plucked, he or she? On such issues, farce and tragedy are separated by the thickness of a membrane.

We of course have no answer to such questions. But what matters is that Othello has no answer; or rather he can give none, for any answer to the questions, granted that I am right in taking the questions to be his, is intolerable. The torture of logic in his mind we might represent as follows: Either I shed her blood and scarred her or I did not. If I did not then she was not a virgin and this is a stain upon me. If I did then she is no longer a virgin and this is a stain upon me. Either way I am contaminated. (I do not say that the sides of this dilemma are of equal significance for Othello.)

135

But this much logic anyone but a lunkhead might have mastered apart from actually getting married. (He himself may say as much when he asks himself, too late, why he married.) Then what quickens this logic for him? Call whatever it is Iago. What is Iago?

He is everything, we know, Othello is not. Critical and witty, for example, where Othello is commanding and eloquent; retentive where the other is lavish; concealed where the other is open; cynical where the other is romantic; conventional where the other is original; imagines flesh where the other imagines spirit; the imaginer and manager of the human guise; the bottom end of the world. And so on. A Christian has to call him devil. The single fact between Othello and Iago I focus on here is that Othello fails twice at the end to kill Iago, knowing he cannot kill him. This all but all-powerful chieftain is stopped at this nobody. It is the point of his impotence, and the meaning of it. Iago is everything Othello must deny, and which, denied, is not killed but works on, like poison, like Furies.

In speaking of the point and meaning of Othello's impotence, I do not think of Othello as having been in an everyday sense impotent with Desdemona. I think of him, rather, as having been surprised by her, at what he has elicited from her; at, so to speak, a success rather than a failure. It is the dimension of her that shows itself in that difficult and dirty banter between her and Iago as they await Othello on Cyprus. Rather than imagine himself to have elicited that, or solicited it, Othello would imagine it elicited by anyone and everyone else. – Surprised, let me say, to find that she is flesh and blood. It was the one thing he could not imagine for himself. For if she is flesh and blood then, since they are one, so is he. But then although his potency of imagination can command the imagination of this child who is everything he is not, so that she sees his visage in his mind, she also sees that he is not identical with his mind, he is more than his imagination, black with desire, which she desires. Iago knows it, and Othello cannot bear what Iago knows, so he cannot outface the way in which he knows it, or knows anything. He cannot forgive Desdemona for existing, for being separate from him, outside, beyond command, commanding, her captain's captain.

It is an unstable frame of mind that compounds figurative with literal dying in love; and Othello unstably projects upon her, as he blames her:

O perjur'd woman, thou dost stone thy heart
And makest me call what I intend to do
A murder, which I thought a sacrifice.
                                                    (V, ii, 64–6)

As he is the one who gives out lies about her, so he is the one who
will give her a stone heart for her stone body, as if in his words of
stone which confound the figurative and the literal there is the con-
founding of the incantations of poetry and of magic. He makes of
her the thing he feels ("my heart is turned to stone" [IV, i, 178]),
but covers the ugliness of his thought with the beauty of his imagery
– a debasement of himself and of his art of words. But what produces
the idea of sacrifice? How did he manage the thought of her death
as a sacrifice? To what was he to sacrifice her? To his image of
himself and of her, to keep his image intact, uncontaminated; as if
this were his protection from slander's image of him, say from a
conventional view of his blackness. So he becomes conventional,
sacrificing love to convention. But this was unstable; it could not
be said. Yet better thought than the truth, which was that the central
sacrifice of romance has already been made by them: Her virginity,
her intactness, her perfection, had been gladly forgone by her for
him, for the sake of their union, for the seaming of it. It is the
sacrifice he could not accept, for then he was not himself perfect.
It must be displaced. The scar is the mark of finitude, of separateness;
it must be borne whatever one's anatomical condition, or color. It
is the sin or the sign of refusing imperfection that produces, or
justifies, the visions and torments of devils that inhabit the region
of this play.

   If such a man as Othello is rendered impotent and murderous by
aroused, or by having aroused, female sexuality – or let us say, if
this man is horrified by human sexuality, in himself and in others
– then no human being is free of this possibility. What I have wished
to bring out is the nature of this possibility, or the possibility of
this nature, the way human sexuality is the field in which the fantasy
of finitude, of its acceptance and its repetitious overcoming, is
worked out; the way human separateness is turned equally toward
splendor and toward horror, mixing beauty and ugliness; turned
toward before and after; toward flesh and blood.

   – But Othello certainly knows that Desdemona exists! So what
has his more or less interesting condition to do with skepticism? –

In what spirit do you ask that question? I too am raising it. I wish to keep suspicion cast on what it is we take to express skepticism, and here especially by casting suspicion on whether we know what it means to know that another exists. Nothing could be more certain to Othello than that Desdemona exists; is flesh and blood; is separate from him; other. This is precisely the possibility that tortures him. The content of his torture *is* the premonition of the existence of another, hence of his own, his own as dependent, as partial. According to me further, his professions of skepticism over her faithfulness are a cover story for a deeper conviction; a terrible doubt covering a yet more terrible certainty, an unstatable certainty. But then this is what I have throughout kept arriving at as the cause of skepticism – the attempt to convert the human condition, the condition of humanity, into an intellectual difficulty, a riddle. (To interpret "a metaphysical finitude as an intellectual lack.")[1]

Tragedy is the place we are not allowed to escape the consequences, or price, of this cover: that the failure to acknowledge a best case of the other is a denial of that other, presaging the death of the other, say by stoning, or by hanging; and the death of our capacity to acknowledge as such, the turning of our hearts to stone, or their bursting. The necessary reflexiveness of spiritual torture. – But at any rate Othello is hardly in doubt that he can ever know whether Desdemona is, for example, in pain (perhaps suffering heartache), and for that reason in doubt that she exists; so again his problem cannot match the skeptical one. – But I ask again: Do we know what it is to be in such a doubt? and know this better than we know how to think of Othello's doubt? Moreover, is it even clear what it would mean to say that Othello does not doubt matters of Desdemona's consciousness such as that she has, or may have, some easily describable pain? If what he imagines is that she is stone, then *can* he imagine that she is in pain? ("Could one imagine a stone's having consciousness? And if anyone can do so – why should that not merely prove that such image-mongery is of no interest to us?" [*Investigations*, §390].)

Is the cover of skepticism – the conversion of metaphysical finitude into intellectual lack – a denial of the human or an expression of it? For of course there are those for whom the denial of the human

---

[1]"Knowing and Acknowledging," *Must We Mean What We Say?* (repr. Cambridge University Press, 1976), p. 263.

is the human.[2] Call this the Christian view. It would be why Nietzsche undertook to identify the task of overcoming the human with the task of overcoming the denial of the human; which implies overcoming the human not through mortification but through joy, say ecstasy. If the former can be thought of as the denial of the body then the latter may be thought of as the affirmation of the body. Then those who are pushed, in attempting to counter a dualistic view of mind and body, to assert the identity of body and mind, are again skipping or converting the problem. For suppose my identity with my body is something that exists only in my affirmation of my body. (As friendship may exist only in loyalty to it.) Then the question is: What would the body *become* under affirmation? What would become of *me?* Perhaps I would know myself as, take myself for, a kind of machine; perhaps as a universe.

I conclude with two thoughts, or perspectives, from which to survey one's space of conviction in the reading I have started of *Othello,* and from which perhaps to guide it further.

First, what you might call the philosophy or the moral of the play seems all but contained in the essay Montaigne entitles "On Some Verses of Virgil," in such a remark as: "What a monstrous animal to be a horror to himself, to be burdened by his pleasures, to regard himself as a misfortune!" The essay concerns the compatibility of sex with marriage, of sex with age; it remarks upon, and upon the relations among, jealousy, chastity, imagination, doubts about virginity; upon the strength of language and the honesty of language; and includes mention of a Turk and of certain instances of necrophilia. One just about runs through the topics of *Othello* if to this essay one adds Montaigne's early essay "Of the Power of Imagination," which contains a Moor and speaks of a king of Egypt who, finding himself impotent with his bride, threatened to kill her, thinking it was some sort of sorcery. The moral would be what might have been contained in Othello's "one that lov'd not wisely, but too well," that all these topics should be food for thought and moderation, not for torture and murder; as fit for rue and laughter as for pity and terror; that they are not tragic unless one makes them so, takes them so; that we are tragic in what we take to be tragic; that one must take one's imperfections with a "gay and sociable wisdom" (in "Of Experience," Montaigne's

[2] Cf. "Aesthetic Problems of Modern Philosophy," ibid. p. 96.

final essay), not with a somber and isolating eloquence. It is advice to accept one's humanity, and one can almost see Iago as the slanderer of human nature (this would be his diabolism) braced with Othello as the enacter of the slander – the one thinking to escape human nature from below, the other from above. But to whom is the advice usable? And how do we understand why it cannot be taken by those in directest need of it? The urging of moderation is valuable only to the extent that it results from a knowledge of the human possibilities beyond its urging. Is Montaigne's attitude fully earned, itself without a tint of the wish for exemption from the human? Or is Shakespeare's topic of the sheets and the handkerchief understandable as a rebuke to Montaigne, for refusing a further nook of honesty? A bizarre question, I suppose; but meant only to indicate how one might, and why one should, test whether my emphasis on the stain is necessary to give sufficient weight to one's experience of the horror and the darkness of these words and actions, or whether it is imposed.

My second concluding thought is more purely speculative, and arises in response to my having spoken just now of "the refusal of imperfection" as producing "the visions and torments of devils that inhabit the region of this play." I do not wish to dispute the evidence marshaled by Bernard Spivack in his *Shakespeare and the Allegory of Evil* showing Iago to be a descendant of the late morality figure of the Vice. I mean rather to help explain further the appearance of that figure in this particular play, and, I guess, to suggest its humanizing, or human splitting off (the sort of interpretation Spivack's book seems to deplore). It is against the tradition of the morality play that I now go on to call attention – I cannot think I am the first to say it out loud – to the hell and the demon staring out of the names of Othello and Desdemona. I mention this curiosity to prepare something meant as a nearly pure conjecture, wishing others to prove it one way or another, namely that underlying and shaping the events of this play are certain events of witch trials. Phrases such as "the ocular proof" and "cords, or knives / Poison, or fire, or suffocating streams" (III, iii, 394–5) seem to me to call for location in a setting of judicial torture. And I confess to finding myself thinking of Desdemona's haunting characterization of a certain conception of her as "a moth of peace" when I read, from an 1834 study called *Folk-lore of the NE of Scotland,* "In some parts of Scotland moths are called 'witches' " (quoted in Kittredge, *Witchcraft in Old and New England*). But what prompts my thought primarily is the crazed logic Othello's rage for proof and for "satisfaction" seems to require (like testing for a woman's witchcraft by seeing whether she will drown, declaring that if she does she was innocent but if she does not she is to be put to death for a witch): What happened on our wedding night is that I killed her; but she is not dead; therefore she is not human; therefore she must die. ("Yet she must die, else she'll betray more men" [V, ii, 6].) Again he claims not to be acting personally, but by authority; here he has delivered a sentence. I recall that the biblical justification for the trial of witches was familiarly from the punishments in Exodus: "Thou shalt not suffer a witch to live." Othello seems to be babbling the crazed logic as he falls into his explicit faint or trance: "First, to be hanged, and then to confess; I tremble at it" (IV, i, 38–9), not knowing whether he is torturer or victim.

I introduced the idea of the trial for witchcraft as a conjecture, meaning immediately that it is not meant as a hypothesis: I do not *require* it for any interpretive alignment of my senses with the world of this play. It is enough, without supposing Shakespeare to have used literal subtexts of this sort, that the play opens with a public accusation of witchcraft, and an abbreviated trial, and is then succeeded with punctuating thoughts of hell and by fatal scenes of psychological torture, and concludes with death as the proof of mortality, i.e., of innocence (cf. "If that thou be'st a devil, I cannot kill thee" [V, ii, 283]). Enough, I mean, to stir the same depths of superstition – of a horror that proposes our lack of certain access to other minds – that under prompting institutions caused trials for witchcraft. *Othello* is at once, as we would expect of what we call Shakespeare's humanity, an examination of the madness and bewitchment of inquisitors, as well as of the tortures of love; of those tortures of which both victim and torturer are victims.

So they are there, on their bridal and death sheets. A statue, a stone, is something whose existence is fundamentally open to the ocular proof. A human being is not. The two bodies lying together form an emblem of this fact, the truth of skepticism. What this man lacked was not certainty. He knew everything, but he could not yield to what he knew, be commanded by it. He found out too much for his mind, not too little. Their differences from one another – the one everything the other is not – form an emblem of human separation, which can be accepted, and granted, or not. Like the separation from God; everything we are not.

So we are here, knowing they are "gone to burning hell," she with a lie on her lips, protecting him, he with her blood on him. Perhaps Blake has what he calls songs to win them back with, to make room for hell in a juster city. But can philosophy accept them back at the hands of poetry? Certainly not so long as philosophy continues, as it has from the first, to demand the banishment of poetry from its republic. Perhaps it could if it could itself become literature. But can philosophy become literature and still know itself?

4

Coriolanus and Interpretations of Politics
("Who does the wolf love?")

SOMETHING that draws me to *Coriolanus* is its apparent disdain of questions I have previously asked of Shakespearean tragedy, taking tragedy as an epistemological problem, a refusal to know or to be known, an avoidance of acknowledgment, an expression (or imitation) of skepticism. Coriolanus's refusal to acknowledge his participation in finite human existence may seem so obviously the fact of the matter of his play that to note it seems merely to describe the play, not at all to interpret it. It may be, however, that this lack of theoretical grip itself proposes a moral, or offers a conclusion, namely that *Coriolanus* is not exactly to be understood as a tragedy, that its mystery – supposing one agrees to something like a mystery in its events – will be located only in locating its lack or missing of tragedy, hence its closeness to tragedy.

But systematically to pursue this possibility would require – from me – following out a sense that this play presents a particular interpretation of the problem of skepticism as such (skepticism directed toward our knowledge of the existence of others), in particular an interpretation that takes skepticism as a form of narcissism. This interpretation does not in itself come to me as a complete surprise since a book I published a few years ago – *The Claim of Reason* – begins with an interpretation of Wittgenstein's *Philosophical Investigations* that takes his move against the idea of a private language (an idea that arises in his struggle against skepticism) as a move against a kind of narcissism, a kind of denial of an existence shared with others; and my book ends with a reading of *Othello* as a depiction of the murderous lengths to which narcissism must go in order to maintain its picture of itself as skepticism, in order to maintain its stand of ignorance, its fear or avoidance of knowing, under the color of a claim to certainty.[1] What surprised me more in *Coriolanus* was its understanding of narcissism as another face of incestuousness, and of this condition as one in which language breaks down under one's sense of becoming incomprehensible, of the sense of oneself as having lost the power of expression, what I call in *The Claim of Reason* the terror of inexpressiveness; together with the thoroughness with which Narcissus's fate is mirrored in the figure of Coriolanus, a figure whose every act is, by that act, done to him so perfectly that the distinction between action and passion seems to lose its sense, a condition in which human existence becomes precarious, if perhaps transcendable. I mention these connections with the philosophical issue of skepticism not because I pursue them further in the essay to follow but only to attest my conviction that a work such as a play of Shakespeare's cannot contribute the help I want from it for the philosophical issues I mention unless the play is granted the autonomy it is in one's power to grant, which means, seen in its own terms. What does this mean? What is a play of Shakespeare's? I shall try to say something about these questions.

Something else also draws me. The way I have been understanding the conflicts the play engenders keeps sending me back over paths of thought that I believe many critics have found to be depleted of interest, or conviction; three paths, or branches of paths, in particular: (1) those that look in a Shakespearean play for something like an idea of theater, as it were for the play's concept of itself; (2) those that sense Christian stirrings and murmurings under the surface of the words; and (3) even those paths of thought that anticipate something you might call the origins of tragedy in religious ritual. I am, I suppose, as drawn to critical paths that others find empty as some poets are to words that others find flat. But to say fully why one is drawn to a work, and its work of interpretation, can only be the goal of an interpretation; and the motive of an interpretation, like what one might call the intention of the work it seeks, exists fully only in its satisfaction.

I expect, initially, general agreement on two facts about *Coriolanus*. First, compared with other Shakespearean tragedies this one lacks what A. C. Bradley called "atmosphere" (in his British Acad-

[1]The *Othello* pages appear in this book as chapter 3.

emy lecture on the play, the decade after his *Shakespearean Tragedy*). Its language, like its hero, keeps aloof from our attention, as withdrawn, austere, as its rage and its contempt permit. Second, the play is about the organization of the body politic and about how that body is fed, that is, sustained. I expect, further, that readers from opposed camps should be willing to see that the play lends itself equally, or anyway naturally, to psychological and to political readings: Both perspectives are, for example, interested in who produces food and in how food is distributed and paid for. From a psychological perspective (in practice this has in recent years been psychoanalytic) the play directs us to an interest in the development of Coriolanus's character. From a political perspective the play directs us to an interest in whether the patricians or the plebeians are right in their conflict and in whether, granted that Coriolanus is unsuited for political leadership, it is his childishness or his very nobility that unsuits him.

In the critical discussions I have read so far, the psychoanalytic perspective has produced more interesting readings than the political. A political reading is apt to become fairly predictable once you know whose side the reader is taking, that of the patricians or that of the plebeians; and whose side the reader takes may come down to how he or she sees Menenius's fable of the organic state, the parable of the belly, and upon whom we can place the blame for Coriolanus's banishment. If few will consider it realistic to suppose that Coriolanus would have made a good political leader, fewer will deny that in losing him the city has lost its greatest hero and that this loss is the expression of a time of crisis in the state. It is a time of famine in which the call for revolt is made moot by the threat and the fact of war and invasion, followed by a time in which victory in the war, and bitterness over its conduct, creates the call for counterrevolt by the state's defender and preserver. In such a period of crisis everyone and no one has good arguments, everyone and no one has right on their side. In Aufidius's great description of Coriolanus at the end of Act IV he summarizes as follows:

> So our virtues
> Lie in th' interpretation of the time; . . .
> One fire drives out one fire; one nail, one nail;
> Rights by rights founder, strengths by strengths do fail.

One might say that just this division of fire and right is the tragedy, but would that description account for the particular turns of just these events, as distinct from the losses and ironies in any revolutionary situation? Even the most compelling political interpretation – in my experience this is given in Bertolt Brecht's discussion with members of his theater company of the opening scene of the play[2] – seems to have little further to add, in the way of interpretation, once it makes clear that choosing the side of the plebeians is dramatically and textually viable. This is no small matter. It shows that Shakespeare's text – or what we think of as Shakespeare's humanity – leaves ample room for distinctions among the "clusters" of citizens, and it shows the weight of their common position in opposition to that of the patricians. And I take this in turn to show that the politics of the play is essentially the politics of a given production, so that we should not expect its political issues to be settled by an interpretation of what you might call "the text itself."

Exactly the power of Brecht's discussion can be said to be its success in getting us *not* to interpret, not, above all, to interpret food, but to stay with the opening fact of the play, the fact that the citizens of Rome are in revolt because there is a famine (and because of their interpretation of the famine). They and their families are starving and they believe (correctly, for all we know) that the patricians are hoarding grain. Not to interpret this means, in practical or theatrical terms, that we come to see that this cluster is of human beings, individual human beings, who work at particular trades and who live in particular places where specific people await news of the outcome of their dangerous course in taking up arms. This fact of their ordinary humanity is the most impressive fact that can be set against the patricians' scorn of them – a fact that ought not to be visible solely to a Marxist, a fact that shows up the language of the leaders as mysterious and evasive, as subject to what one may think of as the politics of interpretation.

Yet we also feel that the pervasive images of food and hunger, of cannibalism and of disgust, do mean something, that they call upon us for some lines of interpretation, and that the value of attending to this particular play is a function of the value to individual human beings of tracing these lines.

---

[2] See Bertolt Brecht, *Collected Plays*, vol. 9, ed. Ralph Manheim and John Willett (New York, 1973), pp. 378–94.

Psychoanalysts naturally have focused on the images of food and feeding that link Coriolanus and his mother. In a recent essay, " 'Anger's My Meat': Feeding, Dependency, and Aggression in *Coriolanus*,"[3] Professor Janet Adelman has given so clear and fair an account of some two decades of psychoanalytic interpretations of food and feeding in the play, in the course of working out her further contributions, that I feel free to pick and choose the lines and moments bearing on this aspect of things that serve my somewhat different emphases.

Twice Volumnia invokes nursing. Early she says to Virgilia, rebuking her for worrying about her husband:

> The breasts of Hecuba
> When she did suckle Hector, look'd not lovelier
> Than Hector's forehead when it spit forth blood
> At Grecian sword, contemning.
>
> (I, iii, 43–6)

And in her first intercession with her son:

> Do as thou list.
> Thy valiantness was mine, thou suck'st it from me,
> But owe thy pride thyself.
>
> (III, ii, 127–9)

Both invocations lead one to think what it is this son learned at his mother's breast, what it is he was fed with, particularly as we come to realize that both mother and son declare themselves to be starving. It is after Coriolanus's departure upon being banished, when Menenius asks Volumnia if she'll sup with him, that she comes out with

> Anger's my meat; I sup upon myself
> And so shall starve with feeding.
>
> (IV, ii, 50–1)

As Coriolanus mocks and resists the ritual of asking for the people's

[3] In *Representing Shakespeare,* ed. Murray Schwartz and Coppelia Kahn (Baltimore, 1980).

voices, his being keeps revolting, one time as follows:

> Better it is to die, better to starve,
> Than crave the hire which first we do deserve.
>
> (II, iii, 118–19)

I say that mother and son, both of them, *are* starving, and I mean throughout, always, not just when they have occasion to say so. I take Volumnia's vision of supping upon herself not to be a picture simply of her local anger but of self-consuming anger as the presiding passion of her life – the primary thing, accordingly, she would have to teach her son, the thing he sucked from her, of course under the name of valiantness. If so, then if Volumnia and hence Coriolanus are taken to exemplify a Roman identification of virtue as valor, they should further be taken as identifying valor with an access to one's anger. It is "in anger, Juno-like," godlike, that Volumnia laments (IV, ii, 52–3); and it is this anger that the tribune Sicinius is remarking as, in trying to avoid being confronted by her, he says, "They say she's mad" (IV, ii, 9). Along these lines, I emphasize Coriolanus's statement about deserving rather than craving not as

> Better it is to *die,* better to *starve,*
> Than crave . . .

as if he is asserting the rightness of a particular choice for the future; but as

> *Better* it is to die, *better* to starve,
> Than crave . . .

as if he is reaffirming or confessing his settled form of (inner) life. I expect that the former is the more usual way of emphasis, but I find it prejudicial.

Coriolanus and Volumnia are – I am taking it – starvers, hungerers. They manifest this condition as a name or a definition of the human, like being mortal. And they manifest this as a condition of insatiability (starving by feeding, feeding as deprivation). It is a condition sometimes described as the infiniteness of desire, imposing upon the finiteness of the body. But starving for Volumnia and her son suggests that this infiniteness is not the cause of human insatiability but is rather its effect. It is the effect not of an endless quantity, as though the self had, or is, endless reserves of desire; but of an endless structure, as though desire has a structure of endlessness. One picture of this structure is given by Narcissus for whom what is longed for is someone longing, who figures beauty as longing. Starving by feeding presents itself to Coriolanus as being consumed by hunger, and his words for hungering are desiring and craving. And what he incessantly hungers for is . . . not to hunger, not to desire, that is, not to be mortal. Take the scene of interview by the people:

> CORIOLANUS. You know the cause, sir, of my standing
> here.
> THIRD CITIZEN. We do, sir; tell us what hath brought you
> to't.
> CORIOLANUS. Mine own desert.
> SECOND CITIZEN. Your own desert?
> CORIOLANUS. Ay, not mine own desire.
> THIRD CITIZEN. How not your own desire?
>
> (II, iii, 66–72)

If you desire to be desireless, is there something you desire? If so, how would you express it; that is, tell it; that is, ask for it? Coriolanus's answer to this paradox is to become perfectly deserving. Since to hunger is to want, to lack something, he hungers to lack nothing, to be complete, like a sword. My speculations here are an effort to do justice to one's sense of Coriolanus as responding not primarily to his situation with the plebeians, as if trapped by an uncontrollable disdain; but as responding primarily to his situation with himself, as befits a Narcissus, trapped first by an uncontrollable logic. Although I shall come to agree with Plutarch's early observation or diagnosis in his *Life of Caius Martius Coriolanus* that Coriolanus is "altogether unfit for any man's conversation," I am in effect taking this to mean not that he speaks in anger and contempt (anger and contempt are not unjustifiable) but that whereas under certain circumstances he can express satisfaction, he cannot express desire and to this extent cannot speak at all: The case is not that he will not ask for what he wants but rather that he can want nothing that he asks. His solution amounts, as both patricians and plebeians more or less note, to becoming a god. What god? We have to get to this.

Let us for the moment continue developing the paradox of hungering. To be consumed by hunger, to feed upon oneself, must present itself equally as being fed upon, being eaten up. (To feed means both to give and to take nourishment, as to suckle means both to give and to take the breast.) So the other fact of Coriolanus's and Volumnia's way of starving, of their hunger, is their sense of being cannibalized.[4]

The idea of cannibalization runs throughout the play. It is epitomized in the title question I have given to these remarks: "Who does the wolf love?" Menenius asks this of the tribunes of the people at the opening of Act II. One of them answers, with undeniable truth: "The lamb." And Menenius, ever the interpretive fabulist, answers: "Ay, to devour him, as the hungry plebeians would the noble Marcius." The other tribune's answer – "He's a lamb, indeed, that baas like a bear" – does not unambiguously deny Menenius's interpretation. The shock of the interpretation is of course that it is from the beginning the people, not the patricians, and least of all Coriolanus, who are presented as lambs, anyway as food for patrician wolves. In Menenius's opening effort to talk the people out of revolt he declares that "The helms o' the state . . . care for you like fathers," to which the First Citizen replies, "Care for us! . . . If the wars eat us not up, they will; and there is all the love they bear us." This fantasy is borne out when the general Cominius speaks of Coriolanus's coming to battle as to a feast (I, ix, 10). And the idea of the warrior Coriolanus feeding on a weaker species may be raised again in the battle at Corioli in his threat to any soldier who holds back, "I'll take him for a Volsce / And he shall feel mine edge," allowing the suggestion of his sword as a piece of cutlery. The idea of an ungovernable voraciousness is furthered by Volumnia's association of her son with his son's tearing apart a butterfly with his teeth. On the other hand, when Coriolanus offers himself to Aufidius at Antium he expresses his sense of having been de-

---

[4] "There seems to be some question whether one's knowing oneself is something active, something one does . . . or rather something one suffers, something that happens to one" (*The Claim of Reason*, p. 352).

voured, with only the name Caius Marcius Coriolanus remaining, devoured by "the cruelty and envy of the people" (IV, v, 77–8). And Menenius, whose sense of justice is constricted, among other things by his fear of civil disorder, is accurate in his fears, in the consequences they prophesy for Rome, and he will repeat his vision of civil cannibalism:

> Now the good gods forbid
> That our renowned Rome, whose gratitude
> Towards her deserved children is enrolled
> In Jove's own book, like an unnatural dam
> Should now eat up her own.
>
> (III, i, 288–92)

All readers of this aspect of the play will recognize in this description of Rome as potentially a cannibalistic mother an allusion to Volumnia; and the identification of Volumnia and Rome is enforced in other ways, not least by Volumnia herself when in the second and final intercession scene she says to her son:

> . . . thou shalt no sooner
> March to assault thy country than to tread
> (Trust to't, thou shalt not) on thy mother's womb
> That brought thee to this world.
>
> (V, iii, 121–4)

It is very much to the point to notice that in Menenius's vision of Rome as an "unnatural dam" an identity is proposed between a mother eating her child and a mother eating herself: If Rome eats up all Romans there is no more Rome, for as one of the tribunes asks, "What is the city but the people?" (III, i, 198).

The paradox and reciprocity of hungering may be found registered in the question "Who does the wolf love?" If the question is asking for the object of the wolf's affection, the more nearly correct grammar would seem to be "Whom does the wolf love?"[5] But this correctness (call it a patrician correctness, a refinement in which the plebeians apparently do not see the good) would rule out taking

---

[5] A point emphasized by the chairman of the *Coriolanus* panel at the Stanford meetings, Professor Harry Berger, in his remarks introducing my paper.

the question also in its opposite direction, grammatically strict as
it stands, namely as asking whose object of affection the wolf is.
(Who does love the wolf?) The answer given directly, "The lamb,"
does not rule out either direction, but as the ensuing discussion
demonstrates, the direction will be a function of what or whom
you take the lamb to be, hence what the wolf. Both directions, the
active and the passive constructions of the play's focal verbs, are
operative throughout the action. I have mentioned this explicitly
in the cases of feeding and suckling. But it is, I find, true less con-
spicuously, but pertinently, in such an odd moment as this:

> CORIOLANUS. Let them hang.
> VOLUMNIA. Ay, and burn too.
> (III, ii, 23–4)

One of the functions in providing Volumnia with this amplification
here strikes me as suggesting her sense of the inevitable reflexiveness
of action in their Rome: Are hanging and burning actions done to
someone, or something "they" are, or will be, doing?

   The circle of cannibalism, of the eater eaten by what he or she
eats, keeps being sketched out, from the first to the last. You might
call this the identification of narcissism as cannibalism. From the
first: At the end of Coriolanus's first long speech he says to the
citizens:

> You cry against the noble Senate, who
> (Under the gods) keep you in awe, which else
> Would feed on one another.
> (I, i, 187–9)

And at the last: Rome devouring itself is the idea covered in the
obsessive images of Coriolanus burning Rome. It was A. C. Bradley
again who at the end of his British Academy lecture pointed up the
sudden and relentless harping, principally after the banishment, on
the image of fire, of Rome burning. Bradley makes nothing further
of the point, but it is worth noting, in view of the theme of starving
and cannibalism, that fire in this play is imagined under the description of it as *consuming* what it burns.

   You may say that burning as a form of revenge is Coriolanus's

projection onto Rome of what he felt Rome was doing to him.
This cannot be wrong, but it so far pictures Coriolanus, in his revenge, to be essentially a man like Aufidius, merely getting even;
the picture requires refining. Suppose that, as I believe, in Coriolanus's famous sentence of farewell, "I banish you!" (III, iii, 123),
he has already begun a process of consuming Rome, incorporating
it, becoming it. Then when the general Cominius tried in vain to
plead with him to save Rome, and found him to be "sitting in gold,
his eye / Red as 'twould burn Rome" (V, i, 63–4), he somewhat
misunderstood what he saw. He took Coriolanus to be contem-
plating something in the future whereas Coriolanus's eye was red
with the present flames of self-consuming. Consuming the literal
Rome with literal fire would accordingly only have been an expression of that self-consuming. Thus would the city understand what
it had done to itself. He will give it – horribly – what it deserves.
Thus is the play of revenge further interpreted.

These various understandings of cannibalism all illustrate the ancient sentiment that man is wolf to man. (The Roman Plautus, to
whom Shakespeare is famously indebted, is credited with being the
earliest namable framer of the sentiment. A pertinent modern instance occurs in Brecht's *Threepenny Opera*.) But the question "Who
does the wolf love?" has two further reaches which we must eventually consider. First, there is the repetition of the idea that devouring
can be an expression of love. Second, if, as I think, there is reason
here to take the image of the wolf as the figure of the mythical
animal identified with Rome, the one who suckled the founders of
Rome (Volumnia is the reason), there is reason to take the lamb it
is said to love (or that loves it) as the mythical animal identified
with Christ.

Before this, I should make explicit a certain way in which the
account of Coriolanus's motivation I have been driving at is somewhat at odds with the direction of psychoanalytic interpretation
summarized and extended by Janet Adelman.[6] She understands
Coriolanus's attempt to make himself inhumanly independent as a
defense against his horror of dependence, and his rage as converting
his wish to be dependent against those who render him so. A characteristic turn of her argument consists of a reading of some lines
I have already had occasion to quote:

[6] In the essay cited in note 3.

> The breasts of Hecuba
> When she did suckle Hector, look'd not lovelier
> Than Hector's forehead when it spit forth blood
> At Grecian sword, contemning.

Adelman reads as follows:

> Blood is more beautiful than milk, the wound than the breast, warfare than peaceful feeding. . . . Hector is transformed immediately from infantile feeding mouth to bleeding wound. For the unspoken mediator between breast and wound is the infant's mouth: in this imagistic transformation, to feed is to be wounded; the mouth becomes the wound, the breast the sword. . . . But at the same time as Volumnia's image suggests the vulnerability inherent in feeding, it also suggests a way to fend off that vulnerability. In her image, feeding, incorporating, is transformed into spitting out, an aggressive expelling; the wound once again becomes the mouth that spits. . . . The wound spitting blood thus becomes not a sign of vulnerability but an instrument of attack. (p. 131)

This is very fine and it must not be denied. But the transformation of Hector's mouth into a wound must not in turn deny two further features of these difficult lines. First, when Hector contemns Grecian swords, he is also to be thought of as fighting, as wielding a sword, so the mouth is transformed into, or seen as, a cutting weapon: The suckling mother is presented as being slashed by the son-hero, eaten by the one she feeds. Suffering such a fantasy would constitute some of Volumnia's more normal moments. Second, the lines set up an equation between a mother's milk and a man's blood, suggesting that we must understand the man's spitting blood in battle not simply as attacking but equally, somehow, as providing food, in a male fashion. But how? Remember that Coriolanus's way to avoid asking for something, that is, to avoid expressing desire, is by what he calls deserving the thing. His proof of desert is his valiantness, so his spitting blood in battle is his way of deserving being fed, that is to say, being devoured, being loved unconditionally. (War and feeding have consistently been joined in the words of this play. A plebeian says: "If the wars eat us not up they will" [I, i, 85–6]. And Cominius: Coriolanus "cam'st to . . . this feast having fully dined before" [I, ix, 10–11]; but again Cominius does not get the connection complete.) To be fed by Volumnia is to be fed *to* her. But since the right, or effective, bleeding depends (according to the equation of blood and milk) upon its being a form of feeding, of giving food, providing blood identifies him with his mother. His mother's fantasy here suggests that the appropriate reciprocation for having nourished her son is for him to become her, as if to remove the arbitrariness in her having been born a woman; and since it is a way of putting her into the world it is a way of giving birth to her. Her son's companion fantasy of reciprocation would be to return Rome's gift, to nurse Rome with the valiantness he sucked from it.

This fantasy produces contradictions that are a match for the fury of contradictions one feels in Coriolanus's position (for example, between the wishes for dependence and for independence). For he can only return his nourishment if Rome – taken as the people – deserves it. Hence the people's lack of desert entails his lack of desert, entails that he cannot do the thing that acquires love; he is logically debarred from reciprocating. The fact that he both has absolute contempt for the people and yet has an absolute need for them is part of what maddens him. (This implies again that I cannot understand Coriolanus's emotions toward the people as directed simply to, say, their cowardice, their being poor fighters. I am taking it that he needs their desert for, so to speak, private reasons as much as public.) The other part of what maddens him is that neither the people nor his mother – neither of the things that mean Rome – will understand his position. Neither understands that his understanding of his valiantness, his virtue, his worth, his deservingness, is of himself as a provider, and that this is the condition of his receiving his own sustenance. (This assumes that he shares his mother's fantasy of the equation of milk and blood – as if there is nothing in her he has not taken in.) The people, precisely on the contrary, maddeningly accuse him of *withholding* food; and his mother precisely regards his heroism purely as toughness, devoid of tenderness; or pure fatherhood devoid of motherhood; and as deserving something more than acknowledging what he provides, more than the delicate balance of his self-account, as if being made consul were indeed something more. ("Know, good mother, / I had rather be their servant in my way / Than sway with them in theirs" [II, i, 107–9].) In these misunderstandings they have both already abandoned him, weaned him, before the ritual of being made consul comes to grief and he is formally banished. This prior rejection, not just once but always, inherently, would allow the understanding of his anger as his mother interprets anger, that is, as lamentation ("Anger's my meat . . . lament as I do, / In anger, Juno-like"). We may not contradict her interpretation, though we may interpret it further. We might go on to interpret it as depression.

I might characterize my intention in spelling out what I call these fantasies as an attempt to get at the origin of words, not the origin of their meaning exactly but of their production, of the value they have when and as they occur. I have characterized something like this ambition of criticism variously over the years, and related it to what I understand as the characteristic procedure of ordinary language philosophy. (One such effort enters into the opening pages of the reading of *King Lear,* chapter 2 of this book.) And do my spellings-out help? Do they, for example, help comprehend Coriolanus's subsequent course – how he justifies his plan to burn Rome and how he is talked out of his plan by his mother? It is not hard to encourage oneself in the impression that one understands these things. To me they seem mysteries. I shall sketch the answers I have to these questions and then conclude by indicating how these answers serve to interpret our relation to this play, which means to me, to understand what a Shakespearean play is (as revealed in this instance).

I pause, in turning to these questions, to make explicit an issue that at any time may nag our consciousness of the play. The mother relation is so overwhelmingly present in this play that we may not avoid wondering, at least wondering whether we are to wonder, what happened to the father. The play seems to me to raise this question in three ways, which I list in decreasing order of obviousness. First, Menenius is given a certain kind of fatherly role, or a role as a certain kind of father, but the very difficulty of conceiving of him as Coriolanus's real father, which is to say, as Volumnia's husband and lover, keeps alive our imagination of what such a figure might look like. Second, Coriolanus's erotic attachment to battle and to men who battle suggests a search for the father as much as an escape from the mother. This would afford an explanation for an otherwise, to me, insufficiently explained use in the play of the incident from Plutarch's Life in which Coriolanus asks, exhausted from victorious battle, that a man in the conquered city of Corioli be spared slavery on the ground that Coriolanus had "sometime lay at the poor man's house," a man whose name Coriolanus dis-covers he has forgotten. The vagueness of the man's identity and Coriolanus's expression of confusion in the Shakespeare – distinct differences from the occurrence of the incidents in Plutarch – suggest to my mind that the unnamed figure to whom Coriolanus wishes to provide reparation is, vaguely, transiently, an image of his father.[7]

Third, and so little obvious as to be attributable to my powers of hallucination, Coriolanus's effort at mythological identification as he sits enthroned and entranced before Rome is an effort – if one accepts one stratum of description I shall presently give of him – to come unto the Father. (I shall not go into the possibilities here, or fantasies, that a patrician matron is simultaneously father–mother, or that, in replacing his father, he becomes his own father.)

I was about to ask how we are to grasp Coriolanus's return and his change of heart. My answer depends on plotting a relation be-tween him and the other sacrificial lamb I have mentioned, the lamb of God, Christ. I say plotting a relation between the figures, not at all wishing to identify them. I see Coriolanus not so much as imitating Christ as competing with him. These are necessarily shadowy matters and although everything depends on accuracy in defining this relation all I can do here is note some elements that will have to figure in the plotting.

Earlier I spoke of Coriolanus's solution to the paradox of hun-gering not to hunger, of wanting not to want, of asking not to ask, as one of becoming a god. Now we may see that Christ is the right god because of the way he understands his mission as providing nonliteral food, food for the spirit, for immortality; and because it is in him that blood must be understood as food. If one is drawn to this as a possibility, one may find surprising confirmation for it

---

[7]This is not meant as an alternative to but as an extension of the fine perception in the last note to Act I, scene ix, by the editor of the Arden edition (Philip Brockbank) that "One name is found in the scene and another is lost." My thought is that both are names held by Caius Martius Coriolanus. I suppose I am influenced in this thought by a further change Shakespeare makes in Plutarch's characterization of the man. In Plutarch Coriolanus speaks of the man as "an old friend and host of mine"; it is at the analogous moment in Shakespeare that Coriolanus speaks of the man as one at whose house he lay. The opening words of Plutarch's Life are "The house of the Martians," where "house" of course means "family," a phrase and passage employed by Shakespeare at the end of Act II where the tribunes invoke Coriolanus's biological descent as if to their sufficient credit for having considered it but to Coriolanus's insufficient credit for election to consul.

in certain of Coriolanus's actions and in certain descriptions of his actions. (I am not interested in claiming that Coriolanus is *in some sense* a scapegoat, the way perhaps any tragic hero is; but in claiming that he is a specific inflection of *this* scapegoat.)

First his actions, two especially. First is his pivotal refusal to show his wounds. I associate this generally with the issue of Christ's showing his wounds to his disciples, in order to show them the Lord – that is, to prove the Resurrection – and specifically with his saying to Thomas, who was not present at the first showing and who made seeing the wounds a condition of believing, that is, of declaring his faith, "Thomas, because thou hast seen me, thou believest: blessed are they that have not seen, and have believed" (John 20:29). (Thomas would not believe until he could, as he puts it and as Jesus will invite him to, "put mine hand into his side"; Aufidius declares the wish to "wash my fierce hand in's heart" (I, x, 27). I make no further claims on the basis of this conjunction; I can see that some good readers may feel that it is accidental. I do claim that good reading may be guided, or inspired, by the overexcitement such conjunctions can cause.) The second action is the second intercession, in which Volumnia, holding her son's son by the hand, together with Virgilia and Valeria appears to Coriolanus before Rome. I take this to invoke the appearance, while Christ is on the cross, of three women whose names begin with the same letter of the alphabet (I mean begin with M's, not with V's), accompanied by a male he loves, whom he views as his mother's son (John 19:25–7). (Giving his mother a son presages a mystic marriage.)

I do not suppose that one will be convinced by these relations unless one has antecedently felt some quality of – what shall I say? – the mythic in these moments. This is something I meant in calling these relations "shadowy matters": I meant this not negatively but positively. It is a way to understand Volumnia's advice to Coriolanus that when he makes his appeal to the people he act out the meaning of his presence:

> . . . for in such business
> Action is eloquence, and the eyes of th'ignorant
> More learned than the ears.
>
> (III, ii, 75–7)

I accept this as advice Shakespeare is giving to his own audience, a certain hint about why the words of this particular play may strike one as uncharacteristically ineloquent.

The second source of confirmation for Coriolanus's connection with the figure of Christ lies, I said, in certain descriptions of his actions. I specify now only some parallels that come out of Revelation. In that book the central figure is a lamb (and there is also a dragon), and a figure who sits on a special horse and on a golden throne, whose name is known only to himself, whose "eyes were as a flame of fire," and who burns a city that is identified as a woman; it is, in particular, the city (Babylon) which in Christian tradition is identified with Rome. And I associate the opening of Coriolanus's opening diatribe against the citizens, in which he rebukes their wish for "good words" from him – glad tidings – accusing them of liking "neither peace nor war," with the message Christ dictates to the writer of Revelation: "I know thy works, that thou art neither cold nor hot; . . . Therefore, because thou art luke warm, and neither cold nor hot, it will come to pass that I shall spew thee out of my mouth" (Revelation 3:15–16). (An associated text from Plutarch would be: "So Martius, being a stowte man of nature, that never yelded in any respect, as one thincking that to overcome allwayes, and to have the upper hande in all matters, was a Token of magnanimities, and of no base and fainte corage, which spitteth out anger from the most weake and passioned parte of the harte, much like the matter of an impostume: went home." Whatever the ambiguities in these words, the general idea remains, indelibly, of Coriolanus's speech, when angry, as being the spitting forth of the matter of an abscess.[8] This play about food is about revoltedness

---

[8] I quote from North's translation of Plutarch's biography of Coriolanus, which is given in an appendix to the Arden edition of *Coriolanus* (London, 1976). The "impostume" passage occurs on p. 133.
Coriolanus's sense of disgust with the people is more explicitly conveyed by Shakespeare through the sense of their foul smell than of their foul taste. Shakespeare does use the idea of spitting twice: once, as cited, to describe Hector's forehead bleeding in battle, and the second time in Coriolanus's only scene of soliloquy, disguised before Aufidius's house: "Then know me not. / Lest that thy wives with spits and boys with stones / In puny battle slay me" – so that both times spitting is linked with battle and with food. As I have implied, I understand Coriolanus's vision of his death in Antium at the hands of wives and boys as a prophecy of the death he actually undergoes there, spitted by the swords of strange boys.

and disgust. *Coriolanus* and Revelation are about figures who are bitter, disgusted by those whom they have done good, whose lives they have sustained.)

Conviction, or lack of it, in these relations is something one has naturally to assess for oneself. Granted that they are somehow at work, they work to make comprehensible what Coriolanus's identification with the god is (they are identified as banished providers of spiritual food) and what his justification for destruction is (the people lack faith and are to suffer judgment) and why he changes his mind about the destruction. It is, I think, generally felt that his mother prevails with him by producing human, family feeling in him, in effect showing him that he is not inhuman. This again cannot be wrong, but first of all he has his access of family feeling the moment he sees the four figures approaching (a feeling that does not serve to carry the day), and second, his feeling, so conceived, does not seem to me to account for Coriolanus's words of agony to his mother as he relents and "Holds her by the hand, silent."

> O mother, mother!
> What have you done? Behold, the heavens do ope,
> The gods look down, and this unnatural scene
> They laugh at. O my mother, mother! O!
> You have won a happy victory to Rome;
> But, for your son – believe it, O, believe it! –
> Most dangerously you have with him prevailed,
> If not most mortal to him. But let it come.
> (V, iii, 182–9)

(I say these are words of agony, but so far as I recall, no critic who cites them seems to find them so. I feel here especially at a disadvantage in never having been at a performance of *Coriolanus*. But I find on reading this passage, or rather in imagining it said [sometimes as by specific actors; Olivier, of course, among them, and the young Brando], that it takes a long time to get through. Partly that has to do with the fact of the repetition of words in the passage; partly with the specific words that are repeated, "O," "mother," and "believe it." It has further to do, I feel sure, with my uncertainty about how long the silences before and within this speech are to be held – a speech that may be understood as expressing the silence with which this son holds, and then relinquishes, his mother's hand.

Suppose we try imagining that he does not relinquish her hand until just before the last sentence, "But let it come" – as if what is to come is exactly expressive of their separating, or, say, that of Rome from Rome. Then how far do we imagine that he goes through the imagining of what is to come, and how long would the imagining take, before he takes upon himself the words that invite its coming?) What it means that she may be "most mortal" to him cannot be that he may be killed – the mere fact of death is hardly what concerns this man. He must mean somehow that she has brought it about that he will have the wrong death, the wrong mortality, a fruitless death. Has she done this by showing him that he has feelings? But Christ, even by those who believe that he is the Lord, is generally held to have feelings. Coriolanus's speech expresses his agonized sense that his mother does not know who he is, together with an agonized plea for her belief. She has deprived him of heaven, of, in his fantasy, sitting beside his father, and deprived him by withholding her faith in him, for if she does not believe that he is a god then probably he is not a god, and certainly nothing like the Christian scenario can be fulfilled, in which a mother's belief is essential. If it were his father who sacrificed him for the city of man then he could be a god. But if it is his mother who sacrifices him he is not a god. The logic of his situation, as well as the psychology, is that he cannot sacrifice himself. He can provide spiritual food but he cannot make himself into food, he cannot say, for example, that his body is bread. His sacrifice will not be redemptive; hence one may say his tragedy is that he cannot achieve tragedy. He dies in a place irrelevant to his sacrifice, carved by many swords, by hands that can derive no special nourishment from him. It is too soon in the history of the Roman world for the sacrifice to which he aspires and from which he recoils.

And perhaps it is too late, as if the play is between worlds. I know I have been struck by an apparent incorporation in *Coriolanus* of elements from Euripides' *Bacchae,* without knowing how or whether a historical connection is thinkable. Particularly, it seems to me, I have been influenced in my descriptions by feeling under Coriolanus's final plea to his mother the plea of Pentheus to his mother, outside the city, to see that he is her son and not to tear him to pieces. The *Bacchae* is about admitting the new god to the city, present in one who is returning to his native city, a god who in company with Demeter's grain brings nourishment to mankind, one who demands recognition in order to vindicate at once his mother's honor and his being fathered by Zeus; the first in the city to acknowledge his divine descent are two old men. My idea is that Coriolanus incorporates both raging, implacable Dionysus and raging, inconstant Pentheus and that Volumnia partakes both of the chaste yet god-seduced Semele and of the mad and murderous Agave. Volumnia's identifying of herself with Juno (specifically, with Juno's anger) may thus suggest her sensing herself as the cause of her curse. It is not essential to my thought here that Shakespeare knew (of) Euripides' play. It is enough to consider that he knew Ovid's account of Pentheus's story and to suppose that he took the story as Euripides had, as about the kind of son (one unable to express desire) to whom the failure of his mother's recognition presents itself as a sense of being torn to pieces.

What is the good of such a tragedy of failed tragedy? Which is to ask: What is this play to us? How is it to do its work? This is the question I have been driving at and now that it is before us I can only state flatly, without much detail, my provisional conclusions on the topic.

They can by now be derived from certain considerations about Menenius's telling of the parable of the belly in the opening scene of the play. Every reader or participant has to make something of this extended, most prominently placed event. Until recent times most critics have assumed that Menenius is voicing a commonplace assumption of the times in which Shakespeare wrote and one that represents Shakespeare's view of the state – the state as a hierarchical organism, understandable on analogy with the healthy, functioning body. It is my impression that recent critics have tended not to dwell on the fable, as though the conservative way is the only way to take it and as though that vision is no longer acceptable, or presentable. But this seems to me to ignore what I take to be the three principal facts about Menenius's telling of the tale, the facts, one may say, of the drama in the telling. (1) The tale has competing interpretations. What the first citizen calls its "application" is a *question*. He and Menenius joke about whether the people or the patricians are better represented by the belly. (2) The tale is about food, about its distribution and circulation. (3) The tale is told (by a patrician) to citizens who are in the act of rising in revolt against a government they say is deliberately starving them; hence the patrician can be said to be giving them words *instead* of food. The first mystery of the play is that this seems to work, that the words stop the citizens, that they stop to listen, as though these citizens are themselves willing, under certain circumstances, to take words for food, to equate them.

Coriolanus's entrance at the end of the argument over the application of the fable confirms this equation of words and food: He has from the early lines of the play been identified as the people's chief enemy, here in particular as chief of those who withhold food; and his opening main speech to them, after expressing his disgust by them, is to affirm that he does withhold and will go on withholding "good words" from them. Accordingly every word he speaks will mean the withholding of good words. He will, as it were, have a sword in his mouth. There are other suggestions of the equation of words and food in the play (for example, the enlivening of the familiar idea that understanding is a matter of digesting) but this is enough for me, in view of my previous suggestions, to take the equation as part of the invocation of the major figure of our civilization for whom words are food. The word made flesh is to be eaten, since this is the living bread. Moreover, the parables of Jesus are characteristically about food, and are always meant as food. The words/food equation suggests that we should look again at Volumnia's intercession speeches, less for their content than for the plain fact of their drama, that they are much the longest speeches Coriolanus listens to, that they cause his mother to show him her undivided attention and him to give her his silence; he is as if filled up by her words. It pleases me further to remember that Revelation also contains a vision of words that are eaten: There is a book the writer swallows that tastes as sweet as honey in the mouth but bitter in the belly (10:10), as if beauty were the beginning of terror, as in, for example, a play of Shakespeare's.

My conclusion about the working of the play, about what kind of play it is, adds up then as follows. I take the telling of the parable of the belly as a sort of play-within-the-play, a demonstration of what Shakespeare takes his play – named for Coriolanus – to be, for *Coriolanus* too is a tale about food, with competing interpretations requiring application, told by one man to a cluster, call this an audience, causing them to halt momentarily, to turn aside from their more practical or pressing concerns in order to listen. Here is the relevance I see in the fact that the play is written in a time of corn shortages and insurrections. The fact participates not just in the imagery of the play's setting, but in the question of the authority and the virtue of portraying such a time, at such a time, for one's fellow citizens; a question of the authority and the virtue in being a writer. I see in Shakespeare's portrayal of the parable of the belly a competition (in idea, perhaps in fact) with Sir Philip Sidney's familiar citing of the tale in his *Defence of Poetry,* or a rebuke of it.[9] Sidney records Menenius's application of the tale as having "wrought such effect in the people, as I never read that only words brought forth but then, so sudden and so good an alteration; for upon reasonable conditions a perfect reconcilement ensued." But in casting his partisan, limited Menenius as the teller of the tale, and placing its telling at the opening of the play, where we have minimal information or experience for judging its events, Shakespeare puts into question both the nature of the "alteration" and the "perfection" of the reconciliation. Since these are the two chief elements of Sidney's defense of poetry, this defense is as such put into question; but hence, since Shakespeare is nevertheless giving his own version of the telling of the fable, making his own story about the circulation of food, he can be understood as presenting in this play his own defense of poetry (more particularly, of plays, which Sidney particularly attacks). It is in this light noteworthy that Sidney finds "Heroical" poetry to be most "[daunting to] all back-biters," who would "speak evil" of writing that presents "champions . . . who doth not only teach and move to a truth, but teacheth and moveth to the most high and excellent truth." But since "the image of such worthies" as presented in such works "most inflameth the mind with desire to be worthy," and since *Coriolanus* is a play that studies the evil in such an inflammation, Shakespeare's play precisely questions the ground of Sidney's claim that "the Heroical . . . is not only a kind, but the best and most accomplished kind of Poetry."

What would this play's defense of poetry be; I mean how does

---

[9]The following remarks on Sidney's tract were reintroduced, expanded from an earlier set on the subject that I had dropped from the paper, as a result of an exchange with Stephen Greenblatt during the discussion period following my presentation at Stanford.

it direct us to consider the question? Its incorporation of the parable of the belly I understand to identify us, the audience, as starvers, and to identify the words of the play as food, for our incorporation. Then we have to ask of ourselves, as we have to ask of the citizens: Why have we stopped to listen? That is, what does it mean to be a member of this audience? Do we feel that these words have the power of redemption for us?

They are part of an enactment of a play of sacrifice; as it happens, of a failed sacrifice. And a feast-sacrifice, whether in Christian, pre-Christian, Nietzschean, or Freudian terms, is a matter of the founding and the preserving of a community. A community is thus identified as those who partake of the same body, of a common victim. This strikes Coriolanus as our being caught in a circle of mutual partaking, incorporating one another. And this is symbolized, or instanced, by speaking the same language. A pervasive reason Coriolanus spits out words is exactly that they *are* words, that they exist only in a language, and that a language is metaphysically something shared, so that speaking is taking and giving in your mouth the very matter others are giving and taking in theirs.

It is maddeningly irrelevant to Coriolanus which party the belly represents. What matters to him is that, whoever rules, all are members, that all participate in the same circulation, the same system of exchange, call it Rome; that to provide civil nourishment you must allow yourself to be partaken of. This is not a play about politics, if this means about political authority or conflict, say about questions of legitimate succession or divided loyalties. It is about the formation of the political, the founding of the city, about what it is that makes a rational animal fit for conversation, for civility. This play seems to think of this creation of the political, call it the public, as the overcoming of narcissism, incestuousness, and cannibalism; as if it perceives an identity among these relations.

In constructing and contesting with a hero for whom the circulation of language is an expression of cannibalism, *Coriolanus* takes cannibalism as symbolic of the most human of activities, the most distinctive, or distinguished, of human activities. (Sidney cites the familiar conjunction: "Oratio, next to Ratio, . . . [is] the greatest gift bestowed upon mortality.") Coriolanus wishes to speak, to use words, to communicate, without exchanging words; without, let us say, reasoning (with others); to speak without conversing, without partaking in conversation. Here is the conversation for which he is unfit; call it civil speech. Hence I conceive *Coriolanus* to be incorporating Montaigne's interpretation of literal cannibalism as more civilized than our more sophisticated – above all, more pervasive – manners of psychological torture, our consuming others alive.[10] Montaigne's "On Cannibals" is more specifically pertinent to this play: its story of a cannibal prisoner of a cannibal society valorously taunting his captors by reminding them that in previous battles, when he had been victorious over them, he had captured and eaten their ancestors, so that in eating him they will be consuming their own flesh – this is virtually the mode in which Coriolanus addresses himself to the Volscians in putting himself at their mercy. And more variously pertinent: The essay interprets cannibalism as revenge; and it claims (in one of those moods of measured hilarity) that when three men from a cannibal society visited Rouen and were asked what they found most amazing about the ways of Montaigne's countrymen, one of their responses was as follows (I shall not comment on it but quote in Frame's translation):

> Second (they have a way in their language of speaking of men as halves of one another), they had noticed that there were among us men full and gorged with all sorts of good things, and that their other halves were beggars at their doors, emaciated with hunger and poverty; and they thought it strange that these needy halves could endure such an injustice, and did not take the others by the throat, or set fire to their houses.

Within the experience of such a vision of the circulation of language a question, not readily formulatable, may press for expression: To what extent can Coriolanus (and the play that creates him and contests with him) be understood as seeing his salvation in silence? The theme of silence haunts the play. For example, one of Coriolanus's perfectly cursed tasks is to ask for "voices" (votes) that he exactly wishes not to hear. Again, the words "silent" and "si-

---

[10] Finding the words/food representation so compelling, I am ignoring here the path along which the circulation of words also registers the circulation of money (as in "So shall my lungs / Coin words" [III, i, 77–8]; and in "The price is, to ask it kindly" [II, iii, 77]). The sense of consuming as expending would relate to Coriolanus's frantic efforts to deny that his actions can be recompensed ("better to starve than crave the hire" – for example, of receiving voices *in return*). Money depends upon the equating of values; Coriolanus, on their lack of equation, on measurelessness, pricelessness.

lence" are beautifully and mysteriously associated, once each, with the women in his life: with his wife ("My gracious silence, hail!"); and with his mother ("He holds her by the hand, silent"). Toward both, the word of silence is the expression of intimacy and identification; but in his wife's case it means acknowledgment, freedom from words, but in a life beyond the social, while in his mother's case it means avoidance, denial, death, that there is no life beyond the social. The ambiguities here are drilled through the action of the play by the repeated calls "Peace, peace" – hysterical, ineffective shouts of this particular word for silence. The play literalizes this conventional call for silence by implying that speech is war, as if this is the reason that both words and war can serve as food. But the man for war cannot find peace in peace – not merely because he, personally, cannot keep a civil tongue in his head, but because a tongue is inherently uncivil (if not, one hopes, inveterately so). Silence is not the absence of language; there is no such absence for human beings; in this respect, there is no world elsewhere.

Coriolanus cannot imagine, or cannot accept, that there is a way to partake of one another, incorporate one another, that is necessary to the formation rather than to the extinction of a community. (As he cannot imagine being fed without being deserving. This is his precise reversal of Christ's vision, that we cannot in ourselves deserve sustenance, and that it is for that reason, and in that spirit, that we have to ask for it. Thus is misanthropy, like philanthropy, a certain parody of Christianity.) The play *Coriolanus* asks us to try to imagine it, imagine a beneficial, mutual consumption, arguing in effect that this is what the formation of an audience is. (As if *vorare* were next to *orare*).

It seems to me that what I have been saying demonstrates, no doubt somewhat comically, the hypothesis of the origin of tragedy in religious ritual – somewhat comically, because I must seem rather to have deflated the problem, implying that whether the hypothesis is true depends on what is meant by "tragedy," what by "origin," and which ritual is in mind.[11] I have, in effect, argued that if you

[11]In the discussion period at Stanford, Paul Alpers noted that I seemed to find something like a comic perspective of the play to be more extensive than just here where I am making it explicit, and he asked how far I wished to go in seeking this perspective. I find this a true response to my reading, but it goes beyond anything I can explore now. I mentioned then what I take to be a starting point to such an exploration, Coriolanus's sense that as he and his mother stand silent together "The Gods look down, and this unnatural scene / They laugh at." Does he feel the gods

accept the words as food, and you accept the central figure as invoking the central figure of the Eucharist, then you may accept a formulation to the effect (not that the play is the ritual of the Eucharist, but to the effect) that the play celebrates, or aspires to, the same fact as the ritual does, say the condition of community. Eucharist means gratitude, precisely what Coriolanus feels the people withhold from him. This is another way to see why I am not satisfied to say that Coriolanus is enraged first of all by the people's cowardice. Perhaps one may say that to Coriolanus their cowardice means ingratitude. As for the idea of origin, we need only appeal to Descartes's idea that the origin of a thing is the same thing that preserves it. What preserves a tragedy, what creates the effect of a certain kind of drama, is the appropriation by an audience of this effect, our mutual incorporation of its words. When the sharing of a sacrifice is held on religious ground, the ritual itself assures its effectiveness. When it is shifted to aesthetic ground, in a theater, there is no such preexisting assurance; the work of art has to handle everything itself. You might think of this as the rebirth of religion from the spirit of tragedy. A performance is nothing without our participation in an audience; and this participation is up to each of us.

   To enforce the necessity of this decision to participate (a decision which of course has its analogue for the individual reader with the script in his or her hands) is the way I understand the starkness of the words of this play, their relative ineloquence, their lack of apparent resonance. The play presents us with our need for one another's words by presenting withholding words, words that do not meet us halfway. It presents us with a famine of words. This way of seeing it takes it to fulfill a prophecy from the Book of Amos (8:12): "Behold, the days come, saith the Lord God, that I will send a famine in the land, not a famine of bread, nor a thirst for water; but of hearing the words of the Lord."

---

laugh because mother and son are too close or too distant with one another? At least the scene is unnatural because it is social, and because the social is the scene of mazes of meaning as dense as poetry, in which its poor, prosaic, half-human creatures are isolated. The comedic perspective I seek presents itself to me as a totalization, or a kind of transcendentalizing, of dramatic irony – where the omen or allusion is not of some specific, future event, but of the totality of the present, of events as they are, without our being able to specify in advance what individuates or what relates these events.

The Political and Psychological

POSTSCRIPT

It may be felt, it should be felt, that my account of Coriolanus's disgust by language has studiously had to avoid a more obvious, or equally obvious, if less explicit understanding than I have given of it. I said that he has a horror of putting in his mouth what (as in his fantasy) comes out of the mouths of others, and I gave that as a reason it is irrelevant to Coriolanus whether the parable of the belly is interpreted with the patricians or with the plebeians as the belly, or as the tongue, or as any other part. What alarms him is simply being part, one member among others of the same organism. But there is a different way of characterizing his reason for alarm, a different manner of taking the parable from the beginning.

This way is one that rather literalizes the parable, one that takes its joking not to turn merely, or primarily, on an ambiguity over whom the belly represents, over who does the providing to whom, but on an ambiguity over what the product is that the belly provides, over what there is to be provided, on this organic view of the state. This further ambiguity concerns what we might think of as the direction in which the giving or returning done by the belly is imagined to happen. Are the belly's process and product directed back toward the body of which it is part, or out toward the earth which it shares, and of which it partakes? In the latter case disgust is a function of imagining that in incorporating one another we are asked to incorporate one another's leavings, the results or wastes of what has already been incorporated.

On this reading two features of the parable of the belly find a better home than I was able formerly, concentrating on words as food, to provide for them: the First Citizen's image or fantasy of the belly as "the sink o' th' body" (I, i, 123), its sewer; and Menenius's offering as the belly's taunting reply to the accusation against it of the rebel parts of the body, what he calls "a kind of smile, / Which ne'er came from the lungs, but even thus –" (I, i, 108–10). I do not insist that you must conceive Menenius here to figure the answering smile as a noise, say a kind of laugh, or a cheer; but only that *if* you find yourself figuring it so, you must be unsure whether the noise comes from above or from below.

The outward direction of circulation is as familiar in this period of Shakespeare as the inward. From *Antony and Cleopatra:* The man at the beginning is saying, "Kingdoms are clay; our dungy earth

169

alike / Feeds beast as man; the nobleness of life / Is to do thus . . .";
and the woman at the ending, "And it is great / To do that thing
that ends all other deeds, . . . / Which sleeps, and never palates
more the dung, / The beggar's nurse and Caesar's." These imag-
inings of the earth as feeding its inhabitants, in reciprocation with
the imagining of its being nourished by the leavings and remains
of those it feeds, for example, by us humans, are in each case here
expressions of a mind in exaltation, hence somewhat reductive of
its environment; minds in a mood that seeks transcendence of the
common lot of humanity. But this means that neither Cleopatra
nor Antony is seeking to deny – the thing it is Coriolanus's mission
to deny – that this circulation *is* common, is even *what* is common,
along the scale of living kinds and the degrees of human ranks. I
suppose that these late Roman plays exist on this axis in what Norman Rabkin has called a relation of complementarity. It accordingly
suggests itself that the two directions of the circulation of nourishment are kept, in healthier imaginations, in healthier appetites, from
crossing; that the imagination of what the mouth receives as food
is normally mediated by passing it through nature, so to purify the
contribution made to the process by other, let us say, human beings.

In suggesting that in Coriolanus the imagination has collapsed
upon itself, that his fantasy is that he is asked to feed directly on
the leavings of others, I am not retracting, but further glossing, his
sense of disgust at the words that exit from their mouths, glossing
what it is he thinks words are, and what food is, or you may say,
the chain of food. Keeping one's critical balance in this matter, not
allowing one's imagination to collapse upon itself, could hardly be
trickier. The very suggestion of the element this postscript invokes
is apt to stifle what the body of my essay takes – correctly, I persist
in thinking – as fundamental in the play, namely the circulation
from mouth to mouth of language. The trick is to let this fact be
challenged, and not overthrown, by the suggestion that language
is at the same time something retained, which perhaps means
hoarded, for expulsion, or banishment, a way of conceiving of
writing, physically altering the world.

The suggestion makes its way, in the part of the world I know,
mostly in slang, or jokes, as when E. E. Cummings has his erring
Olaf say, "There is some s. I will not eat," and in expressions rejecting the words of others by asking what they are trying to hand
you, or by naming the product as the droppings of horses or bulls.

The Political and Psychological

And the idea presents a link with the ideas associating the circulation of food with that of the circulation of words and with that of money (cited in note 10). Here the connection is primarily through the sense of "superfluity," as for example when the First Citizen says, "What authority surfeits on would relieve us. If they would yield us but the superfluity while it were wholesome, we might guess they relieved us humanely; but they think we are too dear; . . . our sufferance is a gain to them" (I, i, 15–22). And the connection of words through grain to money is enforced in the same citizen's longest speech after Menenius enters: "They ne'er cared for us yet. Suffer us to famish, and their storehouses crammed with grain; make edicts for usury, to support usurers." (I, i, 80–3). To my ear, Shakespeare's lines here cite usury not simply as a second historically accurate cause for a second (earlier) revolt, but put as it were the two revolts in apposition, so that usury and hoarding are metaphors for one another. Without insisting on this, I wish to invoke here Marc Shell's rehabilitation of the concept of "verbal usury" for his extraordinary essay on *The Merchant of Venice,* a concept he characterizes as referring "to the generation of an illegal – the church fathers say unnatural – supplement to verbal meaning by use of such methods as punning and flattering."[12] It is as if Coriolanus

[12] "The Wether and the Ewe," in Shell's *Money, Language, and Thought* (Berkeley and Los Angeles, 1982), p. 49. I knew that my debt to Marc Shell went beyond the writing of his I can cite, since, among other matters, he attended the seminar in which I first broached my sense of *Coriolanus* and it was often his questions that kept me moving. But not until after completing not only the body of this essay but also this postscript have I returned to complete my reading of the essays in his *Money, Language, and Thought,* and there I find that I have incurred, or would like at once to incur, a new debt. The second essay of the book, "The Blank Check: Accounting for the Grail," which for some reason Shell did not press upon me on hearing my *Coriolanus* material, suggests to my mind that the story I have told, including its extension into this postscript, has to be extended further to incorporate the scene and action of Shakespeare's *Coriolanus* into a telling of (hence, as suggested by my account, a competition with) the dearth and plenitude as recounted in the legends of the Holy Grail. I assemble a packet of quotations from Shell's essay to indicate my sense of the issue:

> The infinitely large gift and the free gift (one given gratis, without intending to obligate the recipient to reciprocate and without making him feel obligated to do so) may well be impossible in everyday exchange. . . . The hypothesis of the infinitely large gift, for example, appears as the cornucopia, and the hypothesis of the free gift, as Pauline grace. . . . [T]owards the end of the medieval era . . . the first widespread vernacular literature told of a cornucopian grail, an extraordinary gift both infinitely large and free, which was said to be able to lift men out of the ordinary world of exchange into a world in

finds the barest use of words usurious, while the citizens accuse him of a kind of verbal miserliness, depriving them of all credit. The feeling in the citizens' speeches is not alone of their physical pain in suffering want, but of the insufferable *meaning* of this pain, that it is inflicted, that it communicates the contempt in which the patricians hold them. (In saying that grain forms a link between words and money, I take for granted the connection, on either Marxian or Freudian grounds, of money with excrement. The folk character of the connection, hence preparation for its convincingness to me, is present in a joke circulated my way by my father, who once remarked that they must be teaching me chemistry in college because I had learned so well to take money and make dreck out of it.)

In responding to Paul Alpers's query concerning a sense of the comic underlying my entire reading of *Coriolanus* (reported in note 11), I should have pointed to the belly's smile as well as to the gods'

which freedom and totality were possible. . . . The grail legends depict a wasteland to which the limitless production of material and spiritual goods stands as a defining and conceptually unique limit. (pp. 24–5)

Chrétien is a poet-sower who must consider the relationship of the fertility of his seed both to the relative spiritual sterility of his audience and to the material sterility of the wasteland of which he would tell them. Spiritual fertility varies from person to person, so that Chrétien must speak on several levels at the same time. . . . All the grail tales claim the status of riddle. (p. 25)

Like the apostle's inkhorn (*cornu*) . . . the word *graal* operates in the grail tales as a "cornucopia of words," just as the grail itself operates as a plentiful cornucopia of nourishing food. (pp. 26–7)

At the beginning of Chrétien's *Account,* for example, the hero Perceval is presented as a typical hungry adolescent who seeks food from his mother, expects food at the tent he mistakenly believes to be a chapel, demands food from the God he believes to live in the tent-chapel, and finally receives earthly food. Only divine nourishment, however, can satisfy the desire of this questing man. Perceval learns about the kind of food God provides when a hermit tells him on Good Friday that the food he failed to ask about at the grail castle was "real." (p. 27)

The kind of men who do not have good food to go into their mouths do not have good words to come out of their mouths. (p. 29)

The free sacrifice of a woman helps to resolder the broken sword of the realm. . . . [T]here is in many stories this identity of sword and person. (p. 33, and note) laughter. Then what is the joke? Who could laugh at it? Freud has some helpful words:

> There are yet other means of making things comic which deserve special consideration and also indicate in part fresh sources of comic pleasure. . . . Caricature, parody and travesty (as well as their practical counterpart, unmasking) are directed against people and objects which lay claim to authority and respect, which are in some sense *"sublime."* They are procedures for *Herabsetzung* [degradation] as the apt German expression has it. . . . When . . . the procedures . . . for the degradation of the sublime allow me to have an idea of it as though it were something commonplace, in whose presence I need not pull myself together but may, to use the military formula, "stand easy," I am being spared the increased expenditure of the solemn restraint . . . the difference in expenditure . . . can be discharged by laughter.
>
> Under the heading of "unmasking" we may also include . . . the method of degrading the dignity of individuals by directing attention to the frailties which they share with all humanity, but in particular the dependence of their mental functions on bodily needs. The unmasking is equivalent here to an admonition; such and such a person, who is admired as a demigod, is after all only human like you and me.[13]

But the comic pleasure in discovering Coriolanus's vulnerabilities, to us who are neither gods nor just bellies, does not get much beyond the cold comfort of an ironic awareness of the viciousness of his virtue, the uselessness in his usefulness. I think back to my suggestion that the formation of a society depends on there being, on our achieving, a partaking of one another that is beneficial, creative, not annihilating, as if our mutual cannibalism is a parody of what we might be, that we are standing jokes on ourselves, wishing to transcend what would no longer deserve to be transcended if we could mutually give up the wish (as if needing one another's hands meant that human beings are fated to accept what they have so far

[13]*Jokes and Their Relation to the Unconscious*, trans. J. Strachey (New York, 1960), pp. 200–1, 202.

learned to hand one another). Instead we feel deprived, hence vengeful, feel fated as things stand not to get as good as we give. (The comic necessity in these feelings, or tragic contingency, will want pursuing into the bearing of the parable of the belly on the full appeal of the idea of the body politic, as though the belly is smiling at all theorizing that leaves the state, or, say, sovereignty, organic. And does political thinking know itself to be free of this appeal, of, let us say, the idea of the citizen's two bodies, or it may be more; or is it better to think of each of us as of two or more minds?)

In broaching the subject of this postscript, I said that the anality in the play is less explicit than the orality I had confined myself to in the, as it were, body of my essay, implying that its being mostly implicit in the words of the play is hardly a sufficient reason for leaving it inexplicit in a stretch of criticism. But one may well, as Kenneth Burke has, take the issue to be given full explicitness in the play's, and its hero's, name. In the section headed "Comments" that follows, or concludes, Burke's masterful essay "*Coriolanus* and the Delights of Faction," he remarks:

> Though the names are taken over literally from Plutarch, it is remarkable how tonally suggestive some of them are, from the standpoint of their roles in this English play. . . . And in the light of Freudian theories concerning the fecal nature of invective, the last two syllables of the hero's name are so "right," people now often seek to dodge the issue by altering the traditional pronunciation (making the *a* broad instead of long).[14]

But how are we to specify what is "right" about the name? Granted the intentionality of Shakespeare's play's attention to the name, he may in it be seeking a heavenly horselaugh at language's vengeance in distributing one and the same sound equally to a suffix that encodes a name's military honor and to the name of the shape of a sphincter; as if noting a kind of poetic justice. (Another point of justice is perhaps noted in Burke's suggesting "excess" as well as "pride" as a translation of *hubris*.)

Burke is immensely tactful in mentioning the subject, in his essay

---

[14]In *Language as Symbolic Action* (Berkeley and Los Angeles, 1966), p. 96.

here and elsewhere, and while on the occasions of delivering versions of my essays as talks I would allude to the fecal issue as something to be considered, I did not see how to consider it well in unprotected prose. Whatever I wrote down seemed to me either too explicit or too implicit, brazen or hidden. I could understand part of my difficulty to be quite inescapable; one cannot readily rise above the level of one's civilization's sense of humor. As in other matters I take *Walden* as a touchstone for this issue. Thoreau's recurrent allusions in that book to eating and elimination are expressions of his bursting admiration for the capacity of (especially Indian) scriptures to name the organs and functions of the body as plain facts of cosmic rhythms; as facts; without invoking or evading attitudes toward them, as if to suppose them so much as good or bad were presumptuous. It is a capacity to name them, and to make recommendations with respect to them with, let me say, detachment; to name philosophically. Thoreau did not think us Westerners capable of this, as a culture, yet. You might think of philosophical naming as something the serious writing of a culture holds out to it.

It was in coming to see more unprotectedly that Shakespeare's *Coriolanus* is itself exactly in struggle with this question of explicitness and naming, or that it is internal to the way I have proposed taking the play, as a study of the shunning of voices, hence the craving of them, that I was shamed into making my embarrassment (of style, say) more explicit in this note. The implication is that to avoid risking one's critical balance in traversing this play is to avoid a measure of participation in the play's assessments of the balance civilization exacts. Call it the exaction of civility. To what extent can the powers of a city reciprocate in civility and remain powers? To what extent can they withhold reciprocation without naming a state of war, directed inward or outward?

I hope I have sufficiently indicated here why a study of voices goes into a study of the formation of human society, of the recognition of others as, so to speak, *my* others. The idea of a social contract as expressing one's consent to be governed, to be civil, is a demand, as I have had reason to insist, for explicitness, however hard it may be to establish what must constitute an original explicitness. (I have in mind *The Claim of Reason*, pp. 22–8.) For think of it this way. The consent to be governed must express the desire to be governed, governed by consent, hence to participate in the city. To express desire inexplicitly is an act of seduction, hence one that exists only in a medium of prohibition and conspiracy. It may be that human sexual life will continue to require this medium and its struggles for the foreseeable future, say for as long as our politics does not create a more perfect public medium, unfailingly intelligible, reciprocal, and nourishing. Without this, we shall continue to interpret privacy as inexplicitness, and on this ground the private will continue to look like the natural enemy of the political, as in opposite ways it is shown to be, to our distress, in *Antony and Cleopatra* and in *Coriolanus*. Who cares whether the unjust can be happy when we still do not know whether the demand for happiness is survivable?

And the idea of the recognition of others as mine, implying the acknowledgment of human beings as human, things that think, is a matter of putting body and soul together, of connecting perception and imagination I have sometimes said, whatever these are. Philosophers have made problems, as well they might, about what it is to know that others have minds. I am in effect taking *Coriolanus* to raise the question, as well we might, what it is to know that others, that we, have bodies. According to the line of thought in this postscript it is to know that, and perhaps know why, the body has (along with the senses) two openings, or two sites for openings, ones that are connected, made for each other, a top and a bottom, or a front and a back, outsides and insides. But what is the expression of this knowledge, what acknowledges it; I mean, what is the expression of a knowledge of its commonness, for example as between us? Harping on the idea (perhaps as Swift did) seems to miss its commonness, or ordinariness. But how do you know that remaining silent about it isn't denying it? And does Descartes's metaphysical insistence that we are essentially minds deny the universal accident that we are (connected to) bodies? And does Nietzsche's metaphysical insistence that we are bodies deny the grandeur of the mind?

If we say that noting the connection of the body with itself wants tact, we may say that Coriolanus traces the costs of the absence of this tact of civility. While his case is more extreme than ours, our satisfaction in ridding ourselves of him attests to our representation by him, that we make him our agent. Our differences from his case are that we demand less of our honor than he of his and that social divisions among us are less, differences that at best speak of our fortune, or belatedness, not of our credit. So I gather that no one is in a position to say what the right expression is of our knowledge that we are strung out on both sides of a belly, that we are human, that the human is relative to the worm, the rat, the horse. Then the issue is whether we have to know this before we can know the partaking that makes a city good, or whether the city, in its poverty of goodness, can provide itself with individuals, or clusters, who know such a thing, and whether it can then stop and take in what they have to say, whether it can tolerate the voice of its own language.

5

Hamlet's Burden of Proof

IN SPEAKING of a "burden of proof" in *Hamlet* I refer of course to Hamlet's declared purpose in simultaneously testing the Ghost's honesty and Claudius's conscience by means of the play-within-the-play, which stages the story of murder by poisoning. At the same time I allude to the problem of skepticism that has prompted me in each of my amateur forays into Shakespeare, finding, so far, in the cases of Lear, and of Othello, and of Coriolanus, and of Leontes, that tragedy is the result, and the study, of a burden of knowledge, of an attempt to deny the all but undeniable (it may begin, or seem to, as a simple wish to test it) – that a loving daughter loves you, that your imagination has elicited the desire of a beautiful young woman, that however exceptional you may be you are a member of human society, that your children are yours. Lives are founded on such truths, yet something about their acknowledgment – a different thematic something in each case – can seem more horrible to these lives than the denial and disappearance of the world. In turning to the surprising place of skepticism in Hamlet's burden, it is important to me to repeat: the burden of my story in spinning the interplay of philosophy with literature is not that of applying philosophy to literature, where so-called literary works would become kinds of illustrations of matters already independently known. It would better express my refrain to say that I take the works I am drawn to read out in public (beginning with those I have listed of Shakespeare) as studies of matters your philosophy has (has unassessably, left to itself) intellectualized as skepticism, whether in Descartes's or Hume's or Kant's pictures of that inescapably, essentially, human possibility.

In reporting my work in progress toward *Hamlet*, epitomized by the way I am thinking about the crux of the play-within-the-play,

I report first a departure for me in the fact that I use a pair of technical concepts from Freud's writing, that of the "primal scene" and of "primal fantasies." Whenever in the past I have invoked Freud's name it has been simply as the dominant psychologist of the century, the one sweeping our horizons in that line, who claimed that he had been preceded and guided in his insights into the mind's working by the major poets of our culture; and I have sought a mode of thinking and writing that would find, as it were, the membrane between that past of literature and that present of science. I privately called this exchange philosophy. Why this now seems to me not quite enough to invoke in my relation to Freud I shall not speculate about here. Nor about why it is with respect to thoughts about *Hamlet* that this step has seemed to me necessary. Doubtless it has to do with Freud's first speculation about *Hamlet* occurring as a footnote to his analysis of Sophocles' *Oedipus Rex* in *The Interpretation of Dreams;* but also because I take it as some kind of criterion for an understanding of *Hamlet* that one understand the special fascination this play famously exerts upon us.

Freud's most prominent example of a primal scene occurs in the case popularly called after the dream whose deciphering led to the construction of its primal scene – the case of the Wolf Man. The full case, under the title "From the History of an Infantile Neurosis," was first published in 1918. The year before, on the opposite side of the war, in England, W. W. Greg, one of the founders of modern textual scholarship, published what the latest editor of *Hamlet* that I have read, Harold Jenkins in his 1982 Arden edition, calls, with severe impatience, "a notorious article," entitled "Hamlet's Hallucination," in which Greg writes: ". . . the only hypothesis consistent with the King's behavior is that in the dumb-show he actually fails to recognize the representation of his own crime. . . . There is but one rational conclusion: *Claudius did not murder his brother by pouring poison into his ear.* This inference appears to be as certain as anything in criticism can be." I hope Greg is wrong in staking this as a best case for critical certainty, but it does strike me that no one, to my knowledge, has satisfactorily answered Greg's claim.

There seem to be, as Jenkins notes, putting aside the currently disfavored hypothesis of textual anomaly that deletes the dumb-show, only two possibilities besides Greg's: (1) The king did not see the dumb-show. To prove this, and hence to escape Greg's conclusion, precipitated, according to Dover Wilson's account, the years of work that went into his *What Happens in "Hamlet,"* or (2) the king saw and has his conscience caught but was able to suppress the external manifestation of this capture until the repetition of the scene of poisoning accompanied by words. This is the so-called "second tooth theory," the name adopted for such a theory by Greg himself in dismissing it. These claims seem to me essentially weaker than Greg's. All they prove is that this repetitive dumb-show is stageable, performable, while maintaining the assumption that the Ghost is honest. But the very fact that the claims compete with one another, that they are equally acceptable routes to the same consistency, seems to me to emphasize the arbitrariness of each of them. And how could they not be arbitrary, given what they are designed to accomplish – the negative task of excusing, or explaining away, one of the most extraordinary theatrical strokes in our drama, the repetitive dumb-show in *Hamlet*. (I assume the discussion of theater proposed by the stroke is of the relation or argument in theater between the eye and the ear, between representation by action and by words, showing and saying.) And surely the reason for embarrassment over the dumb-show is the one Greg keeps his finger on, that without some such explanation the Ghost's veracity is impugned. But why, at all costs, is that veracity to be preserved? (I emphasize that in questioning the Ghost neither Greg nor I deny that Claudius murdered his brother Hamlet, as he confesses in the Prayer Scene; the question is over the manner of the murder. It is this distinction that sets my argument going.)[1]

I say that the Ghost's veracity wants preserving "at all costs" because the most obvious *positive* explanation for the occurrence of Shakespeare's repetitive dumb-show (that is, one that engages it as an argument about theater) is exactly that it emphasizes the *question* of the Ghost's veracity. Must the Ghost's word be preserved because of some dramatic convention concerning ghosts, or because of some theories contemporary with the play concerning the walking of ghosts – conventions or theories that Shakespeare is presumably incapable of challenging? You might as well say that in writing the revenge play to end revenge plays, Shakespeare had nothing new of interest to offer concerning the idea of revenge. Jenkins concludes

---

[1] This is one of several points at which, with thanks, I modify my manuscript in response to suggestions of Professor Ruth Nevo, made after my presenting of this material at Hebrew University in Jerusalem in March of 1986.

that "the fundamental objection to Greg's case is its pointlessness. With the Ghost's main charge confirmed by the King's solemn confession that he 'did the murder' (III, iii, 54), the precise method of his doing it, for all its picturesque horror, does not affect the essential plot of fratricide and vengeance." But is the author of *Hamlet* really so casual about how death comes, in a play in which no fewer than seven modes of death are meticulously distinguished? Or is the author of *Othello*, or *King Lear*, or *Coriolanus*, or *Antony and Cleopatra*, in which the modes of death may be said to absorb the plots?

It is true that Greg's account lacks sufficient means to convince, that even so highly intelligent and well-reasoned a piece of writing must command a greater scope of speculation if its outrageous conclusion is generally to be accepted. Its scope is constricted in a number of ways: (1) It links the question of the Ghost's veracity to the issue of the Ghost's general mode of existence (as real or imaginary) more tightly than the matter of the dumb-show requires; (2) this helps Greg neglect to ask why, if the dumb-show is Hamlet's invention, he had first to invent the ghost of his father to tell it to him; (3) while Greg explains the remarkable match of the Ghost's story with *The Murder of Gonzago* (saying that the latter suggested the former rather than the other way around) he does not wonder why it is that play, and that mode of poisoning, that should be what Hamlet's mind was after; (4) he does not suggest what difference his revision of the orthodox view of the Ghost's veracity and Hamlet's mentality might make to our sense of the play's subject.

The intuition I wish to follow out further here is one that occurred to Greg in passing. Turning to examine the play-within-the-play Greg notes: "It is such a play as Hamlet might have dreamed." But since Greg has formulated his discovery by saying, "The Ghost's story was not a revelation, but a mere figment of Hamlet's brain," and since his sense of the scene of the show, and of the relation among the characters, is that it is solely Hamlet's behavior during the play that alarms the king, he reduces the point of the dream/play simply to its providing an occasion for that behavior, as if its content is not a critic's (or Hamlet's) business. Here is my clue for Freud's case of the Wolf Man, for such figments of the brain are the exact business of the student of such cases.

In proposing that we look at the dumb-show as Hamlet's invention, let me say his fantasy, and in particular a fantasy that deciphers into the memory of a primal scene, a scene of parental intercourse, I realize that to some it will seem – it ought at first to seem – that I am attempting to preserve the mystery of the dumbshow by a hypothesis no less mysterious than the Ghost itself. But a hypothesis, if it is good, has a way of telling one how to recount matters in a way that provides evidence on its behalf. All I can do here is mostly to list what I take certain lines of evidence for it to be.

That the show is first of all of something indecent, and is meant to bear interpretation, is sufficiently marked in Hamlet's spirits throughout the scene, their being what Ophelia calls "keen," as in his lines to her after the dumb-show, "Be not you ashamed to show, he'll not shame to tell you what it means" (III, ii, 140–1), and his lines to her after the dialogue of the Player King and Queen, "I could interpret between you and your love if I could see the puppets dallying" (III, ii, 240–1). He is aroused, in more than one way. And we already know that the urgency for Hamlet in proving the Ghost's veracity is not alone to convince himself (at least) of Claudius's guilt but to avoid the only other conclusion – that his "imaginations are as foul / as Vulcan's smithy" (III, ii, 83–4). It seems to me that our eagerness to believe the Ghost is fortified by a similar concern over the potentially foul condition of our own imaginations. Moreover, since Hamlet tortures and guides himself to put the Ghost's veracity to the proof, any unwillingness on this matter on our part suggests a claim to superiority over Hamlet's intellect that strains belief, I should say that I simply assume that by his "imaginations" Hamlet is referring not alone to Claudius as a murderer but to the vivid pictures he paints of Claudius as his mother's lover.

That we feel the show and the ensuing play as presented to be of Hamlet's composition has been attested by certain readers on recognizing that there is no good way to place – or, say, to limit – the "dozen or sixteen lines" (II, ii, 535) that he asks to set down and insert in the play. For my hypothesis, beyond this feeling, that Hamlet has written his dream, or let me say, written the memory of a fantasy, I go for evidence to the moment in which we actually see Hamlet produce one of the five pieces of writing the play credits him with – in the scene in which, as the Ghost departs on the injunction "Remember me," Hamlet swears to obey the injunction by entirely replacing the table of his memory with new writing, and does write on his tables. A disciple of Jacques Lacan's, Daniel Sibony, in an article entitled "*Hamlet:* A Writing-Effect" (a useful work, if to Anglo-American academic taste rather heavy with violence and dirty talk – though surely no dirtier or more violent in range than the play *Hamlet*), speculates about the exceptional emphasis on writing in the play but misses what is to my mind the significance of this moment of writing that we are shown, namely that it is incredible as an act of obedience to the Ghost's injunction to remember him. Indeed Hamlet's "tables" speech seems to go out of its way to show that the line (Hamlet calls it his "word") containing the words "remember me" is *not* what he sets down in his tables. Greg admirably says of the "tables" speech, responding to Bradley: "It is not so much a sane fear that madness may drive the matter from his mind, as itself a trait of madness." But what is the method of this madness? I imagine that this enacted absence of obedience means, among other things, and unless we take it that Hamlet is false in swearing to remember the Ghost his father by writing, that the obedience is deferred, and takes place as the dumb-show and ensuing play-within-the-play. (No doubt this reads the gesture of the "tables" speech as itself a fantasy, a stirring of the impulse to write – a fatal matter in Hamlet's hands – with no command yet of the words in store.)

For the Wolf Man's decisive dream to yield a remembered scene of parental intercourse Freud found that its account and associations invited two reversals, from something passive to something active, and from one thing into its opposite. Both of these modes would be implied for Hamlet's dumb-show if we were invited to make one change of character in the scene, or, say, one change of gender, replacing the figure of Claudius with the figure of Gertrude (the reversal of a thing into its opposite). And I imagine that we are, twice, invited to think just this substitution, immediately when the dialogue of the play-within-the-play astoundingly interprets the gestures of the dumb-show as a representation of the king's feeling of approaching death and the queen's killing him (by marrying again). (The later Poisoner would accordingly do his work after the fact, even, conceivably, in a dream, as a denial of the fact.) A second invitation, this time comic, for the substitution of Gertrude for Claudius is tendered when Hamlet, departing for England, says to the feverish Claudius, "Farewell, dear mother" (IV, iv, 52), an identification literal-minded Claudius disputes, with the maddeningly further ambiguous identification, "Thy loving father, Hamlet." Claiming the status of fantasy, hence cipher, for the idea of Gertrude as killer, I do not have to turn aside, as Jenkins, among other critics, is moved to do, the literal possibility that Gertrude is, or that Hamlet thinks she is, the murderer, or an accomplice in the literal murder, of Hamlet's father. What I claim is rather that Hamlet feels her power as annihilating of his own. (Here I should like to record the help of exchanges with Janet Adelman and with Marc Shell on the subject of *Hamlet,* emphasizing most particularly our shared sense that Gertrude's power over the events in Denmark has not been fully measured. Each of us felt that the play-within-the-play was to catch her conscience as well as her new husband's. My expression of this feeling was to say, in the somewhat unbalanced frame of mind that an absorption in Shakespeare's words can sometimes bring on, that in speaking of catching the king's conscience Hamlet was thinking of her, hence that he fantasizes her as the king of that world, the object in view of whose favor of power people kill and return from the grave and drive others mad.) Moreover, my claim is that Hamlet divines that his father experienced Gertrude's annihilating power before him. This is what it means to me that Hamlet's fantasy of the poisoning is not exactly original with him – or, put otherwise, that if it is a fantasy it contains the scene of its own dictation. One's belief in Gertrude's power is surely not lessened if in constructing the primal scene from the fantasy/dumb-show one finds a man collapsing not upon her pouring something into him but upon her having something poured into her (the reversal of passive into active).

One willing to entertain such thoughts will perhaps be willing to consider that when Hamlet claims "to have that within that passes show," his claim is amplified by his capacity to envisage and interpret – to pass through and beyond – the playing of the dumb-show. This means being willing to consider that when Hamlet says, "I know not 'seems'," and describes actions that "indeed seem, / For they are actions that a man might play" (I, ii, 83–4), he is saying more than that he is unreadable to others (and perhaps to himself). That would be saying not very much more than Polonius and Claudius know about human nature, with their knowingness about human indirection. Whereas I understand Hamlet's "knowing not 'seems' " as expressing the presence to him of a world altogether different from theirs. I take it as a preliminary description of his general mode of perception – call it mourning, call it the power, or the fate, to perceive objectively, truly. Here I am assuming the importance of the fact that the beginning business of the play's action is that of mourning, or the refusal and the incapacity to mourn. (And perhaps its ending business is then the learning of mourning. But who is left to use the learning? Who, I mean, besides us?) And I am putting this idea together with Freud's finding, affirmed in Melanie Klein's thought, that the work of mourning is the severing of investment, the detaching of one's interests, strand by strand, memory by memory, from their binding with an object that has passed, burying the dead. But the condition of this work is that you *want* to live. Hamlet is making claim to, or laying hold of, a power of perception that curses him, as Cassandra's cursed her, one that makes him unable to stop at seems, a fate to know nothing but what people are, nothing but the truth of them. His later staring at the skull would accordingly be the occasion not, as traditionally imagined, of some special moral moment of remembering and meditation, but an emblem of the everyday, skeletal manner in which human beings present themselves to him. I think of this in connection with Nietzsche's statement in his autobiography (I mean *Ecce Homo*) that one trait of his nature that causes difficulty in his contacts with others is the uncanny sensitivity of his instinct for cleanliness, or, say, truthfulness, so that the innermost parts, the entrails (we might perhaps say drives) of every soul are *smelled* by him.

How may we understand the dumb-show, so construed, to work at the heart of *Hamlet?* How does it figure the body of the play? Of course I am using it, in such a question, as an image of what Shakespeare thinks a play is; that is, to interrogate *Hamlet* for its testimony as to the work of theater. Here I recommend attention to an exceptionally useful study of Freud's ideas of fantasy by J. Laplanche and J. B. Pontalis in an article entitled "Fantasy and the Origins of Sexuality"[2] in which they specify three primary fantasies, all relating "to problems of origin which present themselves to all human beings." They say: "Like myths, they [these primary fantasies] claim to provide a representation of, and a solution to, the

---

[2]*International Journal of Psychoanalysis,* 1968 (originally published as "Fantasme originaire, fantasmes des origines, origine du fantasme," *Les Temps Modernes,* April 1964, pp. 1833–68).

major enigmas which confront the child. Whatever appears to the subject as something needing an explanation or theory, is dramatized as a moment of emergence, the beginning of a history." Laplanche and Pontalis specify the three primary fantasies as of "the origin of the individual, of the upsurge of sexuality, and of the differences between the sexes," in sum, "of the origin of the subject himself." The primal scene specifically concerns the first of these fantasies, namely the origin of the individual (of the subject as individual). Freud emphasizes in his study of the Wolf Man that the meaning of the primal scene cannot be given at the time of its own empirical origin, that is, at the time the child witnesses it (if there was such a time), but that its meaning is deferred, read back *(nachträglich)*. Now I propose, prompted by Hamlet, to take the fantasy of this origin to be represented by the question: Why of all the ones I might have been am I just this one and no other, given this world and no other, possessed of exactly this mother and this father?

On this deciphering of the dumb-show as primal scene – enciphering young Hamlet's delayed sense of Gertrude's power to annihilate all Hamlets – I see Hamlet's question whether to be or not, as asking first of all not why he stays alive, but first of all how he or anyone lets himself be born as the one he is. As if human birth, the birth of the human, proposes the question of birth. That human existence has two stages – call these birth and the acceptance of birth – is expressed in religion as baptism, in politics as consent, in what you may call psychology as what Freud calls the diphasic character of psychosexual development. In philosophy I take it to have been expressed in Descartes's *Cogito* argument, a point perfectly understood and deeply elaborated by Emerson, that to exist the human being has the burden of proving that he or she exists, and that this burden is discharged in *thinking* your existence, which comes in Descartes (though this is controversial) to finding how to say, "I am, I exist"; not of course to say it just once, but at every instant of your existence; to preserve your existence, originate it. To exist is to take your existence upon you, to enact it, as if the basis of human existence is theater, even melodrama. To refuse this burden is to condemn yourself to skepticism – to a denial of the existence, hence of the value, of the world.

Hamlet's extreme sense of theater I take as his ceaseless perception of theater, say show, as an inescapable or metaphysical mark of the human condition, together with his endless sense of debarment from accepting the human condition as his (which is terribly human of him); as if his every breath and gesture disjoin and join him, from and with mankind. His bar – his lack of "advancement" into the world – is expressed in one's sense (my sense) of him as the Ghost of the play that bears his and his father's name, a sense that his refusal of participation in the world is his haunting of the world. (As if he is a figure in a play.) He overcomes his refusal only in announcing his death.

Conclusions are beginning to gather thick and fast. Since I am not attempting exactly to disburden myself of a proof here, but to clear the place for proof, in particular to present a new picture of the play, one that takes the dumb-show as the play's figure for itself, I welcome the gathering. *Mise-en-abyme* has become a convenient sign for the place of a concept of this figuring process. That the sign is at best the figure of a figure, not the concept itself, so to speak, is shown in considering that the idea of *mise-en-abyme* is of one thing containing another that looks like or copies it, repeats it in miniature. But the way the dumb-show would figure *Hamlet* is exactly not by looking like it.

The play's name for the thing that debars Hamlet from existence is revenge – revenge taken not so much as the competitor or parody of the realm of justice, but as the destroyer of individual identity. I note here merely that Laertes' analogous situation measures Hamlet's difference. The Ghost asks initially for revenge for his murder, a task the son evidently accepts as his to perform, apparently as readily as Laertes accepts the task of *his* revenge. But after telling his story of his death, what the Ghost asks Hamlet "not to bear" is something distinctly different – that "the royal bed of Denmark be / A couch for luxury and damned incest." But is this the son's business not to bear? Here the father asks the son to take the father's place, to make his life come out even for him, to set it right, so that he, the father, can rest in peace. It is the bequest of a beloved father that deprives the son of his identity, of enacting his own existence – it curses, as if spitefully, his being born of this father. Put otherwise, the father's dictation of the way he wishes to be remembered – by having his revenge taken for him – exactly deprives the son, with his powers of mourning, of the right to mourn *him,* to let him pass.

Shakespeare's *Hamlet* interprets the double staging of human birth – which means the necessity of accepting one's individuality or individuation or difference, say one's separateness – as the necessity of a double acceptance: an acceptance of one's mother as an independent sexual being whose life of desire survives the birth of a son and the death of a husband, a life that may present itself to her son as having been abandoned by her; and an acceptance of one's father as a dependent sexual being whose incapacity to sustain desire you cannot revive, which may present itself to his son as having to abandon him. Hence the play interprets the taking of one's place in the world as a process of mourning, as if there is a taking up of the world that is humanly a question of giving it up.

I break off by re-posing the following issue. Freud was so impressed by the apparently universal recurrence in his patients of the primal scene that he allowed himself the speculation that it was a phylogenetic inheritance. Laplanche and Pontalis propose an interpretation of this notion of "inherited memory traces" as, rather than a prehistory, a "pre-structure . . . transmitted by the parental fantasies," an interpretation that goes back to Freud's first theoretical sketches on the subject of fantasy, in which he accords a privileged position to the sense of hearing, understanding this to stand for the legends of parents and ancestors, "the family *sounds* or *sayings,* the spoken or secret discourses, going on prior to the subject's arrival, within which he must make his way." I hope you will be struck by the fit of this account with the fact that Hamlet's fantasy of the dumb-show takes up something he heard from his ancestor's ghost and that it features the mortal vulnerability of the ear. If you are struck by the fit, by the way Shakespeare can interpret Freud's speculation about the inheritance of fantasy as well as Freud can interpret Shakespeare's representation of fantasy – then from whom shall we say we learn of these things primarily? Who first taught us of the legacy of fantasies between generations, of let us say the fantasy structure of human culture, in which the issues of what we call our times occur to us as enigmas and into which the necessity to accept our birth puzzles the will? To recognize that there is no answer to the question of priority between this art and this science would seem to me the sign of philosophical progress.

POSTSCRIPT

It may well be that stable conviction in the proofs offered by Greg, and then by me, against the idea of the actual murder by poison through the ear may well depend on the possibility of establishing how in actuality (as it were) the murder was performed. I think the play does positively tell us how, or sufficiently suggests the manner to us; but I did not want to threaten my negative case about the surface of the dumb-show by taking up the positive case about the murder in the brief span of my paper. Conviction in the positive case depends on a different burden of proof, one that asks not so much for conviction as for considering a possibility. The possibility is that the final scene *shows* us how the murder was done, or at least how Hamlet, following Claudius's preparation, takes it in actuality to have been done, as, after stabbing him with the poisoned foil, he jams the poisoned cup against Claudius's mouth and forces him to drink. Why assume, as some critics have been led to do, that Claudius is some kind of Italian connoisseur of routes of poisoning? What Shakespeare shows us is that Claudius poisons by poisoning a drink. I claim it is enough for Hamlet to know; I suggest it is plenty for us. Hamlet's actions, not just his dreams, are our dreams.

I can imagine that some will wish to speculate about the fact that Hamlet inseminates Claudius; and with Leartes' foil. And further, I guess, that he does so only after he has himself been inseminated by it. These matters seem to me subordinate to one or two others: first, that Claudius is, as it were, killed twice by Hamlet (the second time, with the cup, punning on his "union" with Gertrude), as if to reaffirm the substitution fantasy of the dumb-show that makes Claudius two people (father and mother, at least); second, that Hamlet performs the murder and substitute murder only after announcing that he is dead, thus demonstrating that to take the Ghost's revenge is to become the Ghost.

Conviction that this possibility is to be considered seriously – the possibility that we are at the end shown the mode of murder – depends on a certain view of a particular dramaturgical structure, or discovery, of Shakespeare's, something I shall call deferred representation; Shakespeare's way of presenting in the closing image of a play something denied our sight from the beginning. Every melodramatic tableau may be seen as the reaction to a deferred revelation, but one, so to speak, that has been only empirically invisible. Whereas in the Shakespearean mode I allude to, the closing image takes on a central character's imagination of a scene central to his or her self-understanding, a scene, let me say, metaphysically invisible before this time and place, as if its representation had not been synthesizable before the working of the play to this conclusion. This is roughly how I have described the conclusion of *Othello* (the pair equating marriage and death sheets) and of *Coriolanus* (the scapegoat irrelevantly slaughtered); and how I take the conclusions of *Antony and Cleopatra* (in which the identities of the woman are fused in a fantasy of intercourse as marriage, where intercourse is in turn the fusion of coronation, nursing, acting, and autoerotic managing); and of *The Winter's Tale* (in which the concept of marriage is reconceived as the willingness for remarriage – as, to call upon Nietzsche once more, the forgoing of revenge against time in favor of the happiness in repetition; you may call it the acceptance of days).

So Shakespeare's power to provide a scene – one of deferred representation – with the means of establishing our experience of earlier scenes, as if supplying us with the conditions of that experience, say the conditions of pity and of horror, is the power (of deferred action) Freud attributes to dreams of the primal scene. Some theorists of language and literature, I believe, take Freud's idea to suggest that meaning is always, as such, deferred, deferred accordingly forever. I take Shakespeare's practice (interpreting, interpreted by, Freud's), call it the practice of comedy and of tragedy, to show that, even if you say that some meaning is always deferred, all meaning is not always deferred forever. (To say that total meaning is deferred forever is apt to say nothing, since nothing is apt to count as total meaning; that phrase is apt to mean nothing.) It is no more characteristic of the chains of significance to be theoretically open than it is, at each link, for them to close. As Emerson more or less pictures the matter, the expansion of meaning (like the drawing of a circle around a circle) is discontinuous; each step is a form of life. Shakespeare's dramas, like Freud's, propose our coming to know what we cannot just not know; like philosophy.

6

Recounting Gains, Showing Losses
Reading *The Winter's Tale*

A PART FROM any more general indebtedness of the romantics to Shakespeare, *The Winter's Tale* is particularly apt in relation to their themes of reawakening or revival, as for example entering into the figure of the six-year-old boy of Wordsworth's *Intimations* ode and the ode's idea of the adult's world as "remains," as of corpses. I associate this figure, especially in view of his difficulties over remembering, with Freud's report of a phobia in a five-year-old boy, partly simply to commemorate Freud's acknowledgment that he was preceded in his perceptions by the poets, more specifically because of Freud's consequent perception in this case of adult human life struggling toward happiness from within its own "debris." Now here at the end of *The Winter's Tale* a dead five- or six-year-old boy remains unaccounted for.

Or is this prejudicial? Shall we say that the absent boy is meant to cast the shadow of finitude or doubt over the general air of reunion at the end of the play, to emblematize that no human reconciliation is uncompromised, not even one constructible by the powers of Shakespeare? Or shall we say that in acquiring a son-in-law the loss of the son is made up for? Would that be Hermione's – the son's mother's – view of the matter? Or shall we take the boy's death more simply symbolically, as standing for the inevitable loss of childhood? Then does Perdita's being found mean that there is a way in which childhood *can,* after all, be recovered? But the sixteen years that Perdita was, as it were, lost are not recovered. Time may present itself as a good-humored old man, but what he speaks about in his appearance as Chorus in this play is his lapse, his being spent, as if behind our backs. Then is the moral that we all require forgiveness and that forgiveness is always a miracle, taking time but beyond time? Any of these things can be said, but how can we establish or deliver the weight or gravity of any such answer?

Why did the boy die? The boy's father, Leontes, says on one occasion that the boy is languishing from

> nobleness!
> Conceiving the dishonor of his mother,
> He straight declined, drooped, took it deeply,
> Fastened, and fixed the shame on't in himself.
> (II, iii, 11–14)

But this sounds more like something Leontes himself has done, and so suggests an identification Leontes has projected between himself and his son. The lines at the same time project an identification with his wife, to the extent that one permits "conceiving" in that occurrence to carry on the play's ideas of pregnancy, given the line's emphasis on drooping, as under a weight. But I am getting ahead of my story. The servant who brings the report of Mamillius's death attributes it to anxiety over his mother's plight. But the timing of the play suggests something else. Mamillius disappears from our sight for good when he is ordered by his enraged father to be separated from his mother. "Bear the boy hence, he shall not come about her" (II, i, 59). And theatrically, or visually, the father's rage had immediately entered, as if it was brought on, with Mamillius sitting on his mother's lap and whispering in her ear. What the boy and his mother interpret themselves to be doing is telling and listening to a winter's tale. What Leontes interprets them to be doing we must surmise from two facts: first, that both mother and son have got into this intimate position as a result of mutually seductive gestures, however well within the bounds, for all we know, of normal mental and sexual growth; second, that the idea of whispering has already twice been hit upon by Leontes' mind as it dashes into madness, once when it imagines people are gossiping about his cuckoldry, again as it cites evidence for the cuckoldry to the courtier Camillo in the astounding speech that begins "Is whispering nothing?" (I, ii, 284).

Naturally I shall not claim to know that Leontes imagines the son to be repeating such rumors to his mother, to the effect that he is not the son of, as it were, his own father. We are by now so accustomed to understanding insistence or protestation, perhaps in the form of rage, as modes of denial, that we will at least consider that the *negation* of this tale is the object of Leontes' fear, namely the fear that he *is* the father. As if whatever the son says, the very power of his speaking, of what it is he bespeaks, is fearful; as if his very existence is what perplexes his father's mind.

Why would the father fear being the true father of his children? One reason might be some problem of his with the idea that he has impregnated the mother, I mean of course the *son's* mother. Another might be that this would displace him in this mother's affection, and moreover that he would himself have to nurture that displacement. Another might be that this would ratify the displacement of his and his friend Polixenes' mutual love, his original separation from whom, which means the passing of youth and innocence, was marked, as Polixenes tells Hermione, by the appearance of the women they married. But for whatever reason, the idea of his fearing to be a father would make his jealousy of Polixenes suspicious – not merely because it makes the jealousy empirically baseless, but because it makes it psychologically derivative. This is worth saying because there are views that would take the jealousy between brothers as a rock-bottom level of human motivation. In taking it as derivative I do not have to deny that Leontes is jealous of Polixenes, only to leave open what this means, and how special a human relation it proposes.

To further the thought that disowning his issue is more fundamental than, or causes, his jealousy of his friend and brother, rather than the other way around, let us ask how what is called Leontes' "diseased opinion" (I, ii, 297) drops its disease.

It vanishes exactly upon his learning that his son is dead. The sequence is this: Leontes refuses the truth of Apollo's oracle; a servant enters, crying for the king. Leontes asks, "What's the business?" and is told the prince is gone. Leontes questions the word and is told it means "Is dead." Leontes' response at once is to relent: "Apollo's angry, and the heavens themselves / Do strike at my injustice"; whereupon Hermione faints. Of course you can say that the consequences of Leontes' folly have just built up too far for him to bear them any further and that he is shocked into the truth. This is in a general way undeniable, but it hardly suggests why it is *here* that he buckles, lets himself feel the shock. It is not psychologically forced to imagine that he first extend his assertion of Mamillius's drooping from shame and accuse Hermione of Mamillius's murder, or at least that Shakespeare follow his primary source, the tale of jealousy as told in Robert Greene's romance *Pandosto*, and let Leontes immediately believe the oracle, but still too late; so that news of his son's death and of Hermione's death upon that news comes during his recantation, as double punishment for his refusal of belief. Or again, Shakespeare could have persisted in his idea that Leontes believes the oracle only after he sees that his disbelief has killed, and still have preserved the idea of the shock as the death of both his son and his wife. But the choice of *The Winter's Tale* is, rather, to make the cure perfectly coincide with the death of the son alone. How do we understand Shakespeare's reordering, or recounting?

Think of the boy whispering in his mother's ear, and think back to her having shown that her fantasy of having things told in her ear makes her feel full (I, ii, 91–2); that is, that her pregnancy itself is a cause of heightened erotic feeling in her (something that feeds her husband's confusion and strategy). Then the scene of the boy's telling a tale is explicitly one to cause jealousy (as accordingly was the earlier scene of telling between Hermione and Polixenes, which the present scene repeats, to Leontes' mind); hence the son's death reads like the satisfaction of the father's wish. The further implication is that Apollo is angry not, or not merely, because Leontes does not believe his oracle, but because the god has been outsmarted by Leontes, or rather by his theater of jealousy, tricked into taking Leontes' revenge *for* him, as if himself punished for believing that even a god could halt the progress of jealousy by a deliverance of reason. (Leontes' intimacy with riddles and prophecies would then not be his ability to solve them, but to anticipate them.)

Then look again at the "rest," the relief from restlessness of his brain, that Leontes has achieved at this stage of death and fainting. He says, as he asks Paulina and the ladies in attendance to remove and care for the stricken Hermione, "I have too much believed mine own suspicion" (III, ii, 148) – a fully suspicious statement, I mean one said from *within* his suspicion, not from having put it aside. The statement merely expresses his regret that he *believed* his suspicion too much. How much would have been just enough? And what would prevent this excess of belief in the future? The situation remains unstable. How could it not, given what we know of the condition from which he requires recovery?

He had described the condition in the following way, in the course of his speech upon discovering the mother and the son together:

> There may be in the cup
> A spider steeped, and one may drink, depart,
> And yet partake no venom, for his knowledge
> Is not infected; but if one present
> Th'abhorred ingredient to his eye, make known
> How he hath drunk, he cracks his gorge, his sides,
> With violent hefts. I have drunk, and seen the spider.
>
> (II, i, 39–45)

Of the fabulous significance in these lines, I note here just the skeptic's sense, as for example voiced by David Hume, of being cursed, or sickened, in knowing more than his fellows about the fact of knowing itself, in having somehow peeked behind the scenes, or, say, conditions, of knowing. (Though what Shakespeare is revealing those conditions to be is something Hume, or Descartes, would doubtless have been astonished to learn.) And Leontes has manifested the collapse of the power of human knowing in the "Is whispering nothing?" speech, which ends:

> Why, then the world and all that's in't is nothing,
> The covering sky is nothing, Bohemia nothing,
> My wife is nothing, nor nothing have these nothings,
> If this be nothing.
>
> (I, ii, 293–6)

Chaos seems to have come again; and what chaos looks like is the inability to say what exists; to say whether, so to speak, language applies to anything.

These experiences of Leontes go rather beyond anything I find I might mean by speaking of believing my suspicions too much. So far I am suggesting merely that this insufficiency of recovery is what you would expect in tracking Leontes' progress by means of the map of skepticism. For here is where you discover the *precipitousness* of the move from next to nothing (say from the merest

197

surmise that one may be dreaming, a repeated surmise in Leontes' case) into nothingness. Hume recovers from his knowledge of knowledge, or, let me say, learns to live with it, but what he calls its "malady" is never cured; and Descartes recovers only by depending (in a way I judge is no longer natural to the human spiritual repertory) on his detailed dependence on God. I assume it is unclear to what extent we have devised for ourselves late versions of these reparations. If *The Winter's Tale* is understandable as a study of skepticism – that is, as a response to what skepticism is a response to – then its second half must be understandable as a study of its search for recovery (after Leontes, for example, and before him Othello, have done their worst). That skepticism demands – Cartesian skepticism, Humian skepticism, the thing Kant calls a scandal to philosophy – efforts at recovery is internal to it: It is inherently unstable; no one simply wants to be a (this kind of) skeptic. Skepticism's own sense of what recovery would consist in dictates efforts to refute it; yet refutation can only extend it, as Othello notably found out. True recovery lies in reconceiving it, in finding skepticism's source (its origin, say, if you can say it without supposing its origin is past).

To orient ourselves in finding how *The Winter's Tale* conceives of this search for recovery, let us question its title further. Several passages in the play are called tales or said to be like tales, but the only thing said to be a tale for winter is the tale begun by the boy Mamillius. I have heard it said, as if it is accepted wisdom, that the remainder of the play, after we no longer hear what Mamillius says, or would have said, *is* the play as it unfolds. Supposing so, what would the point be? According to what I have so far found to be true of that narration, what we are given are events motivated by seduction, told in a whisper, having the effect of drawing on the vengeance of a husband and father who, therefore, has interpreted the tale as revealing something about him, and specifically something to do with the fact that his wife has or has not been faithful to him, where her faithfulness would be at least as bad as her faithlessness would be. (This is the match of my way of looking at *Othello*.) Although I find these to be promising lines to follow out as characteristics of our play, they will any of them depend on some working sense of why a play is being called a tale. Is it simply that the play is about a tale, or the telling of a tale, as for instance the film *The Philadelphia Story* is, in a sense, about a magazine story, or the getting and the suppressing of a story? Does it matter that we do not know what the tale is that the play would on this account be about? Three times an assertion is said to sound like an old tale – that the king's daughter is found, that Antigonous was torn to pieces by a bear, and that Hermione is living – and each time the purpose is to say that one will have trouble believing these things without seeing them, that the experience of them "lames report," "undoes description," and lies beyond the capacity of "ballad-makers . . . to express it" (V, ii, 61–2, 26–7). It is uncontroversial that Shakespeare's late plays intensify his recurrent study of theater, so we may take it that he is here asserting the competition of poetic theater with nontheatrical romance as modes of narrative, and especially claiming the superiority of theater (over a work like his own "source" *Pandosto*) in securing full faith and credit in fiction. But what are the stakes in such a competition, if they go beyond the jealousies of one profession or craft toward another? Let us consider that Leontes' interruption of Mamillius's tale itself suggests a competition over the question *whose* tale the ensuing tale is, the son's or the father's, or somehow both, the one told in whispers and beckonings, under the voice, the other, at the same time, at the top of the voice, in commands and accusations.

While evidently I expect considerable agreement that in Leontes' intrusion we have an Oedipal conflict put before us, I am not assuming that we thereupon know how to work our way through the conflict. Freud, I guess like Sophocles, seems to look at the conflict as initiated by the son's wish to remove or replace the father, whereas in *The Winter's Tale* the conflict, on the contrary, seems primarily generated by the father's wish to replace or remove the son. Perhaps this speaks of a difference between tragedy and romance – hence of their inner union – but in any case I do not wish to prejudge such a matter.

Let us for the moment separate two of the play's primary regions of ideas that intersect in Mamillius's whispering of a tale of generation, namely ideas concerning telling or relating and ideas concerning breeding and issue. These are the ideas I shall follow out here to the extent I can, and from which I derive the point of calling the play a tale, something told. To grasp initially how vast these regions are, consider that telling in the play belongs to its theme not alone of relating or recounting, but to its theme of counting generally, hence to its preoccupation with computation and business and the exchange of money. And consider that the theme of breeding or branching or issue or generation belongs to the play's themes of dividing or separation.

The regions may be seen as the poles of opposite faces of a world of partings, of parting's dual valence, as suggested in the paired ideas of participation and of parturition, or in other words of the play, ideas of being fellow to and of dissevering. The play punctuates its language with literal "part" words, as if words to the wise, words such as depart, parting, departure, apart, party to, partner, and, of course, bearing a part. That last phrase, saying that parts are being born, itself suggests the level at which theater (here in a phrase from music) is being investigated in this play; hence suggests why theater is for Shakespeare an *endless* subject of study; and we are notified that no formulation of the ideas of participation and parturition in this play will be complete that fails to account for their connection with theatrical parts; or, put otherwise, to say why tales of parting produce plays of revenge, sometimes of revenge overcome.

Since the region of telling and counting (think of it as *relating;* I am naming it participation) is so ramified, and may yet remain incompletely realized, let me remind you of its range. Reading *The Winter's Tale* to study it, to find out my interest in it, was the second time in my literary experience in which I have felt engulfed by economic terms; I mean felt a text engulfed by them. The first time was in studying *Walden,* another work insistently about pastoral matters and the vanishing of worlds. In *The Winter's Tale* – beyond the terms tell and count themselves, and beyond account and loss and lost and gain and pay and owe and debt and repay – we have money, coin, treasure, purchase, cheat, custom, commodity, exchange, dole, wages, recompense, labor, affairs, traffic, tradesmen, borrow, save, credit, redeem, and – perhaps the most frequently repeated economic term in the play – business. But the sheer number of such terms will not convey the dense saturation of the language of this play – perhaps, it may seem, of language as such, or some perspective toward language, or projection of it – in this realm of terms; not even the occurrence within this realm of what one may take as the dominating thematic exchanges of the action, from suffering loss to being redeemed to paying back and getting even; the saturation seems more deeply expressed by the interweavings of the words and the scope of contexts – or, let us say, interests –

over which they range. If one seeks an initial guess for this saturation or shadowing of language by the economic, or the computational, one might say that it has to do with the thought that the very purpose of language is to communicate, to inform, which is to say, to tell.

And you always tell more and tell less than you know. Wittgenstein's *Investigations* draws this most human predicament into philosophy, forever returning to philosophy's ambivalence, let me call it, as between wanting to tell more than words can say and wanting to evade telling altogether – an ambivalence epitomized in the idea of wishing to speak "outside language games," a wish for (language to do, the mind to be) everything and nothing. Here I think again of Emerson's wonderful saying in which he detects the breath of virtue and vice that our character "emits" at every moment, words so to speak always before and beyond themselves, essentially and unpredictably recurrent, say rhythmic, fuller of meaning than can be exhausted. So that it may almost be said of every word and phrase in the language what William Empson has said of metaphors, that they are pregnant (or are they, or at the same time, seminal?).

I was speaking of the thought that the very purpose of language, it may be said, is to tell. It is therefore hardly surprising, as it were, that an answer to the question "How do you know?" is provided by specifying how you can tell, and in two modes. Asked how you know there is a goldfinch in the garden you may, for example, note some feature of the goldfinch, such as its eye markings or the color of its head; or you may explain how you are in a position to know, what your credentials are, or whether someone told you. (I mean this example, I hope it is clear, in homage to J. L. Austin's unendingly useful study "Other Minds.") In the former case you begin a narrative of the object's differences from other relevant objects; in the latter case a narrative of differences in your position from other positions. (From such trivial cases one may glimpse the following speculation arising: If a narrative is something told, and telling is an answer to a claim to knowledge, then perhaps any narrative, however elaborated, may be understood as an answer to some implied question of knowledge, perhaps in the form of some disclaiming of knowledge or avoidance of it.)

But there is another route of answer to the question how you know (still confining our attention to what is called empirical knowledge), namely a claim to have experienced the thing, most particularly in the history of epistemology, to have seen it. This answer, as it occurs in classical investigations of human knowledge, is more fundamental than, or undercuts, the answers that consist of telling. What makes it more fundamental is suggested by two considerations. First, to claim to have seen is to claim, as it were, to have seen for oneself, to put one's general capacity as a knower on the line; whereas one does not claim to tell by the eye markings for oneself, but for anyone interested in such information. Hence what is at stake here is just a more or less specialized piece of expertise, which may for obvious reasons be lacking or in obvious ways need improvement. Second, knowing by telling, as suggested, goes by differences, say by citing identifying marks or features of a thing: You can for instance tell a goldfinch from a goldcrest because of their differences in eye markings. Whereas knowing by seeing does not require, and cannot employ, differences. (Unless the issue is one of difference in the mode or nature of seeing itself, call this the aesthetics of seeing. Epistemology is obliged to keep aesthetics under control, as if to guard against the thought that there is something more [and better] seeing can be, or provide, than evidence for claims to know, especially claims that particular objects exist.) You cannot tell (under ordinary circumstances; a proviso to be determined) – it makes no clear sense to speak of telling – a goldfinch from a peacock, or either from a telephone, or any from a phone call. To know a hawk from a handsaw – or a table from a chair – you simply have, as it were, to be able to say what is before your eyes; it would be suggestive of a lack (not of expertise but) of mental competence (for example suggestive of madness) to confuse one with the other. As if the problem of knowledge is now solely how it is that you, or anyone, know at all of the sheer existence of the thing. This is why epistemologists such as Descartes, in assessing our claims to know, have had, out of what seems to them a commitment to intellectual purity and seriousness, to consider possibilities that in various moods may seem frivolous or far-fetched, such as that they may now be dreaming that they are awake – a possibility (unless it can be ruled out, explicitly) that at a stroke would put under a cloud any claim to know the world on the basis of our senses. (The difference between dreaming and reality is one of the great philosophical junctures, or jointures, that is not a function of differences; not to be settled by noting specific marks and features, say predicates. It is my claim for Wittgenstein's thought that his criteria are meant not to settle the field of existence [in its disputes with dreams, imaginations, hallucinations, delusions] but to mark its bourn, say its conceptual space.) This is a long story, not to everyone's taste to pursue at length, and not to anyone's taste or profit to pursue at just any time (as Descartes is careful to say). What interests me here is to get at the intersection of the epistemologist's question of existence, say of the existence of the external world, or of what analytical philosophy calls other minds, with Leontes' perplexity about knowing whether his son is his.

Leontes' first question to his son is: "Art thou my boy?" And then he goes on to try to recognize the boy as his by their resemblance in certain marks and features, at first by comparing their noses. That speech, distracted, ends with a repetition of the earlier doubt: "Art thou my calf?" Already here we glimpse a Shakespearean pathos, a sense that one may feel mere sadness enough to fill an empty world. Upon the repetition Leontes compares their heads. These efforts are of course of no avail. Then he rules out the value of the testimony of anyone else, as if testifying that he must know for himself; and as he proceeds he insists that his doubts are reasonable, and he is led to consider his dreams. It is all virtually an exercise out of Descartes's *Meditations*. But while Descartes suggests that his doubts may class him with madmen, he succeeds (for some of his readers) in neutralizing the accusation, that is, in sufficiently establishing the reasonableness of his doubts, at least provisionally. Whereas Leontes is, while in doubt, certainly a madman. What is their difference?

What Leontes is suffering has a cure, namely to acknowledge his child as his, to own it, something every normal parent will do, or seems to do, something it is the first obligation of parents to do (though, come to think about it, most of us lack the knock-down evidence we may take ourselves to possess, in this case as in the case of owning that the world exists). Still it is enough, it is the essence of the matter, to know it for ourselves, say to acknowledge the child. The cure in Descartes's case is not so readily describable; and perhaps it is not available. I mean, acknowledging that the world exists, that you know for yourself that it is yours, is not so clear a process. Descartes's discovery of skepticism shows, you might say, what makes Leontes' madness possible, or what makes his madness representative of the human need for acknowledgment.

The depth of this madness, or of its possibility, is revealed by *The Winter's Tale* to measure, in turn, the depth of drama, or of spectacle, or of showing itself, in its competition with telling or narrative, because, as suggested, even after believing the truth proclaimed by an oracle Leontes is not brought back to the world (supposing he ever is) except by the drama of revelation and resurrection at the end of this work for theater; by seeing something, beyond being told something.

This is confirmed as a matter of this drama's competition with narrative romance, by making the finding of a child who has been empirically lost, in *fact* rejected and abandoned, a matter swiftly dealt with by simple narration: The gentlemen who share the telling of the story of the daughter found say it is hard to believe, but in the event (especially given their use of the convention of increasing one's credibility by saying that what one will say will sound incredible), nothing proves easier. The matter for drama, by contrast, is to investigate the finding of a wife *not* in empirical fact lost, but, let me say, transcendentally lost, lost just because one is blind to her – as it were conceptually unprepared for her – because that one is blind to himself, lost to himself. Here is what becomes, at some final stage, of the great Shakespearean problematic of legitimate succession: Always seen as a matter essential to the flourishing state, recognizing (legitimizing) one's child now appears as a matter essential to individual sanity, a discovery begun perhaps in Hamlet, and developed in Lear.

We are bound, it seems to me, at some point to feel that this theater is contesting the distinction between saying and showing. If the concluding scene of this theater is telling something, it is not something antecedently known; it is rather instituting knowledge, reconceiving, reconstituting knowledge, along with the world. Then there must be a use of the concept of telling more fundamental than, or explaining or grounding, its use to tell differences; a use of the concept of telling as fundamental as seeing for oneself. That there is such a use is a way of putting the results of my work on Wittgenstein's idea of a criterion, because that idea – used to describe, in a sense to explain, how language relates (to) things – gives a sense of how things fall under our concepts, of how we individuate things and name, settle on nameables, of why we call things as we do, as questions of how we determine what *counts* as instances of our concepts, this thing as a table, that as a chair, this other as a human, that other as a god. To speak is to say what counts.

This is not the time to try to interest anyone in why the concept of counting occurs in this intellectual space, I mean to convince one unconvinced that its occurrence is not arbitrary and that it is the same concept of counting that goes with the concept of telling. (Something counts because it fits or *matters*. I think of the concept in this criterial occurrence as its nonnumerical use – it is not here tallying how much or how many, but establishing membership or belonging. This is a matter both of establishing what Wittgenstein speaks of as a kind of object, and also attributing a certain value or interest to the object.) But before moving from this region of parting to the other – that is, from the region of telling and imparting or relating and partaking, which I am calling the region of participation, to the region of departing or separation, which I am calling the region of parturition – I want to note two ways for further considering the question.

The first way is to ask whether it is chance that the concept of telling is used both to cover the progress of relating a story and to cover the progress of counting or numbering, as if counting numbers were our original for all further narration. Consider that counting by numbers contains within itself the difference between fiction and fact, since one learns both to count the numbers, that is to recite them, intransitively, and to count things, that is to relate, or coordinate, numerals and items, transitively; and counting by numbers contains the ideas that recitations have orders and weights and paces, that is, significant times and sizes of items and significant distances between them. In counting by numbers, intransitively or transitively, matters like order and size and pace of events are fixed ahead of time, whereas in telling tales it is their pleasure to work these things out as part of the telling, or as part of a mode or genre of telling – it is why what the teller of a story does is to recount, count *again* – so you needn't be making a mistake if you let lapse a space of sixteen years in your account of certain kinds of things.

The second way I note for considering the connection of counting by criteria with counting as telling (or tallying) concerns what I suppose is the major claim I make in *The Claim of Reason* about Wittgenstein's idea of a criterion, namely that while criteria provide conditions of (shared) speech they do not provide an answer to skeptical doubt. I express this by saying that criteria are disappointing, taking them to express, even to begin to account for, the human disappointment with human knowledge. Now when Leontes cannot convince himself that Mamillius is his son on the basis of criteria such as their having similar noses and heads, and instead of recognizing criteria as insufficient for this knowledge, concludes that he may disown his child, not count him as his own, Leontes' punishment is that he loses the ability to count, to speak (consecutively), to account for the order and size and pace of his experiences, to tell anything. This is my initial approach to the "Is whispering nothing?" speech. Without now trying to penetrate to the meaning of that Shakespearean "nothing," trying rather to keep my head up under this onslaught of significance, I take the surface of the speech as asking whether anything counts: Does whispering count, does it matter, is it a criterion for what the world is, is anything? And in that state no one can answer him, because it is exactly the state in which you have repudiated that attunement with others in our criteria on which language depends. So I take us here to be given a portrait of the skeptic at the moment of the world's withdrawal from his grasp, to match the portrait of Othello babbling and fainting, in comparison with which the philosopher's portrait of the skeptic as not *knowing* something, in the sense of being uncertain of something, shows as an intellectualization of some prior intimation.

And Shakespeare's portrait indicates what the intimation is of, of which the philosopher's *is* the intellectualization, one in which, as I keep coming back to putting it, the failure of knowledge is a failure of acknowledgment, which means, whatever else it means, that the result of the failure is not an ignorance but an ignoring, not an opposable doubt but an unappeasable denial, a willful uncertainty that constitutes an annihilation. These formulations suggest that *The Winter's Tale* may be taken as painting the portrait of the skeptic as a fanatic. The inner connection between skepticism and fanaticism is a further discovery of the *Critique of Pure Reason,* which takes both skepticism and fanaticism as products of dialectical illusion (the one despairing over the absence of the unconditioned, the other claiming its presence), divided by perfect enmity with one another, united in their reciprocal enmities with human reason.

The Shakespearean portrait lets us see that the skeptic *wants* the annihilation that he is punished by, that it is his way of asserting the humanness of knowledge, since skepticism's negation of the human, its denial of satisfaction in the human (here in human conditions of knowing), is an essential feature of the human, as it were its birthright. It is the feature (call it the Christian feature) that Nietzsche wished to overcome by his *affirmations* of the human, which would, given our state, appear to us as the overcoming or surpassing of the human. I said that Leontes loses the ability to count, to tell, to recount his experiences, and now I am taking that as his point, his strategy – to turn this punishment into his victory. Before he is recovered, he *wants* not to count, not to own what is happening to him as his, wants for there to be no counting, which is to say, nothing. Why?

This takes us to that other region of parting, that of departure, separating, dividing, branching, grafting, flowering, shearing, issuing, delivering, breeding: parturition. Without partings in this region there is nothing, if nothing comes from nothing, and if something comes only from the seeds of the earth. Leontes is quite logical in wanting there to be nothing, to want there to be no separation.

The action of the play is built on a pair of literal departures, in the first half (after a short introductory scene) a departure from Sicilia, and in the second (after the introductory scene of Time's soliloquy) a departure back from Bohemia. And the Prologue, so to speak, of the play, the opening scene of Act I, is, among some other things, a recounting of the separation of Leontes and Polixenes. Against which, how are we to understand the range of Leontes', and the play's, final words?

> Good Paulina
> Lead us from hence, where we may leisurely
> Each one demand and answer to his part
> Performed in this wide gap of time since first
> We were dissevered. Hastily lead away.

When were we first dissevered? Who is we? Perhaps we think first of Leontes and Hermione; but Hermione thinks first of Perdita (she does not speak to Leontes in her only speech upon reviving, but says that she "preserved / [Herself] to see the issue" [V, iii, 127–8]); and if Leontes is thinking of Polixenes when he says "first dissevered," does he mean sixteen years ago or at the time of their childhoods? and if he is thinking of Perdita he must mean when he had her carried off, but we shall, perhaps, think of her delivery from her mother in prison; and perhaps we shall think of Paulina's awakening Hermione by saying "come away," speaking of life's redemption of her, and of "bequeathing to death [her] numbness," as her leaving death, departing from it, as a being born (again). As if all disseverings are invoked in each; as if to say that life no less than death is a condition and process of dissevering; as if to see that each of us "demanding and answering to our part" means seeing ourselves as apart from everything of which we are part, always already dissevered, which above all here means – and hence the idea of theater in this theater above all means – that each is part, only part, that no one is everything, that apart from this part that one has, there is never nothing, but always others. How could one fail to know this? I say that such thoughts are invoked in Leontes' concluding words, but to what extent in saying "Hastily lead away" is he, do we imagine, anxious to depart from them as well?

Let us go back to my claim that Leontes' wish for there to be nothing – the skeptic as nihilist – goes with his effort, at the cost of madness, not to count. The general idea of the connection is that counting implies multiplicity, differentiation. Then we could say that what he wants is for there to be nothing separate, hence nothing but plenitude. But he could also not just want this either, because plenitude, like nothingness, would mean the end of his (individual) existence. It may be that each of these fantasies comes to the wish never to have been born. Beyond suggesting a wish not to be natal, hence not mortal, the wish says on its face that suicide is no solution to the problem it sees. If philosophers are right who have taken the idea of never having been born as dissipating the fear of death, the idea does not dissipate the fear of dying, say annihilation. Leontes' nothingness was, as it were, to make room within plenitude for his sole existence, but it makes too much room, it lets the others in and out at the same time. So Leontes, I am taking it, wants neither to exist nor not to exist, neither for there to be a Leontes separate from Polixenes and Hermione and Mamillius nor for there not to be, neither for Polixenes to depart nor for him not to.

It is out of this dilemma that I understand Leontes to have come upon a more specific matter not to count. What specifically he does not want to count is the other face of what he does not want to own, the time of breeding, the fact of life that time is a father, that it has issue, even, as Time, the Chorus, says in this play, that it "brings forth" its issue, which suggests that time may also be, like nature, a mother. Of all the reasons there may be not to wish to count time, what is Leontes' reason?

The last word of the Prologue is the word "one" (in that context a pronoun for "son"); and the opening word of the play proper, as it were, is "nine." It is the term of Hermione's pregnancy, which, as I suppose is by now predictable, I am taking as the dominating fact of the play. Let us have that opening speech of Polixenes' before us.

> Nine changes of the wat'ry star hath been
> The shepherd's note since we have left our throne
> Without a burden: time as long again
> Would be filled up, my brother, with our thanks,
> And yet we should for perpetuity
> Go hence in debt. And therefore, like a cipher,
> Yet standing in rich place, I multiply
> With one "We thank you," many thousands more
> That go before it.
>
> (I, ii, 1–9)

(For fun I note that it is a speech of nine lines, the last not (yet) complete, and that of Polixenes' seven speeches before he accedes to the command to stay, all but one are either nine lines or one line long.) Polixenes' opening speech speaks Leontes' mind, it contains everything Leontes' mind needs (which now means to me, since a working mind, a mind still in command of language, a mind that cannot simply not count), everything it needs to miscount, or discount, to misattribute, the thing it finds to be unbearable to count: The speech has the figure nine as the term at once of pregnancy and of Polixenes' sojourn in Sicilia; it has the contrast between being absent or empty (his throne without a burden) and being present and filled up ("standing in rich place," and especially *time* as filled up, about to issue in something); and it has the idea of nothing as breeding, that is, of a cipher multiplying, being fruitful, the Shakespearean nothing – as noting, as cipher, as naughtiness, as origin – from which everything comes (as Lear, for example, to his confusion, learned).

I observe in passing that the clause "like a cipher / Yet standing in rich place, I multiply" is a latent picture of sexual intercourse, by which I mean that it need not become explicit but lies in wait for a mind in a certain frame, as Leontes' is, the frame of mind in which the earth is seen as, or under the dominance of, in Leontes' phrase, a "bawdy planet." He uses the phrase later in the scene when he concludes "No barricado for a belly. Know't / It will let in and out the enemy, / With bag and baggage" (I, ii, 204–6), another latent fantasy of intercourse and ejaculation. The vision of our planet as bawdy is shared by Hamlet and Lear as a function of their disgust with it, and it is an instance of the way in which the world, in a phrase of Emerson's, is asked to wear our color: Leontes' vision of the world sexualized is a possibility realized in *Antony and Cleopatra,* confronting in that play the vision of the world politicized, where those worlds intersect or become one another; in *The Winter's Tale* the intersection of sexualization is with the world, I would say, economicized.

In Polixenes' opening speech, economicization is expressed in the idea of his multiplying, which in that context means both that he is breeding and that numbers and words in general, like great nature and time, are breeding out of control; and it is expressed in that phrase he uses about filling up another nine months, making time pregnant with thanks, namely that he would still "for perpetuity / Go hence in debt." The ensuing computation by multiplication (adding an inseminating cipher) is meant not to overcome but to note the debt. What the unpayable debt is is sketched in the opening scene, the Prologue. In this civilized, humorous exchange between courtiers representing each of the two kings, each expresses his own king's wish to pay back something owed the other. The debt is discussed as a visiting and a receiving, but in the central speech of the scene Camillo describes the issue between the kings as one in which an affection rooted between them in their childhoods has branched, that is continued but divided. "Since their more mature dignities and royal necessities made separation of their society, their encounters though not personal, have been royally attorneyed with interchange of gifts, letters, loving embassies; that they have seemed to be together, though absent; shook hands as over a vast." In the ensuing play the vast opens, and the debt seems to be for the fact of separation itself, for having one's own life, one's own hands, for there being or there having to be substitutes for the personal, for the fact that visits are necessary, or possible; a debt owed, one might say, for the condition of indebtedness, relatedness, as such, payment of which could only increase it, have further issue.

So we already have sketched for us here an answer to the question why a play about the overcoming of revenge is a play of computation and economic exchange: The literal, that is economic, ideas of paying back and of getting even allow us to see and formulate what revenge Leontes requires and why the revenge he imagines necessary for his rest only increases the necessity for it; and it suggests the transformations required if revenge is to be replaced by justice. Leontes wishes an evenness, or annihilation of debt, of owing, which would take place in a world without counting, apart from any evaluation of things, or commensuration of them, for example, any measuring of visits, of gifts, of exchanges, as of money for things, or punishments for offenses, or sisters or daughters for wives. Payment in such a case would do the reverse of what he wants, it would increase what he wishes to cease; it would imply the concept of indebtedness, hence of otherness. And this sense of the unpayable, the unforgivability of one's owing, as it were for being the one one is, for so to speak the gift of life, produces a wish to revenge oneself upon existence, on the fact, or facts, of life as such.

Nietzsche spotted us as taking revenge on Time, Time and its "It was," as if we are locked in a death struggle with nostalgia. Leontes seems rather to want revenge on Time and its "It will be," not because of its threat of mutability, bringing change to present happiness, but for something like the reverse reason, that its change perpetuates the nightmare of the present, its changes, its issuing, the very fact of more time. This may mean that Leontes' case is hopeless, whereas Nietzsche is led to a proposal for reconceiving time; but then this also meant reconceiving human existence. Nietzsche's formulations will have helped produce some of mine; but a more interesting matter would be to understand what helped produce some of his – doubtless his work on tragedy went into it. This leaves open the question of the relation of telling and retaliation, the question whether narration as such is being proposed as the offspring of revenge, that it is out of revenge for the fact of issuing and unpayable indebtedness that words breed into tales in which evenness is sought, in which recounting, counting again, is imperative, either as retribution or as the overcoming of retribution we know as forgiveness and love.

The opening scene proper of *The Winter's Tale* raises the question why Polixenes, after a visit of nine months, chooses now to leave; it alerts us to consider that Polixenes gives no good answer to this question. He expresses a fear of what, in his absence, may "breed" (I, ii, 12); and when Hermione says that if he'll "tell he longs to see his son" she'll not only let him go but "thwack him hence with distaffs" – that is, to attend to his brood is a reason any woman will respect – but he does not claim this. Furthermore, the victory of her argument comes with saying that, since he offers no reason, as if leaving something unsaid, she'll be forced to keep him "as prisoner, / Not like a guest." When in the next act she is reported, in prison, to receive comfort from her babe, what she is reported saying is "My poor prisoner, / I am innocent as you" (II, ii, 27–8). And Polixenes gives in to her with the words "Your guest, then, madam: / To be your prisoner should import offending" (I, ii, 54–5). Take this as something Leontes hears, or knows for himself, almost says for himself in his identification with Polixenes. The offense for *him* in being her prisoner, her child, would be a matter of *horror,* if she were having *his* child. His logic again, in denying this consequence, is therefore impeccable. (This is not the only time, in noting Leontes' identification with Polixenes, that I allude to the psychic complexities this poses for Leontes. For a further example, if Polixenes is his brother, hence Hermione Polixenes' sister, then imagining that they are adulterous is imagining them incestuous as well. If you take Leontes either as horrified or as jealous of that, hence either as denying or craving it, then the implication is that he feels *himself* on that ground to be the illegitimate and incestuous brother. This idea would be helped, perhaps signaled, by the emphatic lack of mention in the present situation of Polixenes' own wife.)

I am still asking why Polixenes has decided to part now. To the evidence I have been marshaling from his opening speech concerning breeding and time's being filled up and his multiplying and later his not being a prisoner, I add the repeated explanation with which he ends each of his succeeding two substantial speeches: "Besides, I have stayed / To tire your royalty" (I, ii, 14–5) and "My stay [is] . . . a charge and trouble" (I, ii, 25–6). Taken as pro forma, civilized excuses these must receive pro forma, civilized denials from his hosts; and for a long time it seemed to me that he was saying just the thing that would prompt them to urge him civilly to stay. Then the urging gets out of hand, and the leaving becomes no less suspicious than the urging. My better suggestion is by now clear enough, and is contained in Polixenes' word "nine."

He is departing because Hermione's filling up and approaching term seems to him to leave no more room and time for him in Sicilia. It is this, the implication of the fact of her pregnancy, that Polixenes' speech leaves unsaid; and it is this that Leontes in turn undertakes to deny, for, it seems to me, all kinds of reasons. First, out of his love for Polixenes, to reassure him; again, because he feels the same way, that his room and time are being used up by Hermione's plenitude; again, with the very intensifying of his identification with Polixenes, the wish or push to exit, to depart, feels to him like abandonment, as does the imminent issuing, or exiting, or dissevering, of Hermione.

I regard it as a recommendation of this way of looking at the opening of the play that it does not choose between Leontes' love and loss of status as between Polixenes and Hermione, and that it does not deny the sexual implication of the number nine that Shakespeare's telling carefully sets up in coordinating the beginning of Polixenes' visit with Hermione's conceiving. However fantastic it seems of Leontes to imagine that the first thing that happened upon Polixenes' arrival on his shores is that he impregnated his wife, it is not fantastic for him to relate that arrival to an access of his own desire. Another recommendation of this way of taking things is that it does not require a choice between locating the onset of Leontes' jealousy as occurring only with the aside "Too hot, too hot" at the 108th line of the scene and as having been brought on the stage with him. This is now a matter of a given performance, of determining how you wish to conceive of Leontes' arrival at the conjunction of the events in Polixenes' opening speech: He wouldn't have to hear them from Polixenes, for what Polixenes knows is not news for him. What matters is the conjunction itself, the precipitousness of it. Taking the jealousy as derivative of the sense of revenge upon life, upon its issuing, or separating, or replication, I am taking it as, so to speak, the solution of a problem in computation or economy, one that at a stroke solves a chain of equations, in which sons and brothers are lovers, and lovers are fathers and sons, and wives and mothers become one another. Precipitousness

I have also taken as an essential feature of the onset of skeptical doubt, which is a principal cause in my taking Othello's treatment of Desdemona as an allegory of the skeptic's view and treatment of the world. It is a place within which to investigate psychic violence, or torture, as a function both of skepticism's annihilation of the world and of the wounded intellect's efforts to annihilate skepticism.

Still at the beginning of Shakespeare's play, it is nearing time to call a halt. I must reach its closing scene, since that will present this play's vision of a path of recovery, the quest for which is, as I claimed earlier, imposed by the nature of skepticism itself. To prepare what I have to say about this vision of recovery, and as if in earnest of the intention one day to get further into the second part of the play, the Bohemian part, that which after all makes a romance out of a tragedy, I shall pick out two elements of that part that I shall need for a description of the final events – the elements of Autolycus and of the fabulous bear.

In the figure of Autolycus the play's preoccupations with deviousness (both in money and in words – his father or grandfather was Hermes) and lawlessness and economy and sexuality and fertility and art are shown to live together with jollity, not fatality. They are together in his early line, "My traffic is sheets" (IV, iii, 23), meaning that his business is stealing and bawdry; that he sells ballads and broadsheets; that he sells ballads about, let us say, birds that steal sheets; that he steals the ballads from which he makes a living; and that these exchanges have something to do with the providing of sexual satisfaction – all of which it seems reasonable to suppose that Shakespeare would be glad to say of his own art. I emphasize Autolycus as an artist figure, in balance with the solemnity of the Giulio Romano artistry at the play's close, as one of the contributions Bohemia makes to Sicilia, its recounting of existence. It is in Autolycus that, in this play of the play between art and nature, between artifice and issue, we see that the sheepshearing festival is also a business enterprise; it is not in itself, as one might have thought the recovery from skepticism, or civilization; it celebrates the progress of nature no more than the exchange of money and custom, like the play to which it lends its great image. Then Clown enters to Autolycus (it is our first view of him after his going off to perform the "good deed" of burying the remains of the bear's dinner of Antigonous) as follows:

Let me see, every 'leven wether tods, every tod yields pound
and odd shilling; fifteen hundred shorn, what comes the wool
to? . . . I cannot do't without counters. Let me see, what am
I to buy for our sheep-shearing feast?

(IV, ii, 32–7)

The Clown's painful calculation reminds us that all the arithmetical
operations – not alone multiplying, but dividing, adding, and sub-
tracting – are figures for breeding, or for its reciprocal, dying. If
Thoreau had asked the question, What comes the wool to? I am
sure he would at the same time have been asking, What does wool
mean? what does it matter? what does it count for? – as if to declare
that this piece of nature's issue is itself money and that the process
of determining meaning is a process of counting; as if the fullness
of language shown in figuration has as sound a basis as the issuing
of language demonstrated in figuring. (I mention as a curiosity that
the idea of shearing or pruning, as well as that of summing up or
reckoning, is contained in the idea of computing.)

One of Autolycus's ballads he claims to have gotten from a mid-
wife named Mistress Taleporter, evidently a carrier of tales, about
"how a usurer's wife was brought to bed of twenty money-bags
at a burden" (IV, iv, 263–5). It is agreed that Autolycus is mocking
contemporary ballads about monstrous births, and I hope it will
equally be agreed that this, while filling the play up with ideas of
money as breeding, hence of art and nature as creating one another,
is mocking Leontes' idea that birth is as such monstrous; it seeks
perspective on the idea. Further perspective is sought in the following scene, of the sheepshearing itself, in the notorious debate
between Perdita and Polixenes concerning bastards, which expresses
the halves of Leontes' mind: Perdita, like her conventional natural
father, who called her a bastard and shunned her, wants to shun
bastards; Polixenes, in denying a flat distinction between nature
and nature's mending art, benignly concludes that all graftings are
legitimate, as legitimate as nature; typically, he has thus shown a
possibility from which Leontes draws a malignant conclusion, here
that no birth is legitimate, that the world *is* of bastards, to be
shunned and cast adrift.

This brings me to the bear, in whom nature seems to be reab-
sorbing a guilty civilization. His dining on the roaring gentleman,
mocking him, is carefully coordinated in the Clown's report with

the raging, mocking storm, which is seen as having "swallowed" or "flapdragoned" the roaring souls on the ship. But if the bear is nature's initial response to Leontes' denials of it, is there a suggestion that the denial of nature is also nature's work? I take it the play concludes (explicitly, at any rate) not, or not always, that in its citing of "an art / Which does mend Nature, change it rather; but / The art itself is Nature" (IV, iv, 95–6), the implication is that there is also an art that does not mend nature, but that instead changes it into something else, unnatural, or, say, lawful, or rather social, an art not born of nature but, hence, of the human or of something beyond.

This is one of the arguments of which the final scene is a function, summarized in Leontes' cry:

> Oh, she's warm!
> If this be magic, let it be an art
> Lawful as eating.
>
> (V, iii, 109–11)

In proposing that there is a lawful as well as an unlawful magic, which perhaps comes to the idea that religion is lawful magic (thus reversing an older idea), Leontes' words suggest that there is an unlawful as well as a lawful eating. A play like *Coriolanus* a few years earlier was in part built from the idea there is an unlawful, or prelawful, eating, a cannibalism, that Shakespeare names elsewhere as well as the relation of parents to children. (*Coriolanus,* on my view, goes so far as to suggest that there is even a lawful cannibalism, one necessary, at any rate, to the formation of the lawful, that is, to the social.) I note again that *The Winter's Tale* similarly presents lawful and unlawful versions of its ramifying idea of "paying back," with which the first two scenes of Act I and the first and last scenes of Act V open, revenge being the unlawful version of which justice would be the lawful. I propose taking the final scene as, among other things, a marriage ceremony. This means taking Paulina's warning to her audience that hers may seem unlawful business and her invitation to them to leave, as a statement that she is ratifying a marriage that can seem unlawful, where the only unlawfulness in question there would seem to be some forbidden degree of consanguinity. In Polixenes' statement to Perdita,

> You see, sweet maid, we marry
> A gentler scion to the wildest stock,
> And make conceive a bark of baser kind
> By bud of nobler race.
>
> (IV, iv, 92–5)

(which names the convention of grafting as what marriage is, marriage of different stocks and buds), marriage is located as the art, the human invention, which changes nature, which gives birth to legitimacy, lawfulness. No wonder Shakespeare's investigation of marriage has no end.

Since I am not dealing very consecutively with the Shakespearean problematic of incestuousness, which haunts this play, and since I propose no theory of incest – wanting rather to keep the events of the play at the level of data for which any such theory would wish to account – let me register my sense here that we can hardly these days avoid the thought that a play in which the line between nature and law is blurred and questioned is a play preoccupied with incestuousness, taking the incest taboo, with Freud and Lévi-Strauss, as that event which creates the social out of natural bondings. A reason for me not to hurry into this area is that this role attributed to the incest taboo is, in traditional philosophy, attributed, if ambiguously, to the social contract, which may help to explain why the existence of this contract and the new bonds it is said to have created have been the subject of confusion and joking in the history of political theory. It suggests itself that the tyranny of kings, from which the contract was to free us, was itself an expression or projection of something beyond divine right, namely that we require divorce from a contract already in effect, a kind of marriage bond; divorce from the tyranny of the parental or, say, the romance of the familial, a subjugation not by force but by love. Leontes was mad, but the problem he had fallen prey to is real, and remains without a perfect solution.

I said that the bear dining on the gentleman is the play's image of lawful eating, for as the Clown observes, "They [viz., bears] are never curst [i.e., bad-tempered (Arden ed.) or vicious (Signet ed.)] but when they are hungry" (III, iii, 129–30), so that, unlike mankind, things of nature are not insatiable. This is why this dinner can carry comically, why its expression of nature's violence seems the beginning of redemption, or rescue, from the shipwreck of human violence, with its unpayable debts. Near the end of the chapter entitled "Spring," just before the concluding chapter of *Walden,* Thoreau paints the violence of nature in sentences like the following:

> We need to witness our own limits transgressed, and some life pasturing freely where we never wander. We are cheered when we observe the vulture feeding on the carrion which disgusts and disheartens us and deriving health and strength from the repast. . . . I love to see that Nature is so rife with life that myriads can be afforded to be sacrificed, suffered to prey on one another. . . . The impression made on a wise man is that of universal innocence.

In having already described the final scene as a study of theater and proposed it as a wedding ceremony, I am, it will be clear, not satisfied to think of it – as was once more familiar – as a translated moment of religious resurrection, with Paulina a figure for St. Paul, a figure justified by the appearance in the scene of the words "grace," "graces," "faith," and "redeems." It is, however, equally clear to me that an understanding of the scene will have to find its place for this translation. I look for it in a sense of this theater as in competition with religion, as if declaring itself religion's successor. It may be that I am too influenced here by some things I have said about *Coriolanus,* but it strikes me that the reason a reader like Santayana claimed to find everything in Shakespeare but religion was that religion is Shakespeare's pervasive, hence invisible, business. The resurrection of the woman is, theatrically, a claim that the composer of this play is in command of an art that brings words to life, or vice versa, and since the condition of this life is that her spectators awake their faith, we, as well as Leontes, awake, as it were, with her. A transformation is being asked of our conception of the audience of a play, perhaps a claim that we are no longer spectators, but something else, more, say participants. But participants in what? Who is this woman, and on what terms is she brought to life?

She says she preserved herself "to see the issue" (V, iii, 128), meaning the issue of the oracle that gave hope Perdita was in being, and meaning Perdita as her issue, her daughter, to whom alone, as said, she speaks (except for the gods) as she returns to life. Does this mean that she does *not* forgive Leontes? Perdita is equally his issue, and does the odd naming of her as "the issue" accept or reject this? Perdita found is equally the issue of this *play*, called *The Winter's Tale*, as is Hermione awakened. Beyond this, in a general scene of issuing, of delivery, I find myself feeling in Hermione's awakening that the play itself is being brought forth, as from itself, that she *is* the play, something I first felt about Cleopatra and her play, in which her final nested acts of theater are also the staging of a wedding ceremony. Who knows what marriage is, or what a wedding ceremony should look like, after Luther and Henry the Eighth have done their work? And if we are created with Hermione, then we are equally, as an audience, her, and the play's, issue.

Paulina (with her echoing of St. Paul, the expounder both of marriage and of salvation by faith alone) I take as the muse of this ceremony, or stage director; she knows the facts; it is Leontes' faith that is at stake. And the ceremony takes place at his bidding and under his authority:

> PAULINA. Those that think it is unlawful business
> I am about, let them depart.
> LEONTES.   Proceed.
>   No foot shall stir.
>
>   (V, iii, 96–8)

So we, the eventual audience, are here under his authority as well. What happens from now on is also his issue; it is his production. To see what happens to this scene conceived as his creation, and the culmination of his creatings, I put this together with two other authorial moments of his in the early scenes in Sicilia. First with his aside upon sending off Hermione and Polixenes to dispose themselves according to their own bents:

>   I am angling now,
> Though you perceive not how I give line.
>   (I, ii, 180–1)

Taken as an author's revelation to his audience, he is cautioning us that what we do not perceive in his lines will work to betray ourselves. And I put his authority – compromised as authority is shown to be – together also with my seeing him as interrupting his son's

219

tale of generation, another authorial self-identification. Leontes has found the voice in which to complete it, as it were a son's voice, as if he is accepting in himself the voices of father and son, commanding and whispering, hence multiplicity, accepting himself as having, and being, issue. What is the issue?

I have said that not alone the play is the issue of the tale of romance, as from a source, but Hermione as the play. Can Hermione be understood as Leontes' issue? But this is the sense – is it not? – of the passage from Genesis in which theology has taken marriage to be legitimized, in which the origin of marriage is presented as the creation of the woman from the man. It is how they are one flesh. Then let us emphasize that this ceremony of union takes the form of a ceremony of separation, thus declaring that the question of two becoming one is just half the problem; the other half is how one becomes two. It is separation that Leontes' participation in parturition grants – that Hermione has, that there is, a life beyond his, and that she can create a life beyond his and hers, and beyond plenitude and nothingness. The final scene of *The Winter's Tale* interprets this creation as their creation by one another. Each awakens, each was stone, it remains unknown who stirs first, who makes the first move back. The first move of revenge it seems easy to determine; the first move to set aside revenge, impossible. Some good readers of this play who would like to believe in it further than they find they can, declare themselves unconvinced that this final scene "works" (as it is typically put). But I take some mode of uncertainty just here to be in the logic of the scene, as essential to its metaphysics as to the working of its theater. Its working is no more the cause of our conviction, or participation, than it is their result; and our capacity for participation is precisely a way of characterizing the method no less than the subject of this piece of theater.

Does the closing scene constitute forgiveness, Hermione's forgiveness of Leontes? At the beginning of Act V Leontes was advised by one of his faithful lords that he has "redeemed," "paid" more penitence than done trespass, and that he should "Do as the heavens have done, forget your evil; / With them, forgive yourself." This mysterious advice implies that to be forgiven you must allow yourself to be forgiven, accept forgiveness. Has Leontes accomplished this? It seems to be the form in which the revenge against life (as Nietzsche almost said), the weddedness to nothingness, is forgone, forgotten. The romantics saw this revenge, as for example in *The*

Counting and Recounting

Ancient Mariner, as our carrying the death of the world in us, in our constructions of it.[1] The final scene of issuing in *The Winter's Tale* shows what it may be to find in oneself the life of the world.

Is the life of the world, supposing the world survives, a big responsibility? Its burden is not its size but its specificness. It is no bigger a burden than the responsibility for what Emerson and Thoreau might call the life of our words. We might think of the burden as holding, as it were, the mirror up to nature. Why assume just that Hamlet's picture urges us players to imitate, that is, copy or reproduce, (human) nature? His concern over those who "imitated humanity so abominably" is not alone that we not imitate human beings badly, but that we not become imitation members of the human species, abominations; as if to imitate, or represent – that is, to participate in – the species well is a condition of being human. Such is Shakespearean theater's stake in the acting, or playing, of humans. Then Hamlet's picture of the mirror held up to nature asks us to see if the mirror as it were clouds, to determine whether nature is breathing (still, again) – asks us to be things affected by the question.

---

[1] This idea, in conjunction with Coleridge and others, is the topic of my essay "In Quest of the Ordinary," in *Romanticism and Contemporary Criticism,* ed. M. Eaves and M. Fischer (Ithaca, N.Y.: Cornell University Press, 1986).

Index of Names and Titles

Index of Names and Titles

Index of Names and Titles